Entrepreneurial Controls

Entrepreneurial Controls

Financial and Operational Standards for Emerging Businesses

Jack E. Trent
CMA, CTP, CFM, CFE

iUniverse, Inc.
New York Bloomington Shanghai

Entrepreneurial Controls
Financial and Operational Standards for Emerging Businesses

Copyright © 2008 by Jack E. Trent

iUniverse books may be ordered through booksellers or by contacting:

iUniverse
1663 Liberty Drive
Bloomington, IN 47403
www.iuniverse.com
1-800-Authors (1-800-288-4677)

Because of the dynamic nature of the Internet, any Web addresses or links contained in this book may have changed since publication and may no longer be valid.

The views expressed in this work are solely those of the author and do not necessarily reflect the views of the publisher, and the publisher hereby disclaims any responsibility for them.

ISBN: 978-0-595-46326-8 (pbk)
ISBN: 978-0-595-71565-7 (cloth)
ISBN: 978-0-595-90621-5 (ebk)

Printed in the United States of America

To the finest entrepreneur that ever lived and my greatest hero—Dad

To my ever insightful and loving angel—Mom

To my dearest friend, companion and sweetheart—Wendi

Contents

Preface

After reading and reviewing text after text of business guides, small business advice, business magazines and literature I became annoyed and concerned by the lack of discussion and recognition for controls. Many of the "supreme-superior-all-inclusive-all-wonderful" business startup guides do not even mention the terms *control, compliance* or *efficiency* in their index. Some of these unnamed manuscripts are hundreds of pages in length never offering any reasonable reference to the significance of controls or the value they might play in your organization. On the other side of this equation, the materials studied and presented on auditing, fraud management, risk management and internal controls have always been directed to a large corporate audience. It seems no bridge existed between these important bodies of knowledge.

As financial officer, accountant, small business owner and entrepreneur I have often been charged with the task of creating a system of operating standards that would allow for a high degree of flexibility without surrendering security and performance. The problem I had was all the body of internal controls knowledge had been directed toward large, well-established publicly traded enterprises. Most of these companies already had solid internal controls (with the others creating deceptions of success while violating legal and ethical standards). While the principles are the same, the applications of these big business standards often did not apply to smaller enterprises with little capital and even less time to implement a series of sophisticated, complex and often archaic controls.

In working with entrepreneurs as a management accountant I have created a series of instructions, lessons, best practices and guidelines that I had been hoping for some time to assemble into one book.

This book serves as a functional manual for small business owners, offering insight to provide an awareness of and an understanding for the internal controls which can protect them and their businesses from unnecessary risks.

Much of the text is focused on fraud and risk management. Small business owners are often easy targets for con-artists, corrupt employees and other criminals hoping to cash in on ignorance. My desire is that with the proper systems in place many vulnerabilities and risks can be reduced and minimized.

The ultimate measure of success of this text will be measured in my ability to inspire entrepreneurs and small business owners to view controls not as restrictions, but standards that if adhered to, can increase the chances of realizing their goals and objectives.

Always hoping to improve and grow, I welcome your emails with any suggestions, corrections, clarifications or great real-life stories you may have. These emails may be directed to info@jacktrent.com.

Best of success—

Jack E. Trent

Acknowledgements

I extend much gratitude for the persistent and outstanding help of my wonderful wife Wendi. Her literary skills never fail to amaze me. Also for the gifts of Linda Watts and her unparallel skills as an advising editor. The apple never falls far from the tree.

Also, I am indebted to the services of Brainbay Consulting Pvt and Harvestsoft Technologies, specifically under the leadership of Ravi Kumar and Guru P. Chaturvedi who have proven faithful, fair and outstanding entrepreneurs.

I acknowledge and appreciate the work of Durga Krishnamurthi CA. She has been a thoughtful researcher and offered great support.

I also recognize the kind service from the publishing team at iUniverse. They have proven that service can succeed at all levels. I thank Joy Elliott for her tremendous spirit and team attitude. The iUniverse team has demonstrated the power of the entrepreneurial spirit, with that spirit it has revolutionized and transformed even the oldest of industries.

Also many kind thanks to the other entrepreneurs in my life who have inspired and lifted me through so much: Steve and Shannon Berry, for their indomitable spirit and influence; Wendell and Pam Thompson for their triumphant persistence; Mike and Laura Allred for their extraordinary entrepreneurial vision as artists and writers; Russ Beeton for his willingness to take chances and his mastery in accounting; as well as so many other exemplary business people who have shaped my life including Tom Taylor, Tom Stringham, Wallace Harkness, Neil Erickson, Chris Dexter, Reid Olsen, and Glen Olsen. Many other people have exemplified the spirit of entrepreneurialism and I appreciate their examples and stories that have motivated me to pursue my dreams.

To my brothers and in-laws who proved families can work together in an entrepreneurial setting and still go home friends: Jim, Robert, David, Shane and Robb.

Also special thanks to my sweet, supportive and wonderful children, Sadilyn, Annelise and Elijah, for giving me many quiet evenings to write and compile this book.

CHAPTER ONE

Entrepreneurial Controls: Systems Built for Success

Sales are to growth as controls are to profitability and success within your business. If your business is going to succeed, you will find either instinctively, by experience or through research that you need to establish a system of controls. All businesses must develop controls which will enable them to:

- Operate effectively and efficiently;
- Maintain accounting reliability; and,
- Comply with government mandates and standards.

As a small business owner, you already know that sales are paramount to the growth of a company. Yet, what you may not know is that with sales and controls working side by side, growth and profitability can be driven exponentially and the return on your investment can be more readily realized. Many startups from the late 1990's can relate to the horror stories that have been told where companies lost millions of dollars in uncontrolled research and development with little or nothing to show for the investment.

Reality Check:
No Control ~ No Go

A small technology endeavor that accumulated over $12 million dollars of investment money exhausted its resources in just over a year with no product offering, no sales and little to show for the investors. The founders had conceived a revolutionary idea for improving security and communications in the household through a voice-activated system. The sales pitch had netted plenty of interest and money. A potentially amazing ride to the top with a breakthrough in home security products ended in a bumpy ride to the bottom with broken promises and shattered dreams because of the lack of proper controls.

As an experienced management accountant and business consultant, I have seen the mishaps of great business concepts flounder and fail nearly always due to lack of controls.

Aside from driving profitability and growth for your company, internal controls are the single most important method of preventing fraud. Fraud lurks in the shadows of every day business operations and can single-handedly destroy even the most profitable, promising small business.

Reality Check:
Small is Vulnerable

Small businesses are subject to a higher percentage of fraud than large businesses and are hit with greater losses as a group. According to the Association of Fraud Examiners, businesses with 100 or under employees were hit with average fraud claims of $127,500 in 2002, while organizations of over 10,000 employees had average fraud claims of only $97,000.

The disparity is magnified when considering the average business with over 10,000 employees post billions in annual sales and businesses with 100 employees or under only record annual sales in the millions. This represents over 1000% discrimination for small business fraud. Further, this study was conducted during 2002, a year recognized as having unusually high volumes of big business fraud.

These facts contribute to the conclusion that small businesses are more vulnerable to fraud, and that crimes are usually detected later in small business settings than the comparative larger businesses. This disparity is directly correlated to lack of internal controls within small companies.

Source: Association of Certified Fraud Examiners, www.acfe.com.

Thus the objectives of the internal controls system are twofold: to drive profits and to prevent fraud. When a system of checks and balances is established, these controls will help you to maintain order, safeguard your assets and reduce exposure and waste. A business with a properly implemented internal controls system is a system built for success.

The Purpose of Controls and the Pursuit of Profits

Entrepreneur is a term borrowed from the French meaning "enterpriser" or one that undergoes a venture in pursuit of profits at the expense and risk of capital.[1] Our purpose is to provide meaningful insight for this group of managers, operators, innovators and technologists on how best to integrate an effective control system that is right for their individual pursuit of profits.

Often in coping with controls, entrepreneurs complain that these controls are binding constraints which do not allow them to venture freely into higher and unexplored realms of success. The term "controls" seems to be perceived as restrictive rather than as a set of operating parameters that can deliver the desired output and minimize risk through all scales of business. The purpose of a control system is to provide entrepreneurs with the appropriate tools to analyze the business process, thereby picking out trends that point to profitability or lost opportunity.

Controls Should Facilitate Change

In the early 1950's when Dave Thomas was serving his country in the Army before serving hamburgers, he was given an opportunity to be the assistant manager at the Enlisted Men's Club. The sales were minimal and the master sergeant who was Dave's roommate wanted to know if Dave had any ideas on how to boost sales. The Club was serving cold sandwiches at the time and Dave observed that the general customer base consisted of young men in their late teens and early twenties who wanted to snack on comfort food—food that reminded them of home like hot roast beef sandwiches and chicken-in-a-basket. He added these items along with hamburgers, meat loaf and steak sandwiches which boosted sales. He picked out the trend that would enable the Club be profitable, and followed his instinct.[2] What Dave's instinct led him to accomplish can be duplicated by others using a detective control technique where the current situation is analyzed and the solution is created by picking out which trends will lead to profitability potential for the business. In this case, matching the menu offering to the customer base boosted sales and solved the problem.

In a small, dynamic entrepreneurial enterprise, your organization will have the advantage of responding quickly to change after analysis deems these changes necessary. The best control systems are those based on combined feedback from the shop-floor and the top-end management. Keep in mind that if operations do not have the proper controls then implementation and execution of such controls is desirable to procure a successful venture.[3]

Figure 1.1

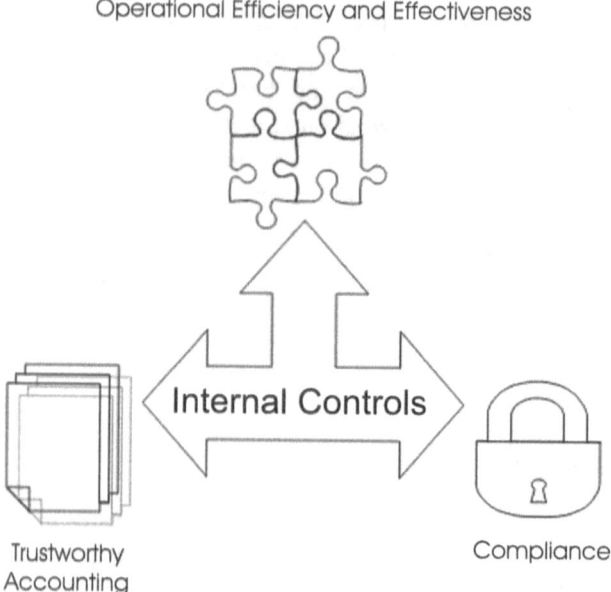

Operational Efficiency and Effectiveness

Internal Controls

Trustworthy
Accounting

Compliance

Internal Controls Introduced

Internal controls have been defined as the focus on the entire business operation at several key junctions including effectiveness and efficiencies of operations, compliance with laws and regulations and reliable financial reporting.[4] We are all annoyed by traffic lights from time to time, especially when late for an appointment. However, if you have ever lived in a society that places little value on traffic laws, you quickly become grateful for the safety that these annoyances cause. When business cultures feel compelled to operate at high speed with little time for compliance, the dangers broaden and the errors intensify with increased speed of operations.

This text will uncover some of the common controls that entrepreneurs and small business owners ignore. Imagine preparing to land and discovering that the Chicago O'Hare Airport is now an uncontrolled airstrip—meaning there are no air traffic controllers to direct traffic. That would be fantastic, right? You could land as soon as your plane came in, no more circling the sky while awaiting your turn on the strip. It would be first come first serve, and your plane could just come right in at any landing strip that was visually open. For any apparent advantage of such an operating system, you can already see the chaos and danger this would cause, especially when airports handle increasingly larger traffic volumes. Try to visualize what a lack of controls will do to your business as it continues to grow. Now visualize a controlled business environment—one that is orderly, safe and protected. These fundamental controls will be explored internally for their efficiency and effectiveness as some key historical components of successful enterprises are reviewed as well.

There are four key control objectives that provide the operating policies for internal controls:

- *Proper authorization:* protocol within policies and procedures;
- *Segregation of duties:* definition of job scope and functions;
- *Adequate documentation and records;* and,
- *Independent checks on performance.*

Proper Authorization

Employees need to be empowered to function within the scope of their responsibilities. These boundaries become sensitive issues when constraints are needed regarding signature authorization, code access, locks, keys, limits and other authorizing tools. You are going to become familiar with many of the different types of authorization required in your business and how to limit unnecessary exposure, at the same time avoiding needless bureaucracy. Often, in a smaller enterprise, few individuals have full access; the intention of this book is to help reduce the burden of access borne by both entrepreneur and employee.

Segregation of Duties

Primary functions within the organization ought to be performed by two or more individuals. A detailed discussion will be presented in a following chapter and provide insight into many of these activities and what can be done to reduce loss from error and extortion. Segregated duties include the recording of financial records, checks, assets, check-writing, and mail among other duties. By setting up simple but vital processes, your risk for loss will be significantly reduced. This book will advise you on precautionary steps that you can take to protect your business over time as it experiences many of the changes facilitated through growth and progress.

Adequate Documentation and Records

Business documentation needs to be kept and preserved carefully, not haphazardly. Your enterprise may rely on this documentation to avoid potential losses due to overcharges, under-billing, warranty issues, design, patent, copyright issues along with a host of other concerns. By taking leadership in supplying proper documentation and its proper storage, a wealth of information will be available to be used for sustaining a knowledge database that can feed future growth and success. All too often lessons of the past must be relearned due to poor documentation controls.

Independent Checks on Performance

Often another vantage point can provide significant insight into your current operations. An occasional review by another professional will open questions and raise concerns that may not have been noticed by your team. Even another member of your staff outside the department in question can provide a quick review for security and compliance with another portion of the business. This book will provide you with some appropriate questions to use as a guide when probing the principal components of your enterprise.

In addition to these objectives, there are subset aspects of controls that will be presented throughout this book including three of the fundamental controls: *preventative, detective* and *corrective controls.*[5]

Preventative controls are those systems designed to prevent an undesirable event which would render an unacceptable risk. An unacceptable risk is defined as any activity which increases risk while not offering compensation in the form of potentially offset gains. Preventative controls can keep invalid transactions from being processed and help to avoid the misappropriation of assets.

When a possible abuse or error of the system has occurred, a feature of a functional control system is to allow detective controls to emerge and uncover the error or missing assets. When properly established, other employees and stakeholders are aware of these system functions and will govern themselves accordingly both in exercising more caution that transactions are properly recorded and processed as well as in preventing abuse, knowing that detection will shortly follow.

After detection, a correction of the problem will need to occur. In response to the detected weakness, immediate action should be taken to resolve the issue. A corrective response is the initial action taken to begin the healing process. For example, one of your supervisors has been caught cheating on his timecard. Upon discovery, the corrective action is to go back and assess all misstated hours and attempt recovery from the employee, thus correcting the situation and restoring the company to its original status. Meanwhile, you can plan a preventative strategy to avert similar situations from occurring in the future.

Implementing Control Systems

In addition to learning about the types of controls available, studying this book will familiarize you with methods for implementing these controls. There are three broad categories for control implementation: *administrative, technical* and *physical.*

Administrative systems are policies and procedures. Included in the text are a number of ideas and templates that can be used for starting the framework of policies and procedures. As manager, you are responsible to see that policies are in place. You can expect that without policies there will be some in the organization that will take advantage of this lack of documentation and claim ignorance to the standard. Case in point: You would have to believe that with as much literature that exists on sexual harassment, common sense would govern employees in avoiding any situation that may create a threatening environment. Nonetheless, without a written policy, you are exposed to certain individuals who claim they did not realize "that behavior" was sexual harassment. Provide the policies and set the expectation that policies are to be followed as procedures of conduct and behavior.

Technical systems will also assist with the functionality of controls in your environment. As you begin to store files of data, research documents, accounting records, and the like, all these records must be governed by controls. In this book you will receive advice on the significance of technology for you as an entrepreneur and be given guidance in taking steps to instill a secure and stable environment.

Certainly physical systems will be required to contain cash, inventory, equipment, physical assets, vehicles, facilities and other tangibles that are used in the course of your business activities. If you have not yet had some challenges in the area of physical controls, you will. This book will describe some inexpensive steps that can be taken to provide a solid platform, one that will allow you to expand and integrate additional resources as assets grow and property values compound. Surprisingly, many entrepreneurs would never dream of leaving a modestly valued collector's coin on their kitchen table at home; yet, many will leave valuable tools on a jobsite unsecured with poor documentation and little or no insurance or labels. Losses can be prevented with a few essential controls in position.

Identification of Internal Controls

Just as the human mind is continually explored and functions defined to optimize its effectiveness, the organization of successful enterprise is continually examined for operations to be effective. On the contrary, you can be oblivious to the actual purpose of an operation for it to be functional. For example, the great Greek philosopher Aristotle "believed the heart was the center of life and considered the brain merely a cooling organ for the blood."[6] Although Aristotle envisioned the role of the brain as nothing more than a radiator for the bloodstream, the brain still functions as it was meant to function. Fortunately, we have a greater understanding for its functionality at present.

Similarly, controls within successful organizations have begun to be dissected and studied. Although still in its relative infancy, controls are becoming better understood and readily implemented. The American of Institute of Certified Public Accountants first defined controls in 1949 as relating to the safeguarding of assets and reliability of managerial policies.[7] Later in 1972, accounting controls were better defined with the initiation of the Foreign Corrupt Practices Act, FCPA; additionally, the integrations of controls for publicly traded companies began to be formalized. Since 1977, all such public companies must report that accounting records reflect fairly and accurately the disposition and usage of all assets. In 1984, these standards were further broadened to include administrative controls and access and accountability to financial documents. In 1985, the Committee of Sponsoring Organizations (COSO) was formed being "sponsored by five major professional associations in the United States, the American Accounting Association, the American Institute of Certified Public Accountants, Financial Executives International, The Institute of Internal Auditors, and the National Association of Accountants (now the Institute of Management Accountants)."[8] Since the emergence of COSO, standards for appraising, monitoring and auditing of assets and performance have emerged, adding value to companies and promoting value for all stakeholders. Focused on the efficiency and effectiveness of operations, reliable accounting, and legal compliance, these principles of controls have intrinsic value and real worth within even the smallest of enterprises.

Centuries of Controls

While businesses have been using controls for centuries, it is only at present that we have identified and can implement such tools to share with the entrepreneurial venture. Self-made business leaders had to learn at a very early period in building their business that there were basic principles of control that could not be bypassed. They found that there were system safeguards that could be established to prevent losses and exploitation and build a successful business.

In the current information era, we are quick to declare our superiority over our ancestors regarding their business involvements. Certainly, imagine the difficulties of protecting enormous assets with only hand-compiled general ledger books (at the time when books were literally books). While they did operate multimillion dollar ventures (billions in today's terms), it is the modus operandi that, although basic, allowed them to accomplish their objectives. Ignoring any preconceived notions on the outcome of their labors, we will focus on the methodology and initial systems of controls which have been successful in the past and continue to permeate today's successful businesses. Ultimately, it will be to help guide your own organization toward success.

Think of your favorite entrepreneur. Whether it's Bill Gates, Steve Jobs, Mary Kay Ash, or any other entrepreneur, you have most likely noticed that these individuals all had unique ways of accomplishing the same task of establishing controls. Some entrepreneurs have a higher instinct toward control requirements, while others tend to rely upon other key individuals to maintain their system of controls.

Drawing from past experiences, this text will direct you to the controls that can and must be duplicated in your own venture in order to thrive. You will learn how to watch for waste through the clues and indicators of a well-governed business. The process involves no advanced technologies, no need for the procurement of a supercomputer, bodyguards or even a gun. Governance is all about creating an environment, a way of doing business. Just as we all have personal ways of directing our life, we function because we adhere to the requirements for oxygen, food, some clothing, medical care (though to some a nice bonus, is a necessity), and occasional rest (as basic elements of human survival). Your business as an entity will need the nourishment of cash flow, the breath of sales, the check up of accounting, and the monitoring of performance.

More than just compliance, the information in this book will strive to demonstrate how internal controls are practical applications of order and optimal management. The statement, "If things seem under control, you are just not going fast enough," may be true as stated by Mario Andretti; conversely, you'll notice that Mr. Andretti has also led a long life. Certainly this was not the result of ignoring racing controls and safety systems. Indeed, a functional control framework should work within your objectives, never against them. Your business can adapt through explosive periods of growth. Controls simply prevent you from exploding.

Chapter Summary

This chapter served as an introduction to the foundation of internal controls, namely, to drive profitability and growth though effectiveness and efficiency, reliable accounting and legal and ethical compliance; and to prevent fraud by protecting assets, maintaining order and reducing waste and exposure. These are the reasons why controls exist. Controls properly understood and implemented should enhance performance, and never limit your success.

You were informed of the four control objectives including proper authorization, segregation of responsibilities, adequate documentation, and independent monitoring of performance; as well as the controls used for monitoring internal performance, which are detective, preventative and directive controls. During the course of this text these objectives will be the overriding theme in creating entrepreneurial controls in your enterprise.

CHAPTER TWO

Leading Programs, Pushing Projects

All successful entrepreneurs quickly master two elements required for the survival of any profitable operation; program implementation and project management. Often success in these areas goes completely unnoticed. There are no closing project parties celebrating the events. There is no one to proclaim and extol the virtues of a newly implemented customer service program. The two foundations of successful operations are often laid without any fanfare or notice at all, yet they must be installed and must establish roots in customer acquisition, retention and profitable operations.

The course of this chapter will help to make you aware and give you some of the basics of Programs and Projects. Often used interchangeably, these are terms that have very distinct functions in the corporate environment and serve very different needs within the organization. The sooner these concepts are understood, the deeper and richer the potential harvest. Entrepreneurs can exert less time performing shallow functions and direct more energy toward digging deeper wells.

What is a Program?

Any operation within an organization's normal course of business is considered a program. This is routine work that is repeated as the day demands.[1] Programs include the myriad of tasks that directly service customers complicated needs and the maintenance needs of the organization itself. Such tasks as sales management, customer services, accounting services, inventory maintenance, and service support would be considered programs. These programs are essential to keeping the business alive with cash flow and prospective customers.

How did all these programs begin and how were they launched? As an entrepreneur, you have the opportunity to see each of these programs emerge from projects (more detail on Projects in a moment). Each program must find its origins as a project regardless of how small that project may be. Mature companies have all but forgotten the humble beginnings of each project that has emerged over time to create sophisticated and advanced series of programs that service daily operations.

These programs are essential to operations and care must be taken at each step in order to ensure customer satisfaction. How many companies have lost a customer because the initial customer service was poor? Remember, you get one shot; and more often then not, if that experience is lousy, you are done. Properly implemented, programs will direct your energy to make the most of that one shot.

Program Controls

Since operational efficiency and effectiveness represent the first component of control, entrepreneurs need to have a focused understanding in each aspect of their programs. This is not to suggest that one individual can or should know all there is to know about a complex business operation. You will have to rely on the expertise of many others' skills to bring an enterprise into a successful position. By working with others, you can design a team that complements and protects the entire staff. Your first control objective is to ensure operational performance.

In order to calculate efficiency and effectiveness you must understand your element. This understanding may be intuitive, but the distinction between efficiency and effectiveness are not usually instinctive. Effective controls are those that hold the power to help a company accomplish its objectives.[2] As an entrepreneur you have goals and the organization needs to respond to those objectives to accomplish what you have in mind. That is the simple beauty of controls. They represent the systems that will put your objectives into action.

What is a Project?

You run your enterprise to achieve specific business objectives. Over the years of running your business, many of your goals and the tasks involved either will evolve or have already evolved into routine and repetitive activities. In some cases these routines may even be consuming valuable resources without contributing to long-term growth. A project is the antithesis of routine work. It is essentially a one-time effort. Typically limited by a timeline, every project has a beginning and an end. A project has been defined as "a complex, non-routine, one-time effort limited by time, budget, resources and performance specifications designed to meet customer needs".[3]

Reality Check:
The Big Dig

One of the most massive state level projects in existence is the Massachusetts Big Dig project, an operation of $14.6 billion and over 25 years in production. Presenting as a behemoth of a project, an operation this large is easy to criticize, being subject to significant weaknesses, learning experiences and other issues that occur over the years. If the estimates are true, and Boston has collectively lost over $500 Million in annual productivity due to traffic congestion and other traffic-related issues, then Boston made a very smart move, investing billions of dollars to establish orderly traffic paths and increase accessibility throughout the city. Ultimately this project payoff will increase annual productivity and fix Boston's limited earning potential.

In review of national projects in the areas of construction, space, and research, there never seems to be an end of fault finders and nay-sayers willing to exploit mistakes, exaggerate losses and fault the leaders. The bottom line of the projects is that their long-term impact offers enormous returns of experience and learning. From Thomas Jefferson and the Louisiana Purchase to the Kennedy space effort, they were all criticized for their largess and spending. These enormous long-term successes have taught great lessons from which we daily reap the benefits. So when some leader is crazy enough to take on new, lengthy, and seemingly visionary projects fraught with challenges, unknowns and risk—then bring it on!

Nonetheless, there is no excuse for sloppy leadership and project mismanagement. While all the issues connected to the Big Dig are yet to be understood, ultimately it seems that Boston will have a reasonable outcome. As both financial and historical center for our nation, Boston has tremendous wealth moving into and out of its center; $14.6 billion really is insignificant if you look at the potential value that will be expanded and the $500 million/year savings from this project.

Retrieved June 27, 2007, from
  http://www.masspike.com/bigdig/background/index.html

Gray, C. F., & Larson, E. W. (2006). Project management : the managerial process (3rd ed.). Boston: McGraw-Hill/Irwin

So how is a project different from other organizational work? A project has a definite objective. For example, you own and operate a bakery. Designing a range of gluten-free donuts would be a project. Every individual contract that a landscape architect undertakes is a project. A project has to a timeline with a definite deadline. When the goal of the project has been achieved the project ends. The results of the project efforts are then integrated into the routine functions of the enterprise and begin to function as programs thereafter. Projects are usually cross-functional. They often require inputs from every department of your business. Being a unique one-time activity, a project needs to be allocated specific resources. Consequently, a project may get bound up in time, cost and result requirements.

Project Scopes

The key to successful project implementation is careful planning and scheduling of resources. In order to achieve your objectives, clearly define your objectives for the project. The outputs expected to be delivered by the project over its lifetime also need to be defined. These outputs are derived through a series of events. Each output must adhere to performance standards. A project scope also incorporates project limitations—the restricted areas which the project at hand will not explore. Lastly, the final output has to be reviewed to ensure it meets intended specifications. In definition, the elements of the scope of a project include project objectives, outputs, events, performance requirements, limitations, communication and review. Further description of these elements follows:

- *Project objectives*: The first step in planning the scope of a project is to set out the reason for doing the project. A project objective will not only define the end-product or products expected to result from the project but also the resources and time required for its completion.

- *Outputs:* The next step is to define the outputs from the project over its lifetime. The first untested product, all its variants and the final prototype are all outputs from the project. Defining what the product is expected to look like at each stage of its development helps to plan the scope of the project.

- *Events*: As we have already mentioned a project is a function of time. Each significant milestone on this timeline is referred to as an event. A table of events gives an estimate of allocation of time resources on the project. These events are constructed around the desired outputs from the project already outlined above. These events should be natural control points in the project. They should be easily recognizable by all the participants in the project.

- *Performance requirements*: Products resulting from a project will need to adhere to some performance or technical standards. These standards may include statutory requirements, safety standards, industry standards or benchmarking standards that the new product has been designed to reach.

- *Limitations*: Limitations can be defined as the things that the project is not meant to do. Defining the limits of a project brings into sharp focus the principal objectives of the project. It prevents spending of resources on the non-priority items and sets the path for achieving the principal objectives. It also helps the final user see what he will receive and what will not be deliverable from a project.

- *Communicate and review*: Planning of the project scope will end with a final review of the project checklist with the type of customer or end user of the products expected to be generated. The communication and review process is important to ensure that all parties involved in the project implementation are in agreement with its goals, objectives and methodologies.

As you can see from the above planning, the project scope will help you break up the project into workable tasks and generate an operational work plan. The affected parties, whether internal or external, should also always remain within this loop to ensure successful communication throughout the completion of the project.

Reality Check:
The Value of a Plan

When I was a financial controller of an electronics manufacturer, there were many occasions in which proper planning would have saved the organization tremendous heartache and money. While leading the implementation of a new Enterprise Resource Planning (ERP) software package, we as a management team had failed to plan appropriately. Not surprisingly, the process took longer and cost more than had been anticipated. Without a master plan, we made the process much more difficult and had to relearn many lessons that had already been taught by other companies on implementing ERP software. Often companies that do not want to undergo the rigorous planning phases will outsource that service with an implementation expert. We opted to implement on our own, and without a rigorous plan.

Not to bemoan ourselves, I only offer these insights to allow you to learn from our mistakes. Create a solid project plan including a clear scope and time-frame, allowing for contingencies, risks and adjustments as needed.

Setting Priorities in Project Planning

Traditionally the success or otherwise failure of a project is defined as a function of whether or not a project satisfies the customer in terms of budgeted costs, time schedules and desired performance requirements or scope. The scope of a project states the specifications of each project element and the name of the person or organizational unit responsible. The time schedule portion of a project plan defines the estimated time required to complete each part of a project. It also maps out the interrelationship between events, meaning which parts of a project must be completed before another can be started. The set of these relationships is called a network.[4]

The relationship between costs and time schedules varies. Sometimes it is necessary to compromise the performance and scope of the project to get the project done quickly or at a lesser cost. Often the cost of a project goes up if it is not completed within the scheduled time. At other times the project may be made less expensive by using cheaper inputs. Sometimes it may be imperative to speed up certain parts of a project by adding labor or material resources and hence driving up project costs.

One of the principal jobs of a project manager is to manage the relationships between these various components of the project plan. In order to accomplish this, a project manager must set out and comprehend the priorities of the project. Interaction between manager, client and upper management is of paramount importance to establish the relative importance of each component. One method of doing this is by drawing up a priority matrix that identifies which components are in short supply, which can be increased, and which can be accepted.

Priorities vary from project to project. In some cases the scope of a project may be reduced in order to meet delivery schedules or alternatively, in order to keep the costs at budgeted values. In an ideal situation there should be no need to compromise on any part, and the project manager can optimize costs, scope and time available. However, perfection is rarely a reality. Most often managers have to make decisions that benefit one component while compromising others. Thus, defining priorities allows the manager to make the right choice at the right time when compromise is necessitated.

Using the priority matrix, you can establish priorities, organize proper communication channels and create shared goals. Further, a priority matrix allows for adjustments in the scope, time, and cost schedules. Additionally, the parameters for troubleshooting are defined and provide a framework of support should unexpected problems occur during the life of the project.

Process Breakdown

Once the scope and output of a project have been identified, the work of the project may be divided into several elements. Thus broken down, an essential structure of the various elements involved in the project is described. This structure helps in identifying all outputs and elements forming the individual parts of the project and in integrating the work involved into the organization's current structure. It also provides a base for establishing control points in the implementation of a project. Basically, this breakdown functions as an outline of the project with an eye on the details. Process breakdown helps the project manager in the following ways:

- Breaking down the project into its component processes in a hierarchical fashion enables evaluation of cost, time and performance requirements at all levels in the organization over the life of the project.
- It provides information to management appropriate for each level.
- It helps assign responsibility to individuals and organizational units, which in turn helps to integrate the project responsibilities into the organization's day-to-day operations.
- Process breakdown also makes planning, budgeting and time scheduling possible. Project costs and output completion targets can be tracked over a time schedule.

Additionally, communication channels can be clearly established with accurate process breakdown. Coordination among various organizational units becomes easier when responsibilities have been clearly identified.

Integrated Activities

An important function of the process breakdown is to integrate the project into current organizational activities. The critical part of this process is to be able to assign responsibilities and allocate duties within the organization's existing functional framework. This structure provides a framework to summarize organization unit work performance, identify organization units responsible for work packages and help with cost control. Basically, the process breakdown enables you with the capacity to assign workloads and responsibilities right down to the lowest organizational unit and create controls points for the project according to each work unit. With the creation of control points, costs and work progress can be easily tracked and monitored. At this stage, these costs do not have to be tracked using monetary units; rather, document all resource allocation in terms of labor, material usage and time.

As the work units have been assigned within the organization function chart, the project at this stage is blended into the regular organizational activities. When a project has been integrated into organizational activity, control can be exercised from two directions: in terms of output delivered as well as responsibility completed.

Project Responsibilities

When a project has been broken down into the smallest possible work units, responsibility can be assigned to individuals and organizational units down the functional chain. Project responsibilities can be tracked through a project responsibility matrix. This chart summarizes the tasks to be accomplished and tracks who is responsible for what on a project. In its simplest form such a matrix consists of a chart listing all the project activities and the individual participants responsible for each activity. More complex charts and matrices may be used to not only identify individual responsibilities but also clarify interfaces between units and individuals that require coordination. They provide a clear and concise platform for depicting responsibility, authority and communication channels.

Responsibility matrices provide a means for all participants in a project to view their responsibilities and agree on their assignments. They also help clarify the extent or type of authority exercised by each participant in performing an activity in which two or more parties have overlapping involvement. By using an authority chart to define authoritative responsibility and communications within its framework, the relationship between different organizational units and the work content of the project are clarified.

The most important step in project planning is, therefore, to clearly define the project. In the absence of a well-defined project plan, many a project is doomed to failure on more than one occasion. Clarity in defining the project goal goes a long way in the effective allocation of responsibilities over the project. A well-planned project allows for a great level of control over its implementation.

Project Risk Management

Risk is inherent to every project. No amount of planning can overcome risk or give you the ability to control unforeseeable events. In the context of projects, risk is defined as an uncertain event or condition that, if it occurs, can have a positive or negative effect on project objectives.

A risk always has a cause and a consequence. This means that if a certain event takes place, it will affect the cost, time schedule and quality of the project. Various types of risks may be encountered during project implementation. Some risks can be identified even before the project starts. Events like change in technical specifications or machinery breakdown may be anticipated but cannot be prevented. Some risks take the form of consequences arising out of project constraints, like cost and time overruns. Risks can take the form of natural disasters or unforeseen calamities like Hurricane Katrina. Some risks can have positive consequences, but for the most part project risks are associated with all that can go wrong with a project. Once risk has been determined, decisions can be made on how best to manage and mitigate the risk.

The chances of a risk event occurring are greatest during the concept, planning and start-up phases of the project. In the early stages of a project, the opportunity for minimizing the impact of a risk event that might occur or the possibility of working around a potential risk is at its highest. Similarly, the cost impact of a risk event is less if the event occurs earlier in the project rather than later. When completion nears the half-way mark and continues to the final stages, the potential cost impact of the risk to the project and the probability of a risk event occurring increases rapidly. Therefore identifying project risk events and determining a response to the risk before the project begins is a prudent approach. Not attempting to manage risk during the project could prove fatal to an otherwise impressive outcome.

Risk management is a process with preventative measures designed to ensure that the surprise element is reduced and that negative consequences associated with risk events are suitably mitigated. It is a proactive approach to planning rather than reactive. Managing risk enables the project manger to make a decision about whether or not to take a risk when a time, cost or technical advantage is possible. Successful project management can improve chances of punctually attaining the project objectives, within the projected costs and meeting performance requirements.

Identification and Assessment of Project Risk

Identification of project risk is the first step in project risk management. Risk management begins with generating a list of all the possible risks that could be encountered during the implementation of the project. An effective risk identification exercise can be achieved by forming a risk management team with members from the core project team as well as other stakeholders in the project. This team's task includes identifying as many likely risks as possible, no matter how far fetched they seem at the beginning. Later on, this list is fine-tuned to produce a more rational and reasonable assessment of the risks facing the project.

The risk management team needs to focus not on the consequences of an unforeseen event but on the events themselves. By first focusing on the larger risks when undertaking a new project, the team can find solutions to mitigate the risks that are associated with an overall impact on the entire project. Risk mitigating solutions can be found only when the actual elements posing the risk are identified.

After the major risks have been identified, then the team may move on to the smaller risks that affect a specific part or parts of the project. Here, the project breakdown structure described earlier becomes a useful tool for describing risks that may occur at the micro level. It ensures that almost no risk event is missed.

Another method used in identifying project risk is to form a 'risk profile' for the project. This can be formulated by asking a series of questions that address traditional areas of uncertainty on a project. These questions are usually drawn up based on past experiences with similar projects. These questions may be organization-specific and/or built up on organizational experience. They may also be industry-specific, addressing questions that affect other organizations involved in the same or similar line of business as well. Generic risk profiles are also available and useful when no specific information is available to the project manager.

As mentioned earlier, the risk management team should consist not only of the core project team but also other stakeholders like clients, vendors, lenders and others. These external agencies will be in a position to provide a perspective on areas that may not be familiar to the project team but which may derail the entire project if the risks facing them are not anticipated ahead of time.

When potential risks have been identified, the list of risks should be analyzed in order to eliminate the highly improbable end of the risk spectrum and also to identify the trivial risks which can be ignored. Managers have to develop methods for sifting through the list of risks and classifying probable risks in terms of importance and need for attention. The most common method of accomplishing this classification process is by analyzing all of the probable scenarios arising out of a particular risk. The team members then analyze the risk in terms of the undesirable event which has been identified as a risk. All the outcomes that may arise out of the event's occurrence need to be contemplated and the magnitude or severity of the event's impact on the project would have to be projected. At this point, the event is evaluated in terms of the probability of actual occurrence. The team then pinpoints a possible time in the project schedule when the event is more likely to happen. Such events create a domino effect and could jeopardize the entire project, leaving the team to study the interaction of the risk event to the project event as well as other parallel projects within the organization.

A useful strategy may include categorizing the severity of different risks into a matrix format. The matrix may be structured around the impact and likelihood of the risk event. High-impact/high-likelihood risks will find themselves at the top of this matrix. In addition to impact and likelihood, impact of detection may also be worked into this matrix. To further clarify the risks, each of the three dimensions of risk analysis can be rated on a scale of one to five. Doing this adds a depth to the risk analysis by adding a quantitative measure to a qualitative decision.

Figure 2.1

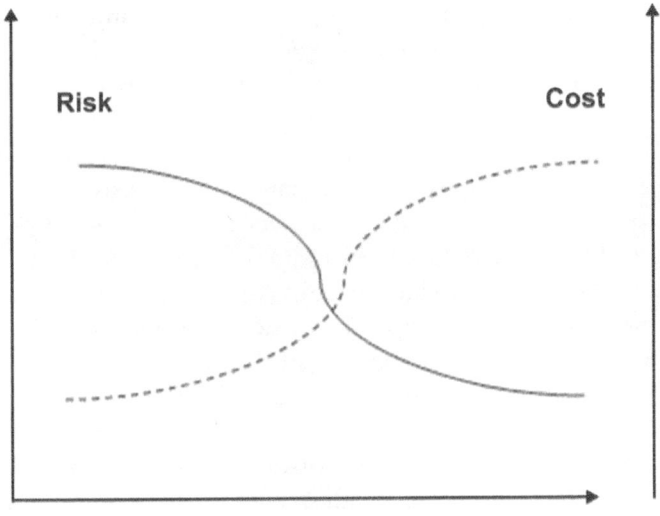

Project Duration

As this illustration suggests, the probability of risk occurrence is highest during the early stages of the project cycle. Even though risk probability decreases as the project matures, the potential financial damage actually increases if risk occurs during the later stages of the project.

Risk Responses

Identification and assessment of the probable risks affecting a project is an important step, yet insufficient without developing suitable responses. These decisions are based on the data provided by the risk management team regarding which response would be appropriate for the specific event.[5] The six possible responses to project risks include *mitigation, avoidance, transference, risk sharing, retention, and monitoring.*

The first logical step in risk management is to mitigate or reduce risk. This can be done both by reducing the likelihood that the event will occur and by reducing the impact that the adverse event will have on the project, if it were to occur.

Risk can be avoided altogether by changing the project plan in such a way that the condition causing the probability of the risk in question is eliminated. Though it is impossible to eliminate all risk events, some specific risks may be avoided before launching the project simply by proper planning. An example of this would be choosing a proven vendor over a newer, low cost supplier.

Another response to risk is to transfer the risk. This is not eliminating risk. Transferring risk simply means passing the inherent project risk to a third party for a price. It ensures that in the event of a risk event occurring, the costs from such an event will not affect project performance. Those costs can be absorbed by the third party involved in the transfer transaction. One method of transferring risk is through a fixed price contract. For example, a contractor factors the costs of possible risks into his initial pricing strategy.

Another method of transferring risk is through insurance. Only some types of risks are easily insurable. These are mostly risks caused by natural calamities and acts of God which are in most cases associated with low probability and high consequences.

Risk sharing is a technique whereby portions of risk are allocated to different parties. This may be done through industry-wide consortiums and other such partnership arrangements. Sharing risk can in some cases cut project costs. Partnerships between owners and contractors have prompted the development of continuous improvement procedures to encourage contractors to suggest innovative ways for project implementation. Usually the costs and benefits of the improved process are shared on an equal basis.

Sometimes a conscious decision has to be made to accept the risk. Some risks are simply unavoidable. In such cases the chance of occurrence is usually rather low and the project owner prefers to assume the risk. In other cases, a budget plan can absorb potential risks. With this scenario, a contingency plan is drawn up to lay out the procedure should the risk materialize.

Additionally, a formal approach to risk management that includes monitoring provides better control over the outcome of the project. Checks and balances are used to track costs and keep budgetary allotments in line throughout the life of the project.

These solutions can be found working separately or concurrently within the scope of the project. The important ideas to remember are that a properly planned response matched to a potential risk will positively impact the project and while risk is inherent to all project undertakings, appropriate responses are a product of proper project design.

Project Leadership

At the front line of a successful project, a dynamic manager can be found leading the way. Diverse in abilities that range from communication to organization and recognition of the different stakeholders in the project, a project manager must coordinate with these different interest groups within as well as outside the organization's functional structure. Of all the interest groups, the core project team must receive priority consideration. This group of individuals is responsible for the success of the project and will work alongside the project manager to produce the intended outcome while at the same time have personal aspirations and differing views on how to best follow through with the project design. An intuitive manager will see these individual competing needs and use these differences to develop strength within the framework of the project team.

Within the company framework, a project manager also competes with other project managers for resources and management support. Often, resources are in short supply and must be shared. Further, a project manager may need to align with functional managers depending upon how the project is organized.

Top management is responsible for approving funding of the project and establishing priorities. They define the measure of success and declare the rewards for achieving it. Their approval is needed for any major decisions that the manager may have to make during the course of the project, whether a course correction or financial adjustment. The manager must therefore be adroit in dealing with the top management.

A project manager may also find allies in project sponsors. These sponsors are the people who champion the cause of the project. Open communication at all stages of product development is especially important with this group. Additionally, constant review and close attention to detail when dealing with sub-contractors, who are major external stakeholders in most projects, will ensure that their contribution impacts the project positively.

On occasion, the project manager may interface with government agencies, vendors and customers during the course of the project execution. Ultimately, a project manager must be able to build a network around all of these stakeholders while giving utmost importance to the needs of the project to successfully follow through and achieve the desired results.

Leading by Example

Co-operative and sustained relationships as described above can be built successfully by using an interactive and visible management style called leading by example. A project manager, by behavior alone, can set the tone for how other people involved in the project carry out their responsibilities. Individuals working on the project get cues on project priorities from the manager's actions, verbalization, and even body language. Likewise, urgency can be conveyed to project stakeholders through stringent deadlines, frequent calls for status reports and aggressive solutions for expediting the project.

A proactive approach to problem solving and the humility to learn from mistakes can create a positive mindset among project players. The project manager also sets the tone for how the team members build relationships with outsiders. Negativity from the leader is reflected by more of the same from project team members. A project manager's performance stands as a benchmark for project team members. Consequently, a lackadaisical manager will not be able to inspire his team to higher levels of performance. Not surprisingly, ethical work habits are the most important of all cues that a manager may communicate to his team members. In many cases, the team members base their actions on how they think their manager would respond in a similar situation. The manager therefore carries the burden of being the ethical soul of the entire project.

Building trust

As previously stated, an effective project manager needs to be an effective leader. One technique to increase effectiveness is to network with team members which lends to team cohesiveness and hence to efficient goal implementation. To sustain these efforts of networking and team building, the manager must, over time, acquire the trust of the project players to be able to exert significant influence over the project implementation. A trustworthy project leader can maintain smooth and efficient interactions within the team.

Trust, being a highly personal trait, is difficult to define and pin-point. It is personified however, through consistency in behavior. Trust is easier to establish through empathy and a burning desire to achieve common good. The willingness to sacrifice personal interests in favor of a higher purpose garners the respect, loyalty and hence, the trust of others. A relationship based on trust and reciprocity can go a long way to sustain a healthy network of project interests.

Leadership Qualities

Fittingly, an effective project manager will show the following leadership qualities:

- Ability to innovate and identify more efficient ways of working while still maintaining stability within the project team.
- A project manager must not get so mired in minutia that he or she fails to step out and see the whole picture.
- A project manager motivates and coaxes individuals while maintaining team cooperation.
- Allow conflicts to settle themselves and sense when to assist with resolution.
- A project manager has to rule with a velvet glove by lending strength to the project team and yet being sensitive and flexible with unexpected occurrences during the course of the project.

The project manager also needs to have the ability to cultivate team members' loyalty to both the project as well as to the bigger organizational goals. A leader can develop each of these skills by focusing on implementing systems that will promote an efficient and effective work environment and being a good communicator as well as learning through personal study and continuing education courses.

Projects in Small Businesses

Having been given explanations of managing risk, what do real-time project risks mean to you as a small business owner and emerging enterprise? There are three governing constraints in projects: cost, time and quality. Since spending more money for projects is usually out of the question and time is always short, quality is usually compromised.

Take, for example, the entrepreneur, Millie, who operates Millie's Interior Decor Services. She recognizes the need for an organized accounts receivables process. She has the software that can create invoices, but no system of ensuring that invoices are created in a timely manner, no rules governing customer credit and no means of monitoring late or slow-paying customers. While the software has most of the tools and adequate file space does exist, the lack of time compromises efficient implementation and the process continues to be delayed. Later, when she realizes she is out of funds, she desperately attempts to catch up and calls customers with outstanding payments only to discover either there was no authorizing purchase order, or that a copy of the invoice was never received.

Creating effective systems that will later become programs are first created through projects. Millie's dilemma is a very common scenario and it stems from the need for creating time to plan a project. Some projects will require the use of advanced spreadsheets, software and Gantt charts. However, most will require only a few steps. In the case of the receivables problem, let's launch the project together.

Project Scope Management
Millie's Interior Decor Services

Objective:

Create a system for accounts receivables from customer credit applications, sales orders, terms, and collections.

Outputs:

1. Customer credit application
2. Sales order acknowledgements
3. Performance of services confirmation
4. Invoicing including progress billing
5. Account collections

Events:

1. Begin July 1: gather 3 drafts of customer credit applications and 3 sales order acknowledgements that can be modeled for use in Millie's Interior Decor Services by July 7th.

2. Create invoice layout by July 9th.

3. Organize folders files and copies by July 10th.

4. Create accounts receivables aging report by July 12th.

Performance Requirements:

Use software package to create form layouts. Work with Phil, the accountant, to get copies of credit applications, sales orders and invoices. Use software and get familiar with aging reports.

Limits:

No funding for software redesign; must use what is in software constraints without modification. Unable to hire assistant, must be simple program requiring less than two hours per week.

Communicate and review:

Demonstrate to my partner, Kris how the process works and train her on filling forms.

This is a project framework. With a little discipline and effort, a clear vision for a customer account process has been created. Now Millie has the tools and a timeframe wherein to operate and accomplish what needs to be done. In coordination with her accountant, Phil, she will pull together several forms to use as templates for her own services. After she has implemented the system she will need to monitor herself and her partner, Kris, as a working program.

Program Management

Using Millie's Interior Decor Services again, we will explore the management process for implementing a customer accounting system.

With the documentation, reports and systems in position Millie and Kris are ready to launch the accounts receivables program. They have decided that the when a new customer is initiated, the other partner is responsible to make sure the customer application is filled. Kris has agreed to process service hours into invoices and Millie has agreed to print weekly aging reports and make collections calls.

In this simple example, you have been given a demonstration of how some planning put Millie in control and helped her to establish a system for customer handling and controls. With the stress of poor cash management reduced, Millie is now able to use her energies positively and direct them in a more productive direction.

The inherent risks to this project and the continuing program that is the result include not following through with each of the steps, possible system failure and communication breakdown. Millie will need to use a file backup system and good technical and accounting support to manage the first two risks. Communication breakdown may be a risk that is accepted and Millie can take steps to insure that she and her business partner follow through with the tasks assigned.

Technology Projects

At times, a company needs to update technology used to assist with business functions such as management and accounting. Abandoning a working, familiar system and moving to the new and unfamiliar can be a daunting task. You may face the risk of migration of your old data incorrectly or losing it altogether. You could tackle this situation by running both systems parallel for a while. You should also ensure you have secured a back up of your old data so that you can retrieve it in the event of a loss.

Any new project faces the risk of untrained personnel or inadequately trained operators. More so in the case of an accounting system installation where the staff is used to working with the old system, there will be some resistance to change. This risk can be controlled by providing lots of appropriate training, and running old and new systems parallel until everybody involved has a good understanding of what is expected of them in facilitating the new system.

External players like vendors, customers and others are also affected by changes to existing systems. The business stands the risk of losing business or in the least, the goodwill of trusted partners if they do not understand the new system. Documenting the new procedures and communicating them to all involved will go a long way in diminishing this risk.

Let us examine a hypothetical situation where you seem to have outgrown your current accounting system and want a complete revamp. You are all set to proceed with new software, but, you ask yourself, *will the changeover be smooth and what risks are involved when one tackles a project like this?*

First of all, you face the risk of choosing an inappropriate system. Begin by making an assessment of what your current system lacks and what you need your accounting system to do as your business grows in the future. Study your current system and what requirements currently exist. Examine the possibility of making changes to ongoing work processes or the way the system is used. Choose the new system you would like to incorporate based on this research.

During this process you will be careful to choose a system that works well for you, and is "built to last". One of the risks you will face is that of obsolescence. This risk can be mitigated by ensuring that the new accounting system has the capability to grow with you.

When you make the decision to change the behind-the-scenes operations whether in financial or management programs, take a logical, steady approach and do your homework. Seeing the latest and greatest at a trade show or in a trade magazine article may trigger your emotions. Be wary of pitches for technology that will ease your workload with 'one touch'. These programs may prove at best to be a distraction. Keep your eyes wide open, even to the possibility that your current system is functioning just fine and focus on growing your business.

Administrative Projects

Meeting customer needs on the one hand while on the other hand increasing efficiencies to remain competitive presents a definite challenge to the owner of any business enterprise. Implementing quality controls will address both sets of problems. A quality management program requires the development of a culture that will instill the belief to your employees and to your customers that customer satisfaction is important. You will need management controls to support this culture and techniques to carry out the steps of quality improvement.[6]

The four major steps in quality control include quality planning, data collection, data analysis and implementation. Keep in mind that putting a quality program in position is a project for the Quality Control Project Team.

Additionally, the process of quality control should address both formal and informal control processes. The informal facilitates active planning and coordination, while the formal documents the planning and keeps the team focused on the objective at hand. The control process involves establishing a company-wide quality improvement team. The task of the team is to communicate philosophy, develop experts to enable use of the appropriate techniques and employ sub-teams to do the same in a hierarchical fashion. Each team will then establish requirements for products and services, detailed process requirements for each product and gaps between outputs and customer requirements. The teams employ appropriate quality techniques, analyze data, and continue to set even higher objectives as the previous ones are met.

Teams should be kept separate for different functions. The objective of these teams is to include all major business functions on the team, for the process of designing both the product and the process concurrently. The practice of putting functional professionals together shortens channels of communication and facilitates quality implementation and training.

While most quality control projects take years to complete, you can choose the extent to which you carry out the project. Developing and implementing quality control within your company is the important thing to remember.

Customer Satisfaction Programs

Customer satisfaction is, without argument, the most important objective of any organization. Customer satisfaction is achieved not only through ensuring production quality but also through ensuring that what you are making is what the customer wants. A customer satisfaction program therefore aims to find a fit between operational output and market requirements. Two factors that could tear down a customer satisfaction program are the delivery systems and changing customer needs. Controls can be put into place to alleviate the risks of these two factors.

Your organization may have all the systems in place to ensure that your product conforms to the highest quality standards yet a breakdown in delivery causes even the best product to fail in the customer's eyes. Whether brick and mortar, e-commerce or a combination of both, this risk can be mitigated through ensuring that your shipping system is efficient and reliable. Where the delivery systems are electronic, you can overcome problems with delivery by ensuring access to high-speed networks and by installing sufficient guards against data theft and hacking.

A dynamic market can also be a risk that could be encountered when striving to achieve customer satisfaction. As newer technologies emerge, demand patterns change within the client spectrum. This necessitates keeping in touch with the latest developments that could affect your customers. Setting up controls to help you keep in touch ensures that you are able to handle customers changing demands as they occur and hence ensure customer satisfaction, always.

Chapter Summary

This chapter demonstrated how Projects and Programs can assist you in taking a structured approach to the changes your organization will need to make as you grow and evolve. View the implementation of each new control as a project; this will give you time to review the impact and effectiveness of the new control.

Once operational, your project is now ready to move from project to program. A program is a routine function of your business. Controls successfully migrated from projects to programs will stand the greatest chance of survival. Remember businesses, just as people, tend to be creatures of habit. As you integrate controls, you will often find an initial outcry of discomfort and complaints. Work with the team to remind them of the long-term benefits and that everyone will be stronger with the support of the resulting changes.

Control projects should be well planned. The greater the control system to be integrated, the more complex and detailed should be the planning. No project flows without challenges. Be willing to accept some struggles along your path of development. All great accomplishments are created through great struggles. Just as John Locke from the television series *Lost* explained, "A struggling moth cocoon would be killed if you were to remove its thin coat; it needs that very struggle to finish its development cycle." As you struggle with your own efforts and learn together with your team, greater will be your achievements in your projects and resulting programs.

CHAPTER THREE

Entrepreneurial Controls for Fraud Prevention

Small businesses are vulnerable. Consider the tendency of a small business owner to steer toward the self-defeating behavior of poorly controlled operations that only survive at present because of the seemingly exceptional advantage that the chaos gives them. For a time, extraordinary margins are posted; yet, when the margins are erased and the inefficiencies are exposed, the company soon flounders, and the owner looks for a quick buyer or closes shop. By recognizing this tendency toward poor controls you as a business owner can avoid these common entrepreneurial mistakes along an already bumpy road to success.

The efforts of this chapter will hopefully ensure that these common mishaps are not repeated by you as you grow your business. Some of these mistakes can lead to costly errors. Increasingly, the most predominant consequence of poor controls is fraud. Fraud is defined as the deception, falsification, lying, embezzling, manipulating, bribing and any other activity that takes personal advantage of another for personal gratification. A study in 2004 revealed that fraud is a fast-growing threat to all business sectors and can be found at all levels within a company.

Reality Check:
Curbing Corporate Fraud

More and more, employees, managers and executives alike are succumbing to the temptation of defrauding the companies they work for. Even more alarming is the fact that over 80% of all fraud cases were committed by people that have no previous criminal history. Perpetrators are seen at all levels, with 12.4% being at the executive/owner level.

Curbing the corporate appetite for fraud begins with making smart choices to tighten controls which can prevent fraud. The checks and balances that are necessitated by internal controls do much to alleviate the temptation that prevails in an easy-come, easy-go uncontrolled work environment. Ethics can help as well, but one of the best ways to curtail fraud is by implementing controls within the business environment.

Source: Association of Certified Fraud Examiners, www.acfe.com

Lack of Controls Invites Fraud

The lack of controls invites fraud into your work environment. There are three factors that make the workplace ripe for fraudulent activity include:[1]

- Motivated offenders
- Available targets
- Absence of control systems

The efforts of this book are to protect your organization in the two latter issues as the first issue of motivated offenders is mostly a product of society. The next issue, available and unguarded targets, presents multiple opportunities for fraudulent activity. Furthermore, the level of potential fraud is proportional to the perpetrator's authority and level of access to property, documentation and assets. Hence, an enterprise with no or poor controls presents a higher probability for fraud. Reducing the opportunity for fraud and creating a culture of fraud awareness will offer long-term results for building a safe and secure business.

Motives for Committing Fraud

The largest motivator for committing fraud is typically monetary gain though sometimes fraud is carried out to make the business appear stronger than it may actually be to obtain higher stock offerings. Either way, deception is the main vehicle where monetary gain is the motive. Unscrupulous employees can sense a weakly controlled business environment and often make plans to take advantage of the situation.

Most white collar fraud begins simply as "borrowing." An employee takes a pen, then notebook, then calculator, then helps himself to more office supplies, and can progress to the point where he is secretly withdrawing self-made promissory notes from the business, and telling himself that he will repay this loan from the business. Self-deception and rationalizations such as "It's only a temporary loan" or "I've earned it anyway" are the most common justifications for fraud.

Rationalization may also include such remarks as "Everyone is doing it" or "The company can afford it" along with other explanations to assuage their guilt.

Other motives for committing fraud include greed, revenge and ego. Employees may feel they have been wronged by their employer and are well-justified with getting even and taking vengeance into their own hands. These feelings often escalate due to resentment against the "system," and since it is corporate America that controls the system, then taking back what should be theirs from the system becomes an open door leading to embezzlement and theft. Some individuals believe they are above the system and not subject to its laws and principles. These personality types are motivated to commit fraud by demonstrating their superior intellect to feed their egos.

Fraud Profile

While everyone is vulnerable to the temptations of fraud and can justify the previously mentioned motives, a certain profile can also be used to determine the possibility of fraudulent behavior. This profile includes the following:

- High school or advanced degree graduate
- Intelligent, competent and highly respected
- Attentive to detail and order
- Complicated lifestyle
- Has long history in same industry
- Uses stolen funds to repay debts
- Does not expect to be caught
- Does not consider himself or herself a criminal
- Average of 4 year history of stolen funds prior to discovery
- Not criminally prosecuted
- Does not repay the organization
- Does not serve prison sentence

As frustrating as it may seem, most common offenders do get away with their corporate crimes due to their lack of prior criminal record and the nonviolent nature of their offenses. Let this profile serve to provide a sense of urgency for implementation of your control systems. Better to prevent losses from occurring than to expect that stolen property will be returned, regardless of the circumstances.

Five Categories of Occupational Fraud

As previously mentioned, fraud is defined as the deception, falsification, lying, embezzling, manipulating, bribing and any other activity that takes personal advantage of another for personal gratification. The term, occupational fraud, more narrowly describes the misuse of employer's funds for personal gain.[2] There are five categories of occupational fraud that you will recognize right away as perhaps obvious; yet, as deeper exploration continues into each category, look for ideas on how to protect your investment, and how to position yourself to reduce such fraud risks as much as possible.[3] The five categories of occupational fraud include:

- *Sales and collections fraud*: sales, cash handling, customer kickbacks, and rebate abuse.

- *Purchases, vendors and payment fraud*: vendor contract manipulation, vendor kickbacks, bribes, purchasing frauds to bogus entities, award manipulation, improper billing, unauthorized purchases and other acquisition schemes.

- *Payroll and personnel fraud*: resume, timekeeping, benefits, health, unemployment, expense report fraud and manipulation. This is perhaps one of the most complicated areas and certainly the source for the majority of lower value, but higher frequency fraud.

- *Equipment and repayment fraud*: purchase, financing and maintenance of equipment used as part of the operations process. This category is usually more vulnerable to highly capitalized industries and public shareholder scams.

- *Inventory, storage and warehouse fraud*: Of course, inventory can become an easy target for theft as well as storage items, but this area continues to plague small businesses with lost revenues and added overhead.

When a company's control weaknesses including document disorganization, lack of segregation of duties, and poor reconciliations function at a high level of disorder, then the fraud resistance level is low. In other words, the more controlled and organized the business environment, especially pertaining to documentation, segregation of duties, and reconciliations, the more resistant the company will be to fraud. Figure 3.1 illustrates a representation of the fraudulent activities which emanate from inside these weaknesses and work their way outwards.

Figure 3.1

Notably, the stronger the core organizational controls, the lower the susceptibility to fraud will be.

Reality Check:
Risky Business

Manage your business so that such a letter is never sent to you:

Dear Mr. Lay,

Has Enron become a risky place to work? For those of us who didn't get rich over the last few years, can we afford to stay? Skilling's abrupt departure will raise suspicions of accounting improprieties and valuation issues. Enron has been very aggressive in its accounting—most notably the Raptor transactions and the Condor vehicle. We do have valuation issues with our international assets and possibly some of our EES MTM positions.

The spotlight will be on us, the market just can't accept that Skilling is leaving his dream job. I think that the valuation issues can be fixed and reported with other good will write-downs to occur in 2002. How do we fix the Raptor and Condor deals? They unwind in 2002 and 2003, we will have to pony up Enron stock and that won't go unnoticed.

I am incredibly nervous that we will implode in a wave of accounting scandals. My eight years of Enron work history will be worth nothing on my resume, the business world will consider the past successes as nothing but an elaborate accounting hoax. Skilling is resigning now for "personal reasons" but I would think he wasn't having fun, looked down the road and knew this stuff was unfixable and would rather abandon ship now than resign in shame in two years.

Source: Watkins, Sherron (August 24, 2001) Letter to Ken Lay, Enron. US House of Representatives.

Internal Controls Procedures

The term "Internal Controls" refers to the management plan of the organization and the systems and procedures in place to ensure the following four objectives:

- To provide accuracy of financial data
- To safeguard assets
- To promote operational efficiency
- To comply with management policies

The absence or a weakness within the internal controls procedures will eventually lead to loss whether through fraud or just the natural course of sloppy business management. Quickly review what should be in place for a tight set of controls to be effective and mentally go over your organization to check off these points. The organizational structure should provide for appropriate segregation of functional responsibilities through controls. Also, a system of authorizations and recording should provide accounting control over assets and liabilities. Organizational responsibilities need to be assigned according to the individual's competence and qualification. Lastly, an effective managerial supervision and review system should be used to gather system feedback and initiate self-correction.

The tone of the control consciousness is set by the management where control procedures and guidelines are developed for the whole organization. Control procedures developed within this framework will achieve specific control objectives. The focus during this part of the process should be on the objectives and not on the procedures. Management monitors the effectiveness of control procedures through exception reports and internal audit examinations to determine whether control objectives are being accomplished.

Components of an Internal Controls System

In addition to understanding the objectives, you need to understand that internal controls comprise the following five components, namely:

- Control Environment
- Risk Assessment
- Monitoring
- Communication
- Information

Each of these components work together to create an internally controlled environment that perpetuates progress and profitability. The core environment is secured as the continuous cycle of risk assessment and control activities keep a tight circle of awareness on what is happening and how the events are unfolding. The flow of information into monitoring activities that is then dispersed by the flow of communication which is also monitored provides safe operating boundaries, protecting company interests and assets.

Following the illustration below are definitions pertaining to each component briefly described and listed above.

Figure 3.2

Control Environment

The control environment is the level of control under which the organization operates. It is reflected in the attitude, awareness and actions of the employees, management and owners towards the control procedures.

The control environment is strengthened when those involved acknowledge that its primary function is to control the climate within the organization. It forms the foundation for all other components of internal control.

Risk Assessment

Risk assessment is the process an organization goes through to identify and analyze the relevant risks that may affect the achievement of its objectives. The purpose of risk assessment is to identify, analyze and manage risks that affect the entity's ability to accomplish its major goals.

Once risks have been identified, management considers their significance, likelihood of occurrence and how the risks should be managed. Management may take steps to put in place plans, programs or actions to address specific risks or it may decide to accept a risk because of cost or other considerations.

Control Activities

Control activities are the policies and procedures established by management to ensure the accomplishment of objectives and mitigation of risks. They ensure that management directives are carried out correctly and in a timely fashion.

Control activities are put in place to achieve specific objectives. These control activities work as a continuous cycle with risk assessment activities to provide security to the control environment.

Information and Communication

The internal control system should be designed to identify, capture and exchange information in a timely fashion to enable accomplishment of the organization's objectives. Management's ability to make appropriate decisions in managing and controlling the entity's activities and to prepare proper financial reports depends on the effectiveness of the information system, including the accounting system.

An effective accounting information system identifies and records all valid transactions; properly classifies transactions for financial reporting purposes; measures the value of transactions in accordance with acceptable measuring criteria; records transactions in the proper time period; and presents the results in the form of financial statements.

Communication involves conveying a clear understanding of roles and responsibilities to personnel. Defining the lines of communication and setting up guidelines enables them to act when the unexpected happens.

Monitoring

Monitoring is a necessary part of internal controls for monitoring involves the assessment of the design and operation of controls and the implementation of corrective action if necessary. Monitoring can be done through ongoing monitoring procedures that are built into the normal recurring activities of an entity. Such procedures include regular management reports and supervisory activities.

Notably, internal audit is considered to be one of these tools. Implementing and supporting monitoring activities which affect an entity's operations and practices such as internal audit should be established and exercised by third parties who include customers, regulators and others.[5]

Signs of Controls

What specifically are the signs of an organization operating under these controls? There are four specific criteria to identify and look for in your organization:

- Financial and operational information will be reliable and trustworthy.
- Operations are achieving your targets for effectiveness and efficiency.
- Enterprise assets are accounted for safeguarded.
- Activities are in compliance with laws and contracts.

Recognizing that these are also all-inclusive categories, successful implementation and attainment of each element is possible at all phases of business. Remember, one purpose of this book is to show you how to look for significant weaknesses and discrepancies in your system, how to make corrections and what to do if or when the problem persists.

These weaknesses and discrepancies can manifest within your business as fraud and therefore a working internal control system is the best fraud prevention. In addition to creating and maintaining internal controls, you need to understand the formal fraud prevention guidelines set by the government that will assist you as you endeavor to keep your business safe.

Introduction to Fraud Prevention Guidelines

In response to escalating corporate fraud in the 1980s, the Federal Government established the United States Sentencing Commission (USSC) Guidelines manual.[6] The USSC identified seven points for organizations to consider while creating an environment that will assist with the prevention of fraud and deception. These points provided the foundation to many later developments in the area of controls and preventative measures. Organizations need to establish the following:

- *Compliance Standards*—policies and procedures capable of reducing criminal activities.
- *Top Level Integrity*—this is the perspective taken by senior management that business leaders lead by example. Cultures are created from the top down with the highest ethical standards required by senior management.
- *Effective Communication*—training programs would include employees in each level of business. This communication should provide education on prevention of fraud and criminal activity.
- *Due Care*—you would not hire a drug addict as a pharmacist's assistant. Screen employees properly in their respective position. If they have had a history of embezzlement and theft it may be best not to place them in the customer returns department.
- *Compliance Monitoring*—through audits and testing making sure policies are followed and procedures are adhered to in order to reduce fraud risks.
- *Enforcement*—consistent means of providing disciplinary action that is applied to all employees regardless of position or history in the organization.
- *Follow Up*—provide a system for employees to voice their concerns about potential threats. Your system should have some whistleblower procedures and protection; these policies can be included in your code of ethics.

Keeping these seven guidelines as ideals when designing your internal control system will help you to safeguard against the many different situations where fraudulent schemes could be attempted or even successfully executed.

Continuing Fraud Education

Within the business environment, different types of fraud exist. Previously, occupational fraud was discussed and you have been shown that care must be taken at all levels to prevent opportunities for these fraudulent activities to be promoted.

Other types of fraud within the business environment include identity theft, management theft, insurance fraud, invoicing fraud, payroll fraud, and cash and credit card theft.

Described as the manipulation and assumption of another's identity to gain advantage, identity theft along with personal fraud is now a growing business fraud area as well. Criminals are using business identities to make purchases, defrauding suppliers with complicated purchasing schemes. Also, with new spoof email capability, thieves can make the authorizations appear to come directly from a given domain source, making detection more difficult. Of course, using business identity for check writing and banking is not new, but it still represents a growing threat to business owners.

Management plays a critical role in fraud prevention within a business. This book was written to help create systems and provide training to reduce vulnerabilities to fraud within the business environment. When a management employee or possible group of management employees conducts a scheme which defrauds the company, you need to be able to detect the theft and respond quickly. Let all employees including management know that they are trusted, but that all activities will be monitored. Honest employees welcome the fact that they are being monitored. When an employee has nothing to hide and is given clear, upfront expectations about standards and code of conduct, there is never a conflict of interest with the use of monitoring.

Insurance premiums on small business remain very high. One of the key reasons for these high premiums is fraudulent claims. Damage left by unscrupulous business owners impact everyone. Unfortunately, theft, fires and other disasters are often initiated even by the business owners themselves who seek to recover business losses or shield themselves from bankruptcy. Insurance fraud is a growing problem which causes the honest business owners to suffer from the consequences of these poor choices made by the dishonest few. When you purchase insurance, it is often in your best interest to shop for a policy with a high deductible. This will help to reduce your premiums and still protect your business in the event of a major catastrophe. Additionally, a higher deductible will often reduce your number of claims and help keep your policy premiums from accelerating. This may mean you will not be able to report every small stolen item or broken window, but a higher deductible, in the long run, establishes you as a low risk/high yield account for your insurer, and they will be motivated to keep your business in their portfolio.

Disorganized businesses are often exploited with false invoices and requisitions. Invoicing fraud is a concern that can be prevented with careful planning and proper controls. One area that should be high on your controls priority list is your purchasing department: most especially with the documentation and payment process. Get organized and this threat can be greatly reduced. For example, require two or more signatures for every purchase order to ensure that the power to purchase is a shared power. This one procedure will eliminate the temptation to use business orders for personal use or gain.

Corrupt or simply lazy employees may take advantage of a weak controls system in payroll processing and commit payroll fraud. From monitoring hours, documentation and signatures, to termination records, get organized and protect yourself from this crime. The simplest way to put prevent this type of fraud is to invest in an automated timecard system. Automated timecard systems can be purchased for a few hundred dollars and will link employee timecard activity to a personal computer, allowing you to directly access the recorded time punches. In my experience, I have seen thousands of dollars saved per month in this important tracking system. Another good suggestion is to look at sharing liability with a Professional Employee Organization. Often for a modest fee your business can tap into extraordinary services which sometimes will include advance expertise in such areas as workman's compensation, benefits administration, and payroll taxes.

As more and more businesses carry less and less cash, cash theft risk is decreasing. Yet, with this transition comes the increase in credit card theft at the employee level. Make sure all customer credit information is kept extremely secure. Stolen credit card information will not only make you liable for potential bank losses, but the negative publicity can be extremely embarrassing and disruptive to your business.

Reality Check:
JetBlue Crash-landing

A crash-landing for JetBlue's PR was caused by uncovering an employee credit card theft ring. Four JetBlue employees and a city corrections officer were charged with stealing credit card numbers from JetBlue passengers. The "JetBlue 5," as they have become known, used the card numbers to go on a "spending spree" that included "restaurants, liquor stores, and shops including Bloomingdale's and Victoria's Secret."

Sadly, three of the alleged culprits were Customer Service Representatives and one was a flight attendant. As for the city corrections officer, what was he thinking?

Learn from JetBlue's mistakes and make proper controls paramount when accepting credit cards for payment at your place of business.

Source: Meghann Marco, www.consumerist.com, May 1, 2007

Application of SAS 99 in Small Business Fraud

While private business is finally realizing the importance of implementing controls as a preventative measure against fraud, publicly traded companies have long been regulated through accounting standards and are required to pass rigorous external CPA audits. The Statement on Auditing Standards or SAS 99 was created in an evolving document by the AICPA (American Institute of Certified Public Accountants) and is seen as a seminal document on fraud control.[7] Considering the standards of the publicly traded companies along with everything else that has been discussed will positively impact your policies in building an environment of fraud awareness:

- *Professional Skepticism:* look at all documents presented with a questioning mind. Do not take on face value that information from other employees is complete or accurate. Mistakes are made and occasionally misrepresentations are intentionally made. Accept that people can change over time and need it is important to remain constantly vigilant.

- *Assessing Fraud Risks:* business owners should have knowledge of the risks involved in both their industry and their personal situation. With multiple locations, checks and balances should be in each location. Any accusations of fraud should be documented and archived. Should vulnerability exist that could have made the accusation a potential reality, steps should be taken to fill the gap. Management should be communicating regularly to employees on the awareness of fraud and reasons for using controls.

- *Significance of Fraud:* risks should be identified in areas and probabilities of the risk becoming reality then placed. In your small business situation look at receivables with your own eyes, and ask: *what is the probability that someone could deposit a check intended for the company into a personal account? If the same person is receiving checks and making deposits, what safeguards do you have that all activity is legitimate? What adjustments can you make?*

- *Management Overrides:* time is short and you must have something done right away. Before you skirt around the policies you have put in place to save time just this once, you should ask: *Are you authorizing individuals to bypass the procedures you put in place to protect the business? If they bypass this once, how likely is it to continue? Does your example show others that controls are only required when it is convenient?*

- *Transaction Concerns:* On a regular basis, check and double check transactions that have been recorded. While reviewing transactions, keep in mine: *Are there unusually large transactions on the books? Are you aware of and have a process to qualify all approved vendors? Who frequently are entries made into the accounting system?*

Review of Fraud Evidence Using SAS 99 Benchmarks

SAS 99 uses auditing benchmarks whereby auditors review discrepancies and relationship issues. These benchmarks can be relevant to your situation as a small business owner and will increase your awareness level of your record-keeping system. As you review your books, keep in mind these auditing benchmarks:

- *Unauthorized balances:* If you do not understand any number on your balance sheet or income statement, ask questions. Do not simply assume your accountant or bookkeeper is in control. Leaving the books to "them" may prove costly. As the business owner, you are ultimately responsible for any discrepancies even if your accountant or bookkeeper makes the mistake.

- *Authorization to access assets and systems:* Employees with excessive access to some or all systems and assets of the business pose a threat. Only authorize employees to the access that is necessary to complete the relevant tasks at hand. You want to allow access to most items on a temporary basis with the understanding that authorization is for one-time use and that the authority will end with the completion of the task. (For example: keys to be returned, or password and authority changed at end of task).

- *Rumors of corruption:* Take rumors in your enterprise very seriously. Do not dismiss simply as gossip. Never find yourself the source of rumors, but if such comes to your attention—take action and investigate. In a small business you may not have the luxury or resources for misplaced trust.

- *Missing or altered documents:* Pay attention to checks and purchase orders before signing. Any unfamiliar vendors on checks may be worthwhile to research what the company had purchased, who authorized the purchase and to find a proof of receipt. Many small businesses are scammed by bogus invoicing schemes.

- *Missing, inflated or outdated inventory:* Small businesses often lack inventory control. Ironically, for many contractors and manufacturers this will be your quickest undoing. Verify your inventory levels, even if only performed on a spreadsheet with a hand count. Better to have a trustworthy process now than to wait until your enterprise can afford the latest industry application software.

As we continue to migrate toward stricter accounting controls for public companies and larger non-profit organizations, private enterprise will continue to see an increase in the need for governance and controls. Much of this is motivated by the banking community. Bankers expect borrowed assets to be well-handled to maximize the company's ability to repay the funds. In recent years, more banks have been requiring loan recipients to generate CPA-documented, compiled, reviewed and audited financial statements. Expect this trend to continue. Organize yourself that such financial documentation is readily available.

AICPA Controls Program

Additional information for specific guidelines pertaining to the process and procedures that should exist in an antifraud control program has been established by the AICPA through the document, *"Management Antifraud Programs and Controls."*[8] The first six items deal with the culture of the business and how to create a culture of integrity and honesty and an example of what behavior is acceptable. Again, to educate you as a small business owner in your endeavors to prevent fraud, these procedures are presented for your review. They include:

- *Tone at the Top:* Corporate officers and directors need to create an attitude of ethical integrity at the highest levels. This behavior should model standards for the rest of the entity and should be set as an expectation for all employees to follow. "Lead by example" and "practice what you preach" are the guiding principles in setting your tone at the top. Do not expect others to do what you are not doing yourself.

Reality Check:
Tone at the Top

"Mr. Sears had a clear choice. Instead of respecting the integrity of the government's procurement system, he chose the financial interests of his company over the best interest for America," stated Paul McNulty, US Attorney.

Michael Sears, former CFO of Boeing Company, pled guilty on November 15, 2004 to aiding and abetting acts affecting a personal financial interest. From

September 23, 2002, through November 5, 2002, Sears aided and abetted Darleen Druyun, then the Principal Deputy Assistant Secretary of the Air Force for Acquisition and Management, in negotiating employment with Boeing while she was participating personally and substantially as an Air Force official overseeing the negotiation of a $20 billion lease of 100 Boeing KC 767A tanker aircraft.

Michael Sears was contacted in September 2002 by Darleen Druyun's daughter, herself a Boeing employee. In a series of E-mails to Sears the daughter outlined her mother's intention to retire from the Air Force and the type of position her mother would accept after retirement. As a result Michael Sears and Darleen Druyun met in a private conference room at the General Aviation Terminal of Orlando Airport on October 17, 2002.

When top officers concede to corruption, a culture of fraud often permeates the entire organization.

Source: Department of Defense, Press Release, February 18, 2005.

- *Positive Work Environment*: When employees have positive feelings about their environment and their contributions they are more likely to stay clear of fraud and corruption that would shed negative light upon themselves. Create a positive peer pressure environment which will encourage employees to be honest and fair. Remove negatives from your enterprise. Ask yourself the following questions about your workplace:
    - Are employees afraid to deliver bad news?
    - Do others perceive that there are inequities in behavioral standards?
    - How do employees generally feel about their workplace?
    - Do you operate autocratically or diplomatically in decision making process?
    - Are wages fair or considered below average?
    - How open is communication?
    - Do employees have support if they voice a contrary opinion?
- *Hiring and Promotion Guidelines*: To increase chances of creating a positive environment and avoiding fraud, management needs to create some hiring and promoting standards. Prior to hiring, background checks should verify criminal records, academic and professional credentials. Regular performance reviews will offer important insights into the feelings and concerns of staff members.

- *Ethics Training:* All employees should be exposed to routine discussions and formal ethics training. This should include discussion about what to do in the case of suspected fraud, how to communicate potential threats, and who should be responsible for that information. Periodic updates should be extended to all employees. This is an investment in the long term health of your enterprise. There is no reason to create long, drawn-out meetings. Make training sessions brief and clear.

- *Disciplinary Action:* Any allegations of fraud should be given a quick and thorough response. The manner in which the enterprise handles the treatment of fraud will set the expectations of how seriously fraud will be prosecuted. Any flaws found in controls should be reviewed and removed. Send clear signals to the entire operation that any illegal activity, irregardless if it is in favor of the business, will not be tolerated.

- *Code of Conduct:* All employees should be required to sign a code of conduct statement acknowledging they are both aware and understand the behavioral requirements and restrictions in the organization. This does not need to be a lengthy dissertation on ethics, just a clear message stating they will be fair, ethical and honest in their affairs of the business.

Reality Check:
Code of Conduct Sample

No set formula, no prescribed requirements for any elements in an organization's code of conduct exist. Well-crafted codes of conduct should include elements of ethics, disclosure, compliance, confidentiality and reporting standards.

- *Measure Fraud Risk:* The organization needs to consider what specific risks the organization may encounter. Estimates should be made as part of the risk management strategy, including worst case scenarios. This may often paint a bleak and frightening picture; however, it is part of creating your survival package. Remember, risk does not go away if it is ignored. Often it can become more of a reality than if the risks are acknowledged. Quantify risks as nearly and clearly as possible. The objective is risk recognition, probabilities are then weighed to determine if the event is possible or not. While the following Reality Check may or may not have any bearing on your life, in your business it has real significance. Remember all business activities entail risk, which is acceptable. Just be aware of those risks and the probabilities of their occurrence.

Reality Check:
Risk versus Reward

Let's assume your dear Uncle has passed away and would like you to have a portion of his estate. To gain the inheritance he has written in his will that you must be present at the funeral over 100 miles away in order to collect your portion, $10,000 inheritance. The drive, as will every automobile use, may include a fraction of a percentage that you will be involved in an accident that will completely destroy your car, valued at $20,000. However, you have insurance in just such an event with a $500 deductible. You have effectively transferred this risk over to the insurance company of $19,500, in exchange for a semiannual fee.

Now you can calculate that on 100 miles your probability of the event is less than 0.002% (based upon one accident every 500,000 miles). Multiplied by the balance of the uncovered deductible, your risk rate is $0.10. So you reason, for a dime's worth of risk, it is well in your best interest to attend the funeral and collect the $10,000 inheritance.

- *Mitigating Risk*: As mentioned in the prior inheritance example, your risk of a total loss on the vehicle has been mitigated by the offsetting insurance. The risk of fraud is reduced by putting systems and controls in place, reducing the possibility of mismanagement to an acceptable level. Reducing risks through controls, transferring risks to insurance companies are types of risk mitigation.

- *Monitoring Internal Controls*: Do not assume because you have properly set controls they will remain in that position. The process should also include intervals of monitoring to ensure that controls function as designed. Because we are creatures of habit, it is sometimes easier to function in the environment without the newly establish controls; not surprisingly, old ways resume and once again controls are non-existent.

- *Audit Committee*: While establishing committees may seem to be a large organizational function, it does not need to be such an involved process. A committee can be composed of two people with a shared vision. In this situation, your internal audit team should have access to all information and authority to make inquires into questionable activity. Your internal audit activities should be flexible and able to adapt to your business situation. At the entrepreneurial level, the auditing team should be nimble, cost-effective and direct. Do not preoccupy yourself with great formalities and bureaucratic rhetoric.

- *Management Integrity*: In publicly traded entities, as with all companies, management may sometimes have different agendas and personal desires that conflict with the organization. Make certain your managers adhere to the policies. Follow the "do as I'm doing" principle of leadership.

- *Internal Auditors:* This is a specific component of the internal audit committee. As you evolve, you may be required to pass an external audit from an accredited CPA firm. If you are already having internal audits, this will provide significant gains over a company with few controls and practices.

- *Independent Auditors*: This is the external agency referred to above. This level of auditing is a required component of publicly traded companies and large funding requirements. Prepare accordingly, a foundation of control will accelerate this process and voluntary auditing of this nature will keep your business running smooth.

- *Fraud Examiners*: If fraud is suspected and evidence demands investigation that may be out of your skill set, include the opinion of an expert in fraud detection. Use caution and care prior to any accusations, such could be subject to slander and civilly punishable allegations if unsubstantiated with some compelling evidence. Never attempt to gain a confession on your own from an employee without proper knowledge or consent.

This extensive list of procedures acts as a guideline for publicly traded companies. Just because you are small does not mean you are exempt from developing a plan to prevent fraud.

Fraud Squad for Entrepreneurs

Most large organizations have advanced teams for dealing with developing fraud prevention procedures. While the more elaborate systems of teams and committees are necessary in these large companies, some of the simple elements should be implemented into all sizes of companies. While there is no system that guarantees the prevention of all crimes, what is expected is due diligence in preventing fraud. Subjective in nature, the phrase "due diligence," found in the rules upheld by the Securities Exchange Commissions, essentially sets a "best efforts" expectation. Since your organization is most likely not subject to Securities Exchange Commission rules, due diligence will refer to your best attempts at preventing fraud.

Creating a charter for fraud prevention is a valuable document for your internal controls team. This charter ought to include three components:

- *Fraud investigation*: Investigations into fraud and unethical behavior and any violations of the code of conduct are highest priority activities and as such the enterprise will take all reasonable action to prevent further abuse or expansion of the alleged activity.

- *Fraud squad*: The fraud team should create a network of professionals that can help respond to allegations. This would include using Accountants, CPAs, Fraud Experts, and Police Investigators to find timely resolutions to the problem at hand.

- *Protective measures*: Recommendations for corrections and deficiencies are to be taken seriously from all levels of the entity. From the most junior member of the organization, when vulnerabilities are exposed, they need to be documented and analyzed for their risk potential.

Control Self Assessment

Formally evaluating and identifying areas in need of control within an organization is an important process to understand in addition to everything else that has been presented for fraud prevention; this process in larger organizations is known as the Control Self Assessment (CSA). You will now become acquainted with the concepts and tools used in the CSA and with some techniques that you can apply directly to your company. The CSA includes groups of individuals who take different methods of surveying their work environment to help management close the gaps found in the current controls system. There are a number of positive outcomes achieved by going through the CSA process:

- Management becomes involved in the internal controls process.
- Soft controls are identified.
- Members of the team are willing to take responsibility for control and establish personal ownership of the control system.
- Control teams can focus on areas of weaknesses rather than attempting more generic strategies.
- Validation for the need of controls will be established.

There are three major programs for executing the CSA and each has its own advantages and disadvantages. By becoming familiar with each technique you can use the method that will best help your organization develop a controls system. The three most common CSA methods include team workshops, surveys and management analysis.

Facilitated Team Workshops

In a team workshop setting, use a format to study the business process from several different angles. An objective-based format discussion will center on what the business is attempting to accomplish with current controls. Then the discussion will try to pinpoint the risks that are not fully or effectively controlled by existing controls. The objective of the workshop is to ensure that the controls are working reasonable well and that exposure to risks is minimal. The team workshop may be conducted on a risk-based format, which starts with identifying the risks likely to be encountered in the process of achieving the business goals. Through this process, all the risks, threats, obstacles, and possibilities are listed, and control procedures are examined to verify that they cover all but the minimal, acceptable levels of risk. In this process you will go through the entire goal-risk-control cycle, like you would at the time of installing new control procedures.

Another focus for a team workshop may be the controls themselves, and how effective they are in the current environment. In this exercise, the risks and controls are identified before the workshop, and the team only discusses how the controls take care of the risks while taking you closer to achieving your business goals.

Using a process-based format, your objective is to determine the difference in what you need from the control system, and what you are actually getting. This means selecting a set of activities that constitute part of a process or processes, taken from the beginning to the end. These processes are then studied in detail, including intended aims of the process, underlying risks and control procedures. The discussion in the team workshop using this format will delve into the process in great detail, and is a valuable tool when one or two processes need a complete overhaul with the objective of working toward process improvement, and is not restricted to control systems alone.

Surveys

A CSA program using surveys comprises preparing a questionnaire aimed at the intended participants of the controls improvement initiative. It is useful when the participants are geographically separated and cannot be brought together for a workshop. The questions have to be designed carefully and intelligently and require only simple yes/no types of answers so that the data generated from them can be easily analyzed and used to finalized plans to facilitate change.

Management-Produced Analysis

This tool is often used along with other initiatives in a business-wide control systems assessment program. It is mostly carried out by teams in support roles who analyze current control procedures. The intent of this analysis is to increase understanding of given characteristics of controls. This input can then be used by other CSA initiatives to improve the control environment.

All CSA initiatives assume that there is a control system in place, that the team involved in the CSA is aware of risks and control concepts, and that the team has good communication skills. The reports generated by CSA techniques may be used to strengthen the existing control procedures and also to review them from time to time.

Chapter Summary

This chapter has captured the urgency of fraud prevention within your company. The most effective way to accomplish this task is by implementing a flexible, managed control system that functions within your organization and takes the guesswork out of operations and management activities.

Fraud is the most prevalent when a lack of controls is evident. Unscrupulous employees can sense this vulnerability and more often than not, will exploit this weakness. Preparing an internal control system will assist you in preventing fraud within your organization.

Tools such as a Fraud Squad and the CSA, and your internal controls team will be effective in helping you to create an environment of fraud awareness. By mirroring techniques used in big business, you can harness the power of controls that will benefit your company and protect your assets from fraudulent activities.

As a small business owner, you need to take a proactive stance in the fight against fraud. The key to curbing fraud in your company is the internal controls that you implement within your organization from top to bottom.

CHAPTER FOUR

Design and Implementation of Operational Controls

Overwhelming is an understated description of the task to drive innovation, sales, operations, service and support in addition to monitoring all of these activities as well. This kind of pressure can drive some to teeter on the edge of insanity. To make the whole chore less burdensome, the next few paragraphs will break down some basic fundamentals for creating operational controls. Before continuing, keep this simple truth in mind: *There is no single all-inclusive formula for managing a business.* Your company is unique and must be directed and governed accordingly. If you do not know your weaknesses, this book will hopefully expose them and demonstrate how they can be exploited either intentionally or blindly by others to your detriment.

Growth is not accidental. An overnight success is always years in the making; it's just that no one sees the "behind the scenes" process of becoming the overnight success! Whatever size you plan to grow, the key element will be your plan and internal controls need to be a formidable part of that plan.

The first several chapters have introduced the many concepts of entrepreneurial controls and risk management in terms of their broad application. You are now going to be given specific steps to create your own system of controls. A review of these control processes will be beneficial when tackling systems that are new to you. Keep in mind that you will need to make some time to plan, strategize and implement changes.

As you look around your office, inventory, customer counter, service center, manufacturing floor, and any other location where you conduct business, ask the questions that are directed to you in this chapter. The first step to being in control is exploring all processes and identifying weaknesses. Once you know where weakness exists, you may decide that the remedy cost is much higher than the risk of threat. At this point, accepting the risk is a perfectly acceptable option if the cost of implementation exceeds the cost of prevention.

> **Reality Check:**
> **Balance: A Fine Line**
>
> If you operate a flower shop and conduct a few hundred dollars in cash daily, then it may not be in your best interest to hire an armed guard service to make cash deposits. In fact, such a service may actually draw unwanted attention to your operations and make it a target for armed robberies. Point being, the cost of prevention must be lower than the risk exposure.
>
> However, in that same flower shop it may be worth spending a few thousand dollars for a point-of-sale electronic system, especially if you have more than two employees. Finding a balance for your security needs and with your budget is a fine line. As you create priorities, you will find ways to maintain balance between necessary controls and excessive regulation.

This chapter will also delve into various documents throughout your organization. Additionally, good practices will be reviewed along with other common but vulnerable systems. Next, you will take a "tour" of your operations: from the sales process through purchasing (where much time will be spent); then on to inventory, warehousing, production, quality controls and customer support. Each subject will be examined for strengths and weaknesses; then, advice will be given on avoiding the common pitfalls while creating a controlled environment.

Document Control

Control systems may sound like they are all about documentation and recording and you may be wondering if they are going to bury you in a pile of paper. Take heart as nothing could be further from the truth. A good control system aims at setting a path for growth while organizing data into ordered information systems which will help reinforce measured growth.

One of the first steps to building better control into your business is to get a grip on the documents that your business maintains and the flow of paperwork throughout your operations. This process is called document control. It includes the management of documents to a higher degree of reliability for security, version, visibility, availability and, most importantly, with a controlled and reliable audit trail.

Process and Theory

So what must document control achieve? All of the business documentation should be accessible at any level, based on appropriate roles and need-to-know information for decision making purposes. A list of the key points in document control includes the following ideas:

- The system must establish a framework for document controls over the period of the document life cycle. It should cover controls over document creation, change management, management approvals, and regulatory filings as well as include real time as well as historical reporting.

- Document control should be a dynamic process involving all levels and areas. As changes are made in the process and process controls, the documentation systems and procedures must also be altered to reflect these changes. Isolation of document flow can lead to compliance and quality failures and create gaps between documented objectives and process implementations.

- The control process should provide an audit trail. This means every point of control in the business process must include an act of evidencing the control procedure.

- Changes to documented procedures and processes must trigger appropriate organizational training processes.

- Facilitate document control in offline and email environments. As process documentations, SOP's, supplier contracts are collaboratively managed, it is critical that offline and email based document controls are implemented. In many cases, documents must be worked on by remote suppliers without requiring access to your document management environment.

It is critical that all these documentation changes and approvals are captured in your system in offline environments.

Paper Flow in Practice

Increasingly, the term "paper flow" refers less to actual paper and more to the document handling process through the document's life cycle. Typically, high volume transient documents will not require the same levels of control as will high value permanent documentation. For instance, the life cycle of routine emails within departments is very short, and such correspondence does not need to be highly "controlled". It helps to have a policy on what email can, and must be discarded and what needs to be preserved as part of a paper (or non-paper) trail. On the other hand, mission statements and business policy documentation have a high permanence and need to be stringently protected.

Having a tight control mechanism for all documents would not be appropriate; however, having no control mechanism for any documents is unimaginable. Certain documents like key processes, specifications, submissions to regulatory bodies, standard contract terms and strategic plans naturally demand a greater degree of attention. The ability to know when particular features appeared in a document, why; who approved any changes in a document, and who was advised of the new version is often essential. It is not essential to know this all the time for every document. However, the ability to locate that information instantly, with total confidence in its reliability when it is required, is absolutely necessary.

Achieving Effective Document Control

The advantages of effectively controlling your documentation are numerous. While the why is obvious, the how may be a bit ambiguous and therefore frustrating. By breaking down the process into four main purposeful activities, you will be able to successfully organize your documentation to fit your needs. A document control system should:

- *Enable creation, approval and filing of all documents*: Choose a system that covers the entire document life-cycle, allowing the existing documents to be available for re-use as well as integration into historical records and storage systems.

- *Be auditable*: Your system needs to incorporate controls that leave behind a visible audit trail.

- *Be mobile*: If your business operates from many locations, or you have mobile field workers, you should look into a system that can provide documentation functions on site, whether through email or PDAs or on dedicated networks.

- *Be accessible*: Choose a system where documents are easily accessible to provide feedback to the quality processes.

By planning your system with these four points in mind, the end result will be a document control system that will accommodate all the document needs of your business. This step is imperative because a well-designed document control system lays the foundation for a strong controls environment.

Managing Confidential Documents

Every business generates records and documents that are sensitive in nature and require some level of confidentiality and secrecy. Employee and customer records, customer financial data and vendor information form a part of these sensitive records. Leakage of this information or poor handling of these select documents can have serious legal, financial and business repercussions. To maintain confidentiality of important documents, your company should establish a storage and disposal program by implementing the following steps:

- *Review all documents and records generated by your company.* These could include payroll records, customer lists, tax records, personnel information, vendor information, memos and scratch paper, general wastebasket contents, computer data and microfilm.

- *Set up retention schedules for documents.* You may be able to consult with industry trade organizations to learn about legal retention timelines.

- *Determine how the confidential information will be stored and destroyed.* Simple recycling is not always effective, because the data may not be rendered unreadable for some time after being picked up or dropped off at a recycling center.

Documentation and Human Resource

Human resource documentation comprises mainly employee information and payroll information. You should keep a personnel file for each of your employees, containing every important job-related document, including job applications, offer letters, employment contracts, benefits and salary information, government forms, performance evaluations, and disciplinary actions.

As a rule, most employees or former employees have the right to inspect certain types of documents from their personnel files. You can be present for this inspection to make sure nothing is added, removed or altered. Generally, you should treat personnel files as you would any other private records. Limit access to those with a need—or a legal right—to the information. A reasonable policy might allow access to you, the employee, and the employee's supervisor or manager, as necessary, to make personnel decisions.

Sales and Revenue Controls

An objective and accurate sales forecast is one of the founding principles for all budgeting within the organization. It is also one of the most difficult and complicated from which to secure reliable data. There are many advanced forecasting and sales modeling tools available; however for the new enterprise with little history, such tools are helpful but less reliable, since they are based upon trend analysis.

Gaining measurable control over the sales functions takes a combination of many elements including the sales organization, product, pricing, distribution and sales methods. In order to lay the framework in this most critical aspect of your business you will need to ask tough questions and anticipate necessary adjustments in your strategy.

Sales Plan

In creating your strategic and operational plans, you will need a sales plan along with a forecast. As you prepare for operations, your sales plan must be credible and attainable, with forecasts based upon product delivery which include delivery of each component of the sales cycle. The most challenging portion is estimating future sales based upon current product, market conditions, pricing, as well as subjective data including customer demand. The three types of methods for establishing a sales forecast are:

- Analytical
- Judgmental
- Statistical

The figure below illustrates the different forecasts in relation to the sales plan. These forecasts are of a revolving nature and need to be revised at regular intervals.

Figure 4.1

Analytical Forecasts

This broad category includes advanced tools from market share simulation to end-use projections. A listing of these tools includes:

Market Simulation: This involves a model of the existing market and modifying input based upon a variety of conditions. It is a powerful tool, but usually more costly.

Product Line Analysis: This takes a look at your sales channels and the distribution methods based upon region or sales partner niche.

End-Use Analysis: This works well if you are in an industry where the number of products to be sold per year can be forecasted based upon historical data. This works well with larger purchases for which the government tracks and provides data such as homes, automobiles and larger appliances. Since the majority of enterprises fall outside these parameters, it may not be of benefit to your organization.

Market Share Analysis: This is similar to End-Use Analysis where one must have access to data for the market as a whole if this information can be accurately estimated this can be a great foundation to build a credible sales plan. Often trade journals and magazines contain articles pointing out different sectors of your industry. It would be well worth researching these publications to find credible market information.

Judgmental Forecast

This process gathers data from several sources including executives, sales staff, and customers:

- *Executive opinions:* The first group, executive opinions, is based upon experience, market conditions, product position and history. The questions for gathering data from this group are fairly subjective questions about what executives think of their forecasted sales and the reasons for their answer. Often it becomes more of a guessing game, but some key members of a company may know their market very well. Because of its subjective nature, this forecast should be weighted with the others to test for feasibility and probability.

- *Sales staff opinions:* The next group to approach for sales forecasts is the sales staff themselves. Each sales member should know his or her market fairly well, with the exception of new product introduction into a new market. If the survey is limited to a new product in an existing market, the sales team should be able to build up some estimates. The sales staff is closest to the actual sales event and is in a sensitive position to know of current market dynamics. They are also responsible for fulfilling these targets and are often conservative by nature, self-preservation being a driving force. However, one should be wary that sales staff may tend to increase projections beyond reality when market conditions are strong, and may understate potential when market conditions are soft. Further, when compensation is tied to this estimate, then these estimates may be quite low because better perceived performance (low estimated sales/high actual sales) will bring higher compensation to the sales team.

- *Customer forecasts:* The third class and perhaps most important, is a forecast from customers. The data will be specific to your product and as much of their own forecasting has been made, in the cast of wholesalers, this may offer valuable indicators for your own market. Some wholesale customers may also provide you with a sales forecast in order to ensure that your operations are prepared to service their demands; this also provides an opportunity to resolve issues that may limit potential sales due to an unknown constraint, such as a product missing certain features, undesirable product pricing or product support issues. Of course, for retailers dealing with end-use customers, such forecasts are most likely not an option.

Statistical Forecasting

This category of sales forecasting requires a variety of mathematical methods requiring a skilled technician and software to arrive at forecasts based on sales efforts, campaigns, and other variables. Time series analysis creates a computer-modeled trend based upon extrapolated data looking at seasonal patterns, cyclical trends and random fluctuations. A correlation analysis looks for patterns of sales behavior based upon similar trends from correlated resources plotted against an index or correlated set of data. In the entrepreneurial world, statistical methods, though the most accurate in terms of setting expectations, are usually not the most cost-effective nor most available as the other requirement, history and trend data, are often elusive and hard to track.

Regardless of how your plan is constructed, the key is to create a sales plan, as this plan will provide financial control for the organization as a whole; for after determining a sales plan, a budget can be created and accountability will be assigned and limitations will be put in place.

Other helpful tools for collecting potential customer information as you determine your sales plan include: trade journals, state governments, libraries, publications such as Business Week, universities and economic development centers. From the US government you have U.S. Bureau of Economic Analysis, *www.bea.gov* one of the most extensive sources for consumer data available in the United States. Other sources include U.S. Department of Labor, *www.dol.gov*, and many other industry-specific government websites.

Sales Organization

Having an assigned and responsible individual to manage sales is critical to the success of any venture. This individual must understand and accept the burden of sales production and will be essential in planning, forecasting and growing your business. Often in small startup situations, this person is also the President. There are many benefits to the President making active sales calls and helping to close deals. If there is a match for his or her skill set, there could be a high degree of success resulting in many long-term customer relationships.

The bottom line to your success in sales is to have a responsible and dedicated individual over sales. Many startups attempt sales as a team effort; for those that have survived, they know this is a common mistake. One person must bear the burden for making the sales materialize. Others may play secondary positions but the responsibility must rest with a key member of the team. Young companies often make great sacrifices to recruit and retain sales talent; it is not uncommon for the highest paid employees of an entrepreneurial venture to be among the sales staff. This level of compensation is not to be envied but accepted as a part of the risk and responsibility that the position also carries.

Sales Performance Standards

Prior to closing the sales process, agreement on the sales plan must be made. The sales manager needs to concur that estimates are accurate at which point these estimates become the sales target for the predetermined sales period. The formation of these projections is based upon the best tools available to the organization and it becomes a cornerstone for all other enterprise activity. Sales targets must be fair to both the sales staff, not overly optimistic to create unreasonable pressure, as well as fair to the business, not overly conservative that little or no growth is projected although more can be reasonably anticipated. Sales projections and forecasts are to be reviewed at least on a monthly basis, allowing management to make shifts in activity in response to market conditions.

The purpose of these targets is to provide management with the ability to control the sales effort. There is no other aspect as vital as your sales if you have no targets and objective goals, you have no sales controls. Without sales controls, you business is shooting in the dark, a dangerous and unproductive activity. If sales are not happening as required, behavior and strategy will need to be modified, yet without a clear objective, there can be no strategy.

Sales Process Benchmarking

In order to achieve the desired results, the organization is going to need to set forth the effort corresponding to the target objective. For each of the questions below your enterprise will have its own targets and standards based upon your product and market. Moving through this list will be a good exercise in developing controls and will ensure that your Sales Executive has parameters by which to monitor progress. Just as operational duties are closely monitored and regulated, sales positions should also be judged by their entire performance. Review the follow questions with your sales team:

- *Internal Sales Criteria*
  - What are sales calls per orders made ratio for existing customers?
  - How many new customers are made per call?
  - What is the per dollar promotional effort made to number of inquiries made?

- o   How many prospects are on each sales queue?
- o   What is the average order size?
- o   Why does the company lose prospective sales?
- o   What is the number of units or volume sold per customer?
- o   What is repeat sales ratio? What are you doing to improve this?
- o   How is follow-up performed and measured?
- *Representatives*
  - o   Who are your agent dealers and representatives?
  - o   What efforts are made to support these representatives?
  - o   Are profits sufficient to motivate representatives?
  - o   What feedback can each representative provide about their market?
  - o   What is your target number of representatives?
  - o   What efforts can be made to obtain new agents?

Sales Quotas

Armed with an achievable sales plan and executive buy-in, sales executives understand the obligation of a quota. Your sales team must be well-equipped to meet these objectives and convinced that the sales targets are attainable. When compensation is commensurate with the efforts required and a well-formed plan is established, sales staff should respond favorably to sales quotas and understand their significance to the organization.

Quotas should be based upon weekly, monthly, and yearly expectations. While some may contend that once a quota is reached the sales staff may reduce their efforts. This may well be appropriate as the now burden falls on operations to delivery promised goods and services. Yet, if a sales team relaxes, what generally happens is an overall slowdown and it takes time to get the sales engine running again.

Point being, sales is what drives profitability and if that sales process slows down or stops, so will operations. Consider the old Aesop fable, the tortoise and the hare: Which animal won the race? However you chose to measure your sales performance, the bottom line should maintain activity toward sales formation.

Reporting Sales Activities

As an entrepreneurial venture, you have little time for needless data and reports. However, one reporting area that cannot be shortchanged is the Sales Report. This should be an objective sales sheet providing core information that will lead up to monthly sales objectives. My experience has taught me that weekly and monthly reporting provides data that will give solid benchmarks for senior management to set expectations. The sales executive should have the resources available to generate this report. Even using simple spreadsheets can deliver valuable insight to the number of calls, prospect listings, sales targets, anticipated closings and current sales. Sales executives should base performance upon planned quotas. I have also learned that any variation from these targets should be agreed upon by the executive team, not left to the sole discretion of the sales executive.

One simple format that yields high results is a weekly sales meeting with your executive team. This meeting should usually last no more than an hour and should include items from the sales report. Senior management should be close to the issues confronted in sales. If sales losses are the results of poor quality, lack of features, service issues or other components of the sales cycle, the executive team should be informed and make adjustments as needed. This forum should include enough details in the report to measure progress and current sales position. Set up a weekly appointment for the executive staff to meet, placing sales at the foremost of their agenda.

Sales Performance: Excuses vs. Results

Occasionally there will be a need for revisions to quotas and projections. This is part of the program, and a learning element in the business. There are many factors which are out of the hands of sales staff such as natural disasters, economic recessions, or other tragedies affecting the achievement of sales targets. Controls of sales rest upon accountability, and remember, that which you cannot count, you cannot measure. Ensure the targets and objectives for sales are very clear. Weekly, monthly and yearly sales targets should be identified and signed off as accepted by the sales executive.

Reality Check:
Performance is Everything

One mistake common in all young organizations is to become attached to a single person. If your most promising employee fails to live up to his or her promise, let them move ahead with their life, and you with your business. Harsh realities of survival demand results; you will lose customers and profitability and no one will hear your cry as your business sinks into obscurity with the weight of an underperforming or worse, nonperforming employee.

In the case of sales, if your sales executive is not achieving results, make sure time is taken to review issues. When reasonable barriers are removed and sales still languish, do not hesitate to redirect the sales executive either within the organization or to a new position elsewhere. Your business most likely does not have limitless cash reserves to provide secure salaries to whomever, especially when your survival depends upon the potential sales from a well-salaried employee.

Pareto Principle

The Pareto principle seems to apply to all types of performance related issues. This principle is claims that 80% of all results are performed by 20% of the expended resources. In sales the top 20% of your performers will produce 80% of your results.

If you suspect that your sales performance is not reaching into the top 20% of your efforts, make a change. You simply don't have time to waste on average performance. As an emerging business, you must ensure that you have the top 20% working for you and that the other individuals falling into the 80% category are working for your competitors.

Pricing Controls

It is too easy to misprice yourself out of a sale. Prices set too high result in purchase barriers, especially for a new venture. Yet, for the entrepreneurial venture the tendency is to lowball the price in an effort to attract customers. Prices that are too low often raise flags about poor quality and sales can be lost due to those concerns among potential customers.

Both cost and competition need to be considered when creating pricing. This can be done in an orderly format if you have created an environment through researching and identifying both the costs involved as well as your competitors pricing. Outside influences such as inflation, local and international market, consumer price index and unemployment will impact your pricing and should be considered generally.

Your objective is to apply your knowledge to your market in order to accomplish winning the sale with maximum returns. The key to pricing is to remember that there is little room at the bottom and lots of room at the top. This suggestion may sound upside down, but it is a very realistic view of how the market actually works.

Marginal Cost Pricing

The traditional costing method of marginal costing looks at the incremental costs of producing your product or service. Core costs include raw materials, direct labor, variable manufacturing expenses, variable selling expense and variable administrative expenses, fixed expenses directly applied to the product and the sum of total direct costs.

Equipped with knowledge of your marginal costs, you can now add on indirect costs and your profit margin to establish your pricing model. If the enterprise is selling below these costs, it is not making a profit and it is best not to undersell your product as you will eventually run out of capital.

Often margins can be reduced if there is idle product capacity at which a greater reduction of the profit from the sale may be made and still meet margin requirements. This situation will present new issues however, as price reductions often become expected and the customer soon becomes resistant to the "regular" pricing. Further spread of the discount to other products augments the demand for reduced pricing resulting in margins that become eroded and diminished. Stay in control of product pricing and cautiously weigh the occasional discount with the implications of revised customer expectations.

Total Cost Pricing

Total cost pricing varies from marginal cost pricing in that it adds a fixed percentage or rate on to the raw materials and labor, adding overhead including, administrative, sales and advertising, research and development as a percentage of materials and labor markup. Total cost pricing is one of the most common and easiest-to-use pricing systems employed. Since it is based on the full costs of the operations, including target profit margins, it helps to insure the gains from set margins are realized.

There are a number of disadvantages with this total cost model. First, this method of pricing may not recognize optimum profit potential. For example, if there is greater demand and margins have been left at a lower rate, there may be missed revenues. Second, this pricing often fails to account for higher volume activity where reduced margins may be warranted while still meeting total profit expectations. And third, this model does not recognize the differences of profits earned with different margins. In other words, some products may be operating at a much lower margin due to very low volumes while others are operating with a higher base.

Purchasing Controls

There are five key areas that flow through the purchasing process. These areas include vendor selection and vendor inspections; purchasing, purchase requisition, and purchase orders; receiving and inspection; claims; and accounts payables.

The purchasing process is fraught with risk, fraud and embezzlement, and provides a unique opportunity for numerous illegal and unethical situations. The establishment of strong controls and systems could avert severe consequences when proper controls are lacking and unethical individuals seize the opportunity and exploit the weakened position of the company.

Vendor Selection

Vendors need to be selected fairly with appropriate policies to ensure that pricing, quality and delivery terms are satisfied. The purchasing department or the team member in charge of purchasing should be responsible for locating qualified vendors who can provide materials to operations as needed to fulfill customer demands. The following criteria should be part of your purchasing program:

- *Pricing*: While very important, there may be other factors that qualify or disqualify vendors. Lowest pricing may not represent the lowest cost to the business. For example, purchasing from the lowest price vendor with a history of late deliveries may end up costing the organization much more than the amount saved.

- *Availability:* Does the supplier carry stock; pull inventory; or custom-make your order? Can you rely on the vendor to deliver as promised?

- *Capability:* Does the supplier have adequate resources to fulfill this order? Do they have the facility, stability, financial resources to deliver?

- *Quality:* What quality systems are in position to ensure on time delivery? Are they ISO 9000 or do they have some other third party quality verification?

- *References:* Can the vendor provide credible customer references that have current working relationships with this supplier?

Using these five factors during vendor selection will lead you to find the vendors best-suited to supply your business and assist you in keeping your customers happy.

Vendor Inspections

For certain critical suppliers it may be in your best interest to arrange for onsite inspections. This is particularly true of custom contract material. These inspections will provide valuable insight into not only general quality but the attitude and philosophy of management. In addition to onsite inspections, you may require a vendor to provide pertinent information during the decision-making process, before establishing a purchasing relationship. A sample vendor application form has been included with this text and is a draft that can be applied to various business situations and modified as appropriate to your situation to qualify vendors to do business with you. (*See Appendix A-4:* Sample Vendor Application Form).

Using the vendor qualification form you can then create an approved vendor list (AVL). This controlled list documents who the approved vendors are for your company as well as who made the approvals and when. Ensure that a supervisor or someone other than the purchasing agent signs off on the approval as this protocol is part of the system of checks and balances.

Purchasing Process

Once the vendor base is established, we need to set guidelines for how the purchase is to be requested and fulfilled. In the traditional purchase process, a requisition form is sent to the purchasing department by a supervisor. This may take the form of a request for specific products by the production manager or inventory manager. Or it could be a computer-generated requisition based on current inventory levels and production plans.

For example, in a manufacturing plant you will find that requisitions are issued by production departments and sent to the production manager for approval. In a retail organization, overall authorization to purchase product lines may be given to individual buyers by the marketing manager. The authorization limits may be built into a computerized purchase order system, with exceptions on specific limits to be authorized directly by the marketing manager. Store managers also may be given authority with specific dollar limits, to purchase a limited amount of goods.

Key terminology used in purchasing can help to define safe and prudent guidelines for developing a purchasing policy. You may choose to implement these terms and their usage into your own company purchasing policy:

- *Economic Order Quantity (EOQ)*—This is the reorder quantity with the lowest total cost for procurement. These costs are comprised of administrative costs, handling costs and possession costs.

   Q = optimal order quantity

   C = cost per order event (*not* per unit)

   R = monthly (annual) demand of the product

   P = purchase cost per unit

   F = holding cost factor; the factor of the purchase cost that is used as the holding cost

   H = holding cost per unit per month (per year) ($H = PF$)

   Total cost = purchase cost + order cost + holding cost, which corresponds to:

   $$Q = PR + CR/Q + PFQ/2$$

   While this may be more than you care to know about EOQ, you can see that it is influenced by *costs per order* (How much does each order cost, purchasing agent time, administration and markup?), *demand* (What supplies are our current sales demanding?), and *holding costs* (What are the costs associated with holding this inventory, warehousing, cost of capital, attrition, etc.?).

- *Just-In-Time (JIT)*—This is the method of timing materials deliveries to occur at the time the item is required for production and sale. The purpose is to reduce stock inventory down to its lowest possible levels. The concept was originally accredited to Henry Ford and later perfected by the Japanese, to minimize space and warehousing needs.[2]

Two terms that are used in conjunction with JIT method are the *reorder point*, and the *safety stock*. The reorder point is the point used to calculate the reorder quantity. The safety stock is the minimum quantity required on-hand to satisfy demand during a given period. It is the buffer that is needed to protect the enterprise from being out of inventory and losing orders due to the inability to fulfill the orders. Understanding these terms will help you to fully apply the JIT method as your purchasing policy if you choose.

When utilizing JIT, purchase orders, both manual and computer-generated, are reviewed by the purchase department before being forwarded to an approved vendor. In a just-in-time manufacturing process, an agreement is signed with the vendor where the vendor agrees to supply merchandise as and when required by the business's production schedule. A long-term supply contract is negotiated by specifying price, quality of products, estimated quantities and other variables. In this case, specific purchase orders are not issued; instead the production plan is communicated to the supplier with the specified delivery dates. The production plan takes the place of a purchase order.

Purchase Requisition

Purchase requisition may come from any agent within the enterprise. The important part is to create a formal process for which purchasing agent respond to needed material. This will help reduce fraud and misunderstanding, purchasing agents may request items needed for their own use, but this is typically limited to office supplies and materials rather than production materials. Any production inventory and materials should be generated from the inventory or project management team.

One highly successful variation for small businesses to create is to allow purchasing agents to also perform the duties of project managers. This is limited to a job shop based projects, purchasing can be held responsible to minimize inventory, price and lead times.

In the appendix is a draft of a purchase requisition, this document includes some of the standard elements, purchase requisitions should be modified to meet your organizations needs. This document forms part of the business audit and marries with inventory receiving and inspection and invoice prior to payment release. (*see Appendix A-5:* Sample Purchase Requisition)

Purchase Orders

A purchase order is normally issued on a pre-numbered form to avoid duplication of order numbers. Among other information, the purchase order should contain details of the quantity and prices of goods ordered, quality specification and delivery date. Other common elements of a purchase order include descriptions regarding terms, shipping, quantity, cost, tax exemptions and other details. Later, this purchase order will be used by the delivery department to decide whether or not to accept a consignment. The accounts department uses the purchase order to ensure that the purchase was duly authorized and that the invoice is correct.

The actual purchase order itself is the next step in the purchase process. One requirement that serves a unique purpose in working with smaller suppliers is the requirement for a signed confirmation; either the vendor could sign and return the purchase order, or send over an email sales acknowledgement. Regardless, the purchase order should be confirmed and acknowledged. Too many issues caused by miscommunication can result in delays, surprises and frustrations. (*See Appendix A-6:* Sample Purchase Order)

Receiving and Inspection

The receiving department should ensure that the goods received have been authorized purchases, by verifying the purchase order as identified by the number on the vendor's invoice. The goods received should meet order specifications and should be physically counted. A record should be made of the goods being received. Entries for initial receipt of goods may be made by using any of the following methods:

- Pre-numbered receiving documents.
- Computerized record, obtained by scanning all goods received.
- Department direct receiving.
- Just-in-time receiving.

When the receiving process results in the preparation of a pre-numbered receiving document, a copy of the purchase order is reviewed to determine whether the purchase was authorized. One effective control that can be used here is to blank out the order quantities from the copy of the purchase order. This way the quantity counted and recorded is the receiving document and becomes an independent check over the quantity of purchase order and goods received. The receiving department therefore must independently count the goods received. The pre-numbered receiving documents ensure that all goods received have been recorded chronologically, and in the correct period.

Automated scanning improves control and efficiency of the receiving process. Products with bar codes can be directly scanned into the system. Then the receiving department only has to take a few sample counts to verify accuracy. This should be accompanied by a visual check of the goods for quality and breakages or damages if any. The comments of this inspection should be entered into the system. The system should be able to generate a numbered list of goods received and comments about quality in a sequential manner.

When shipments are directed to departments, the department must approve payment for the invoice raised. This method is utilized when there are certain supplies that are specifically allocated for a department.

In the case of goods received from a regular vendor for a just-in-time process, no documentation needs be prepared to record the receipt. Payments will be made according to production within the contracted period.

Reality Check:
Purchasing Scams, a Personal Note

Some con artists take advantage of small businesses (and sometimes even very large businesses) when the purchasing department and corporate payment processing is disorganized. In my own experience, I recall several occasions when I was receiving invoices for various products and services ranging from communication services to offices supplies and had reason to suspect a fabricated order.

One scam I remember must have taken some homework as the scammers first had to locate the name of a buyer within the business. With this information, they would then send boxes of product to the business (very cheap, poor quality) with a PO referencing the purchasing agent's name. At first glance, these products may cause you to think that the order is legitimate; but I caution you, always suspect a shipment that does not include proper documentation and *never* pay an invoice without proper documentation and without ensuring that there is a legitimate business need to support the order.

Other, more brazen scam artists simply send out invoices hoping to be paid. Sometime later a "collections" agent will call demanding payment for advertising services, for example. Yet, there were never any advertising services provided and upon further investigation nor was the collections firm legitimate. Again, proper documentation and confirmations will save your enterprise a great deal of money over time as these are not once-in-a-lifetime hoaxes, rather frequent occurrences in everyday business dealings.

Claims

Claims will have to be made for any discrepancies raised during the process of receiving a delivery. Commonly, claims are made for variations in quantity or quality. Quantity issues will become apparent at the time that the invoices are compared with the receiving document and purchase orders. Upon thorough inspection, any quality issues should be recorded in the system at the time of receipt.

Claims procedures should provide for periodic review and tracking of claims status. The purchasing department should be given authority and trained to have the competency to decide whether the defective goods should be returned or replaced. The accounts department should be kept in the communications loop on all such claims.

Quality Control

Probably the most familiar usage of the term control is when it has been placed with its most common partner "quality." Quality control is critical during the receiving process and the delivery process.

There is a governing principle regarding quality and on-time delivery; learn it well as the price for failing to learn this lesson is your reputation and good name: *Customers will forget and forgive a late delivery, but they will never forget nor forgive a poor quality shipment.* Referring back to my electronic manufacturing days, I am reminded of the times where customers had demanded product to be delivered and the quality process was compromised in place of an on-time delivery. In all cases, defective product was never forgiven. In contrast, customers will forget a late delivery or two (although it's important not to abuse the relationship) and with next month's orders, there will be new pressures and new customer demands to handle and new opportunities to deliver quality product on time.

Traditional Quality Controls Standards

As a business, you always strive to deliver to your customers a 'quality' product. Quality is indeed a subjective term that can mean many things to many people depending upon the circumstances. In technical usage, quality can have two meanings: firstly, the characteristics of a product or service that must exhibit the ability to satisfy stated or implied needs and secondly, a product or service free of deficiencies.[4] "Quality control" refers to a system of evaluating tools used to bring to light needed corrective responses or the operational techniques and activities used to fulfill requirements for quality. It is the act of guiding, or the state of a process in which the variability is attributable to a constant system of chance causes.

Traditionally quality control standards encompass the following concepts:

- *Statistical Control*—This consists of random sampling on the production line to ensure that the output conforms to prescribed performance standards. Variances are continuously tracked and manufacturing processes are corrected in time to avoid faulty production.

- *Product testing*—Under this method of quality control a sample of the product is subject to intense testing for stresses much greater than it would be subject to in actual usage. It is expected that this testing will show up any defects in the manufacturing process. Simple changes to the process can often deliver dramatic results in terms of product quality.

- *Total Quality Management*—The philosophy of Total Quality Management (TQM) aims at embedding awareness of quality in all organizational processes. It goes beyond merely achieving customer satisfaction to encompass maximization of organizational objectives as well.

When quality control falters, your company can lose its' competitive edge and business will diminish. The following discussion tells the woeful tale of the Xerox Corporation which, due to weakened controls, lost its way. They had to learn to run lean and mean before they were able to get back on track and in the black.

Reality Check:
Quality Fix with a Vengeance

Well into the 1990s, Xerox Corporation carried a fabled reputation for manufacturing innovation, by building printers and copiers that combined both high-precision machinery and cutting-edge information systems with a 90,000 headcount.

Yet, by the decade's end, Xerox had lost its way. The "Document Company" could not even straighten out its own billing problems. But Xerox's highly disciplined commitment to a lean Six Sigma program helped save it. This statistically rigorous analytical method breaks down processes to measure and isolate error. Redundant steps are eliminated, and broken steps are fixed.

The road back has been painful, with headcount down by 36,000 to around 60,000 today, but Xerox is profitable again, thanks partly to its conviction about quality. "It takes strong leadership to succeed with Six Sigma. We've gone at it with a vengeance," says CEO Anne M. Mulcahy.

The Businessweek, Small Biz, August 28, 2006

Accounts Payables

In a traditional document-based purchase system, the accounts payable department matches the vendor invoice, the purchase order and the receiving document to determine the correctness of the purchase, and to authorize the payment. If the entire order matches, the invoice can be set up as a payable invoice with a scheduled payment date based on the business's line of credit with the vendor.

Accounts payables should coordinate with purchasing on matters regarding pricing differences between the purchase order and the invoice and whether there was authorization for these differences; to investigate discrepancies in quantity and to issue debit invoices for differences in billing, if any. Accounts payables then transfers the supporting document to the treasury department or the cash desk with an authorization to pay the invoice. All documents should be recorded by the authorized person immediately upon receipt.

There should be procedures in place to ensure that the person making the payment verifies the documentation before paying. All paid invoices and other documentation should be cancelled as 'paid' to avoid duplicate payments. For this same reason, payments should not be made against a copy of an invoice unless the treasury has been authorized by accounts and purchasing to do so, except in certain cases.

Inventory Controls

Accounting for inventories can be a major concern for you not only because this represents a significant investment of money but also because inventories are a vital part of the production process. Inventories have been defined in the Accounting Research Bulletin No.43 Chapter 4, as "those items of tangible personal property which are held for sale in the ordinary course of business, are in the process of production for such sale, or are to be currently consumed in the production of goods or services to be available for sale."[1] Inventory therefore includes produce on a market shelf ready for sale as well as unprocessed raw material in storage at the production facility. Inventory presents many hurdles to management because of its complex nature in terms of diversity of items of inventory, high volumes of activity and use of varied accounting valuation methods.

Additionally, inventory valuation lends itself easily to fraud. Many fraudulent activities involve inflating inventory. Inventory is easily transportable, and can be easily moved from location to location, thus exposing it to security risks. Inventory is often maintained at several locations, many of which may be remote from the business's headquarters. Inventory may become obsolete due to technological advances even though there are no visible signs of wear. Defective inventory can go undetected. Also, determining the valuation of a particular item of inventory can be difficult. Returned goods, if they exist, will need to be separately identified and valued differently.

Inventory Control Philosophy

A good inventory control system will ensure the following:

- Authorization for all purchases.
- Inventory-related transactions are recorded on time, accurately and completely, within the accounting portion of the system.
- Received inventory to be properly accounted for and independently tested to verify adherence to company standards.
- An up-to-date cost accounting system to properly identify costs that are assigned to production and analyze variances from budgets, as well as investigate and properly allocate costs to inventory and cost of goods sold.
- An inventory system that will serve as a basis for management reports and managing inventory.
- All products should be systematically reviewed for obsolescence and appropriate action to be taken once a product is outdated.
- Regular management reviews of inventory to minimize excessive inventories and reduce losses due to technological obsolescence.

The underlying philosophy for inventory control is that your bottom line depends on having proper inventory available to deliver what you have promised to your customers in terms of quantity and quality. Strict inventory guidelines will enable you to deliver or to plan delivery to your customers in a reasonable amount of time for a reasonable profit.

Inventory Counting Systems

It is one thing to have a perfect recording system on paper, but the proof of its accuracy can only be verified by physically checking on the stock position. This is called "taking a count". Inventory counts are a very good control over the inventory management system. Inventory counting may be periodic or a continuous cycle counting method may be used:

- *Periodic Count*: This means to take a physical inventory of all the items in storage on a given date or at given intervals such as monthly or quarterly.

- *Continuous Cycle Count:* Each item of inventory or a group of items is counted together. Inventory counts are taken continuously, throughout the year. When one item or group of items is completed, the next one is taken up and so on until the entire inventory has been counted. With this cycle complete, the process is begun again, starting with the first item to be counted in the cycle.

Keeping a close watch over your inventory is vital to successfully follow through with sales and counting your inventory is another control that perpetuates profitability. Using a perpetual inventory system allows an organization to know not only the current stock of its inventory but also to identify products that need to be reordered, unsold stock that has been sitting idle over a long period of time, or products that may have become obsolete.

In order to reduce the risks involved in an inventory system, there must be sufficient control mechanisms when recording inventory. The inventory system should record receipts and sales of inventory promptly. The receipts and sales should be properly authorized before being recorded and only authenticated records must enter the inventory system.

Obsolescence and Spoilage

Computerized inventory systems provide a wealth of information for a company to systematically review its inventory for potential obsolescence. Some procedures that are effective in searching for possible obsolescence are as follows:

- *Monitoring procedures*: Monitoring sales or age of products by product lines and comparing the sales with past performance and expectations for the current period.

- *Tracking procedures*: Tracking the impact of the competition's new product introductions on the sale of your products.

- *Comparison procedures:* Comparing budgeted sales with actual sales.

- *Reviewing procedures*: Periodically reviewing the number of days worth of sales currently in inventory at any given point of time.

- *Adjustment procedures*: Adjusting for poor quality of inventory based on reports from periodic cycle counts.

- *Projection reviews*: Reviewing current inventory in light of projected new product introductions.

Potential losses due to spoilage (sometimes referred to as shrinkage or dumpage) can be similarly reduced by using a well-designed inventory system. To curtail shrinkage, it is essential that feedback from inventory counting regarding the deterioration in the quality of the inventory is entered into the inventory accounting system and that there are controls to ensure that such information is promptly acted upon.

Customer and Vendor Consigned Inventory

In production and retail situations, it is not uncommon for customers to consign inventory to a manufacturer of some or all the materials they desire to produce. Vendors may also issue materials on consignment for retailers to display and receive payment after the sale has been made. In either case, receive materials as you would if you were making a material purchase.

Indeed, any shortfalls with vendors or customers will come against your organization. Shortages need to be documented and submitted to customers within 48 hours of product receipt. Timely processing will ensure communication is well maintained and that discrepancies are resolved. As you can imagine, many sore situations have been caused by misunderstandings involving consigned inventory. This is particularly painful when, for example, in a manufacturing facility you are responsible for $10 of value-added work per unit, but the missing components (which you failed to document) are over $80 each.

Material Cost Controls

Direct material is defined as material applied to a particular job, product or process and its associated costs. If you are involved in either retailing, construction or manufacturing you know very well the significant of materials controls. Here are some reasons to motive you to make materials controls a very high priority on your controls project list. A materials controls system will:

- Reduce the risks of theft and fraud.
- Prevent production down-time.
- Cut materials waste and inefficiency.
- Reduce the capital needed for funding inventory.
- Scale back extended inventory.
- Produce a solid basis for product pricing.
- Estimate inventory more accurately.

When creating a pricing model, direct material costs seem like a fairly straightforward task. This model includes material used for the sale of product. In creating your cost value for materials you will also need to consider the following significant variables. Each of these variables may have greater or lesser impact on your pricing model. Again, this underscores the value of a strong inventory system and tight internal controls of the materials handling process. These variables that need to be considered are:

- *Scrap*: Some level of scrap exists in every manufacturing process, it is your responsibility to reduce scrap rates and ensure that operations function within your controls. Tolerances for different processes vary; use your control team to coordinate efforts with operations to create realistic scrap rates.

- *Samples and testing*: Sales and marketing will need demonstration units, testing will require products for various tests and studies. Ensure that these costs are visible and that each unit is used as requested.

- *Discounts:* Suppliers often provide volume incentives as well as early payment discounts; these can be factored into your operations as a reduction in materials costs.

- *Freight*: Include costs of inbound materials costs. In our environment of rising energy prices you will continue to see freight costs pushed upon you by suppliers. Make sure you factor this into your cost model.

- Packaging: Often overlooked, the costs of packing boxes, wrapping supplies, tape are direct product costs.

Being aware of these variables will help you to more accurately create the cost value of your materials, see the impact this cost has on your pricing model, and give you a clearer picture of how your pricing model needs to be designed.

Materials Forecasts

There are three common techniques for setting materials requirement standards when forecasting your materials needs. These techniques include:

- *Engineering studies*—Includes evaluating the design and required material quality and quantity.
- *Past experience*—History of costs under similar situation.
- *Controlled test*—Test runs providing simulated standards.

Typically, engineering studies and evaluations are used for anticipating materials needs. Experience and testing can provide corroborative evidence for requirements.

Labor Cost Controls

Labor costs are broken into direct and indirect costs. Direct labor is work that is directly traceable to the manufacturing process for the production of goods and services directly related to the customer use. Direct labor costs include all benefits, such as holiday, retirement and other expenses as well as all taxes and other labor-related activity.

Indirect labor is all other activities that do not directly affect customer product or services. These include human resources, overhead management, administrative and other activities not directly involved in meeting customer orders. Direct employees can often perform indirect labor work, such as training or special activities and allow for some flexibility in your labor accounting system.

Once you have hired your first direct employee, you become very familiar with how expensive and challenging it is to keep employees involved in activities that are productive and generating revenue in a tight market area. The following action items will help to secure your labor expenses:

- *Limit employees*: Use the n-1 rule to help you to determine how many employees you actually need.

N-1 Rule for Employee Hiring

$$AC = n - 1$$

AC = Actual employees on the job

n = number of employees requested

For example, if you need 3 people for a given job, n equals the variable, in this case $n = 3$, and 3 less 1 is 2. Use 2 people on the job. While you will have complaints and some resistance, realize that this is healthy for optimal efficiencies. It is much cheaper to pay a bit of occasional overtime (when under customer duress) than to have hiring and firing waves. Also, limiting layoffs to only extreme situations will keep your unemployment insurance rates down as well.

- *Use an automated time clock.* For a few hundred dollars you can purchase an electronic clock that will connect to your personal computer. You may trust all your employees, but people can make errors and 99% of the time, those errors will not be in favor of the business.

- *Use your past data for estimated time standards on current projects.* While the past is not usually an indication of current situations, you can gain realistic estimates of what is needed based upon your experience.

- *Keep records of labor production and activity.* Learn from your successes and failures. Without knowing your time standards, you are guessing and your success depends upon hunches rather than evidence.

- *Create labor categories that can be used to track time standards.* If you have not been tracking labor, you are in for a surprise for what you estimated would take three hours may end up taking over twelve or more. Without this knowledge, you could be losing money. Most entrepreneurs are optimists with unrealistic time frames and tend to bid low on time requirements. This can be a major setback on labor-intensive projects.

Once you have secured pragmatic expectations for your employee needs, you will more easily be able to determine your hiring needs and develop a plan to control your labor costs. Remember that over-hiring is just as detrimental as under-hiring and uncontrolled labor costs are one of the top reasons a mismanaged business closes its doors.

General and Administrative Cost Controls

Another area where constant vigilance is required is in the area of overhead expenses. Categories of General and Administrative (G & A) expenses include such overhead as salaries, fringe benefits (like a company car), rent, communications, repairs, depreciation, travel and entertainment, dues and subscriptions, utilities, insurance, offices supplies and other nominal expenses related to running a business.

Without proper control over G & A, you will continue to be bogged down and struggle with inadequate profits to fund operations and growth. Be vigilant with your G & A expenses, as these expenses can quickly add up and run out of control. Here are some ways to reduce these expenses:

- Have paychecks approved by supervisors and assure that each check contains the proper deductions.

- Compare your efficiencies with *best industry practices*. You can do this by looking at some of your top competitors; many will be public companies with records available for you to make interpolations regarding your own enterprise.

- Monitor bad debt expenses closely. Customer collections should maintain a very high visibility with at least weekly reviews and aging reports.

- Monitor dues and subscriptions closely to ensure only required services are used. There are many industry groups and coalitions that can benefit your company; limit your involvement to one or two. Remember that these groups are nice, but may not necessarily be contributing to the growth and profitability of your company.

- Charitable contributions should only be made when you have evidence that you are profitable and you know you can afford to make the donation. Remember, you do not need extra tax write-offs when you are losing money, you need profits.

- Telephone, cell phone, internet, fax lines and other communications devices should be limited to only those tools needed for profitable use and use should be limited to business use.

- Insurance expenses can vary tremendously for businesses. By obtaining three bids each year, you will have a realistic view of your insurance current costs and needs and can make adjustments as necessary.

- When you are starting out you want a professional, clean location, and lease rates should reflect your conservative position. The temptation to lease extra space for your "future needs" often backfires and ends up costing more in inefficiencies and waste. Here the n-200(t thousands) sq ft rule applies:

n-200 Rule for Facility Usage

$$FN = RN - 200(t)$$
Actual Facility Needs = FN
Requested Needs = RN
t = Thousands position (1 per each 1000 sq ft)

For example, your operations team says they need a minimum of 5,000 square feet to operate effectively. Using the "n-200" rule you will figure $5,000 - 200(5) = 4,000$ square feet. So the actual facility need equals 4,000 square feet. The request was 1,000 square feet too big. An extra 1,000 square feet of rented space could be enough to kill your profits every month and hold back growth. Keep things tight for you do not have the luxury to waste lease space. If you do lease more than you need, sublet and recover some of those expenses.

- Be frugal on all office expenses and repairs. Unless your business is programming or highly intensive engineering you do not need all the latest and most expensive computer gear. Keep office equipment simple and you will keep costs down.

- Equipment lease rates should be limited to larger acquisitions. Consolidate as much as possible. Depending on the tax consequences, often it is best to purchase equipment as an operating lease.

- Interest expenses should reflect best market rates. Often small businesses incur debt burdens which are difficult to service when rates begin to rise. Debt is a powerful tool. Only use debt when absolutely necessary for the energy required to service the debt tool can often be draining and devastating. Banks generally recognize when your performance ratios are down. Sensing a liability waiting to happen, the bank may call your loan (nearly all small business loans contain numerous "call provisions" where the bank reserves the right to call the note due). If you have ever had loans or lines of credit called, it is a very nerve-racking experience. Develop a good relationship with your banker and branch manager to keep lines of communication open and lines of credit available.

- Officer salaries may or may not reflect market rates. Pay what you are able. Officers of a new enterprise understand that high salaries are often not part of the entry equation. In the beginning, if you cannot pay for talent, you can always train for talent.

Improving Administrative Efficiencies

Many opportunities exist that can be used to cut costs in the area of efficiency. Efficiency will reduce duplication of efforts, lower waste and search time *(... how many organizations lose thousands of dollars in productivity looking for tools and materials that were simply misplaced?)* Take a look at a number of these details and see where your organization can improve:

- *Keep the scene clean*: Removing old documents, re-appointing unused supplies, reducing scraps and reorganizing space can add real money to your bottom line. As an entrepreneur you may think you do not have time to get organized, yet review your productivity once you have a cleared work space. The top-down trickle effect management principle applies here with standards of cleanliness as with all attitudes pertaining to every aspect of your business environment: the level of cleanliness that you maintain in your office space will also set the tone for the level of cleanliness the whole organization will maintain.

- *Eliminate document duplication*: Store used documents in a secure location, then move ahead. Avoid extra or unnecessary copying or document duplication. As a word of caution, keep in mind that most small businesses actually do not keep enough of the proper documentation. If you happen to be on the other side of copy compulsive, remember one secure hard copy and soft copy along with a media backup is sufficient for even the most rigorous audit.

- *Cross-train employees*: Office and administrative staff should know how to perform many functions. Just as the manufacturing environment has undergone great progress using just-in-time techniques, make your office a JIT area. Employees should be skilled to handle workloads of those that are absent. Again, use care that proper segregation of financial controls remains in tact.

- *Balance employee hiring with actual work loads*: Remember the n-1 rule for production staffing can also apply in the office environment. Managing some complaints about too heavy work of a load is much better than handling complaints from your investors and bankers that you are losing too much money.

Taking these suggestions into consideration, examine your current situation and make a commitment to improve your efficiency at the executive level.

Chapter Summary

This chapter begins with offering some suggestions and methods for documentation control, later addressing the types of documents to protect and some practices for keeping the various sensitive documents that surround you at work.

The foundation of budgets and organizational planning, the sales plan, was introduced and discussed. The sales plan should be your highest budget priority. If you create only one forecast, create a sales forecast. This will help set goals that will guide your enterprise, keeping you focused and motivated.

Product pricing structures and systems and the techniques used for establishing product prices were then introduced. This topic led the discussion into purchasing controls at the vendor level. You became familiar with approved vendor lists including methods for vendor selections. An exploratory look at how purchase orders are made included familiarity with some of the systems governing the purchasing cycle. The area of quality controls was explored briefly as well.

Next, materials and inventory levels were reviewed. Knowledge was shared on how to purchase and manage operational concerns in areas of direct materials and direct labors. This material led to the discussion of keeping controls in inventory levels and materials best practices. Direct labor costs were analyzed, and the "n-1 rule" was introduced.

Finally, we studied G & A expenses and highlighted a number of focus and audit points. Included in the discussion were lease rates and the "n-200" rule of space efficiency. The chapter concluded with methods to improve administrative efficiency and specific areas for audit and consideration.

CHAPTER FIVE

Accounting Controls

Through the course of this chapter you are going to become familiar with practical security, monitoring and accounting tools. These are real world scenarios taking you through the process of sales and explaining the specifics of cash handling, sales, inventory, and collections.

At each point along the way, keep in mind what is happening in your business and how can you upgrade controls, when such changes make sense and what tools will allow you to grow your business to the next stage.

Duties of Accounting

Your accounting staff may begin with just yourself in your emerging business, however you will soon find that the daily whirl of business activities requires some assistance. You hire your first bookkeeper and from this position emerges an accountant, then a treasury, staff accountants, receivables and payables clerks, controllers and financial officers. Although your present needs may seem far from needing a complete accounting department, you will find each function is also required in smaller enterprises. Thus responsibilities exist regardless of size.

In entrepreneurial settings many of these duties are merged, that is acceptable but you must be familiar with the risks implied and equipped with the knowledge to know which duties must be separated from the same position (i.e. check writing and check signing). The following is a review of some of the major functions and responsibilities within an accounting department in a large organization:

- *Accounting Manager:*
    - o Oversees all general accounting activities and staff.
    - o Prepares financial reports and ensures the quality of bookkeeping and documentation.
    - o Supervises Accounts Payable and Accounts Receivable Clerks.

- *Controller:*
  - Creates and implements accounting policies and procedures.
  - Administers plan for control of operations, profit planning, investing, financing, sales forecasts, budgets, costs standards.
  - Compares performance with operating plans and interprets results, administers tax policies and government reporting.
  - Ensures quality of data entry and orders recorded.
  - Provides management with timely and valuable information to perform their functions.
  - Establishes pricing guidelines with sales and marketing works with outside accounting assistance.
- *Treasury:*
  - Responsible for raising capital, debt and cash management and fund balance activities.
  - Oversees long term financial planning, forecasts and company-wide cash practices.
  - Liquidity management, ensuring cash is available for present and future requirements.
- *Credit Manager:*
  - Processes customer credit requests, financial terms, limits and credit parameters.
  - Assists in the collections of delinquent accounts.
- *Purchasing Manager:*
  - Purchases supplies, inventory and capital goods for operations.
  - Negotiates pricing, delivery and terms with suppliers.
  - Evaluates vendors and reorder points and stock levels.

By being aware of how a large accounting department is organized, you can adjust these duties to fit your own company's needs.

Petty Cash Controls

From repair parts to reward donuts, there will always be a need for petty cash. Each business's petty cash needs vary depending on the types of transactions, but typically a small business with a million dollars in sales or less should have no more than $300 available in petty cash. Although it may seem intuitive to keep funds locked, sad experience reminds us that we don't always follow our instincts. We may believe that we have established an environment of trust within a business; however, the very nature of cash in easy reach is sufficient reason to store petty cash in a closed container within a safe. This can prevent cash from slipping away and save the petty cash custodian from any unwanted and potentially embarrassing situations. An ideal, and often free, container is an extra deposit bag with a close-able zipper (usually available from your local banker … just ask nicely!).

The petty cash should be maintained by a petty cash custodian, the individual who is assigned to account for funds used and to make records of receipts for expenses. There should be a petty cash journal, ideally an inexpensive notebook to be used to write down who, when, how much and for what purpose funds are used. Since many of these purchases are expensible, you will want to ensure that you have an accurate record of these transactions.

Petty cash should always be just that, petty, so be sure to keep funds in this account to a minimum. If you can operate with $100 or less, then do so. Keep a low profile with the petty cash fund because the amount of petty cash on hand will not be kept secret as your operations will require you and others to use these funds. In short, less money on hand will reduce any unwanted interest in access to petty cash.

Safes and Safe Deposit Box Controls

There are many occasions when a safe may be a great investment. One simple and inexpensive solution may be a gun safe. These safes are often mass produced, and can be secured to your business floor to prevent removal. There is no fool proof system of controls and preventions for keeping cash and other assets secure onsite, but a gun safe works well for this purpose and also makes a fitting place to store blank checks and copies of other miscellaneous corporate documents. If a safe is not yet a viable option for the business, a large locking file cabinet is another option. Keep in mind, however, that even the best brands are easily accessible with a screwdriver. Yet, when used in combination with an electronic security system this may be an acceptable solution for a young operation with still nominal sales.

For security in an offsite location, consider a safe deposit box at your local bank. Original documents and important contracts may be more secure offsite in the event of theft or fire. Keep copies onsite in a gun safe or locked file cabinet as well as instructions for obtaining the originals if you are not available when the information is needed.

Cash Drawer Controls

For retailers with a cash drawer or register you will need to follow some guidelines to reduce your cash shortage risk. First rule in cash drawer management: only one cashier at a time. There should be no exceptions. When servicing customers as a team working from a single register, one person should be assigned to the cash drawer and should be the only individual responsible for entering orders. This person will be certified and trained to the specific features, functions, and processes for the cash drawer. Using one certified cashier reduces the likelihood of confusion in cash totals at the end of the day as well as errors such as voids and over-rings. The protocol for opening and closing the register needs to include counting and recording all cash and checks in the drawer. A simple form should include the number of notes and bills in each category: Hundreds; Fifties; Twenties; Fives; Ones; Quarters; Dimes; Nickels; Pennies; and Other (make a place for the interesting coins and $2 bills floating about). This checklist should have two columns for listing opening as well as closing totals.

When multiple team members share a cash register, each team member should be certified to use the cash drawer and the protocol for each new shift per cashier should include counting and recording the cash totals at the beginning and at the end of the shift. As stated before for single use, a simple form should include the number of notes and bills in each category. This checklist should have two columns for listing opening and closing totals as well. Although this may seem like common sense, it is a process that requires strict observance to protect immediate cash flow.

When two or more cash registers are used, make sure to duplicate the same process for each register and use only one certified cashier per register or per shift. Duplicating this process for each register will keep your records organized.

Cash registers should be equipped with a closing function. If you do not have a register with this capacity, it is well worth the several hundred dollars spent to save you from headaches that can come from too many shortages. Since credit cards are an integral portion of this process, totals from credit cards should be readily accessible at the end of the shift allowing employees to calculate their totals.

The cash transaction should never be allowed to transfer through the register without proper recording. Any errors such as voids, over-rings or miss-rings need to be registered and recorded on an end-of-day tally sheet. Voided transactions should be approved by sales manager and cashiers should never ring up sales to relatives or close relations. Cash drawers should only open to finalize payment for purchase whether cash, check or credit card is used.

The closing process for the cash drawer should include a tape total printed for that register along with the report for cash items listed individually. The credit card report can be included in the daily batch report. End-of-day reporting will vary based upon the card reader and merchant account and verification process. Credit card terminals will be able to print out a listing of each individual transaction and an end-of-day settlement sheet.

Figure 5.1

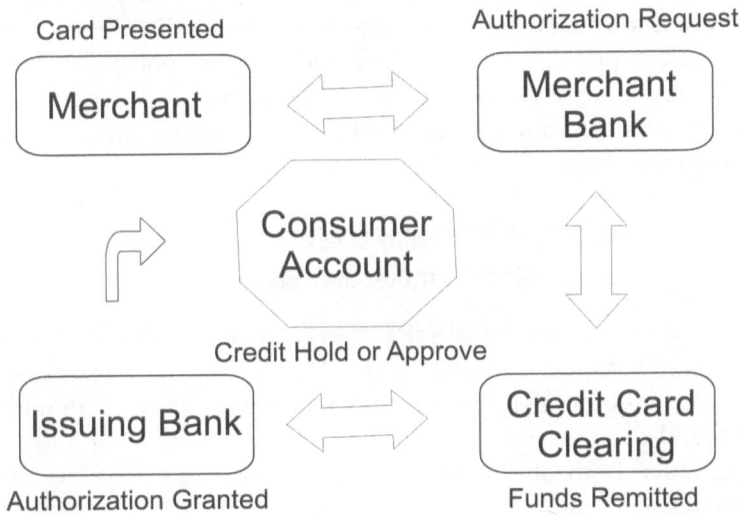

Credit Card Clearing

Card Presented

Merchant

Authorization Request

Merchant Bank

Consumer Account

Credit Hold or Approve

Issuing Bank

Credit Card Clearing

Authorization Granted

Funds Remitted

Point-of-Sale Computerized Cash Register

This process is simplified with the use of a computer-operated POS (Point-of-Sale) system. There are many different software tools available ranging from general use to industry specific programs. You may find it well worth the investment to use a POS system. Do your homework to be sure that the program fits your needs and goals.

When starting up your operations, a fancy, expensive system may just be increased overhead and you could possibly use a basic process as was explained earlier until you reach a certain goal for sales that would justify upgrading and automating your system. If you have the capital and you have budgeted for a POS system from the beginning, that situation is ideal. Still, the most important rule of cash drawer management remains to allow only one certified cashier access either for the entire daily operation or per shift or per register.

Refunds

As an emerging business, your return policy must insist that receipts and original merchandise tags in new condition accompany all product returns. A signed receipt noting the customer's name, phone number and reference to the returned product should accompany all return requests. In addition to customer information, the sales manager needs to approve the final refund.

Many small businesses have time limits for returns and also specify how returns can be credited. For example, in a small specialty shop, you may have a policy that states a return is only eligible for exchange or in-store credit. Or you may choose to simply not accept returns at all. The latter is a good policy for discouraging shoppers from the buy-try-return or exchange routines. This type of policy also commands respect for your products and services and encourages customers to commit when they buy.

Reality Check:
Track Your Customer Returns

One retailer reported a continual variance from a distant plant and warehouse. The amount of customer credits were very large which the manager attributed to employee turnover and merchandising decisions. During an inspection, auditors found that customer returns from the plant were being sold in a local flea market. Most of the inventory sold in the flea market was quality new styles sold below retail.

Further inspections revealed that the customer credits were increasing annually; moreover, records supporting customer returns could not be produced. To make matters more interesting, employees had stacks of customer returns in their work areas. Employees were allowed to purchase any returns and the plant manager said most returns were not repairable.

After review of rejected material, it was noted that the majority of the product was first quality returns, many without any defects. Management had simply been left without controls and a division-wide fraud had spread from management to many employees.

To avoid this scenario in your own company, track your customer returns and the supporting documents—a return can still be a valuable asset.

Source: Trobaugh, Don. April, 2004. Internal Auditor.

Before you begin to sell your products, set up a process for managing refunds. Any increase in refunds should quickly alert you to a potential problem which could be as simple as a defective product, or as distressing as a scheme by criminals to return inferior product with switched labels or knockoffs or unsellable merchandise. Your suppliers have a policy, and you should too.

One sensitive area that continues to plague small businesses is credit card fraud and unauthorized refunds. Pay particular attention to refunds directed to different cards. Because customers do sometimes return product purchased without the original credit card but with original merchandise tags, you will need to create a policy that will prevent charge-backs to wrong accounts. Keeping records of all credit card receipts will help you in the event that you need to verify a purchase. Automated systems will keep these records electronically and save you time in the verification process. You should never authorize a refund without proper identification

Credit Card Security

Credit card control is maintained on two levels: corporate credit cards you use for purchases for your business and customer credit cards for purchasing goods and services offered by your company. Each transaction carries certain specific risks and their control is vital for financial integrity.

Corporate Credit Cards

When not in use, corporate credit cards should be locked in the company safe or kept by owner of the card. As a rule of thumb, treat credit cards as cash. Although there are concessions for false charges, it is much better to prevent losses than to assume that your bank will grant allowances for credit card fraud. As such, credit cards kept in the safe should be maintained in a similar fashion as with petty cash, where a corporate credit card journal is kept for recording the date, time and with whom the credit card left its secure position and for what purchase and/or purpose the card is being used.

Purchases online should be made only at encrypted and well-established trade sites. Some form of antivirus and anti spyware should be in place prior to any online purchases. Some reliable antivirus tools are available to download at no cost such as AVG antivirus and AdAware by Lavasoft. If there are any concerns about network security, it is best to call the order in and place the order directly with a customer service representative.[1]

Customer Credit Cards

Though you would like to think that no one would be involved in defrauding your customers, there are unscrupulous employees who can fly under your honesty radar who may be tempted to retain credit card receipts and other valuable information to either sell or attempt to use themselves for purchases. If any card information is to be retained, ensure that access can only be granted to those who authorized to have that access, namely the owner and the sales manager.

Too many times small businesses create uncontrolled liability by having handwritten notes with credit card data lying around in order to be able to fill the next customer order; this is particularly true of corporate accounts that wish their orders to be filled on a routine or frequent basis. Take the time to keep this information in a secure location such as the company safe or a locked filing cabinet.

Reality Check:
Customer Privacy

Customer credit card information should be handled with the understanding of your fiduciary role as custodian of that credit card data. The news media presents constant headlines of companies that have lost sensitive customer data or information that has been stolen and then used for identity thefts on some third world server.

Consider comments such as this made in this press release "... the specter of such fraud was raised on June 17 when MasterCard disclosed that someone had penetrated the computer network of Atlanta-based CardSystems Solutions, which processes transactions for more than 40 million cards of all brands, including MasterCard and Visa. The hacker gained access to names, account numbers, and verification codes." It is enough to almost want to return to a cash-only system to avoid these kinds of problems. However, the convenience of credit cards in our fast-paced society would be hard to give away.

Source: Brenner, R. & Carter, A. (2005). The Truth About Credit Card Fraud. BusinessWeek, June 21, 2005.

Checks and Check Copies

Checks have to be safeguarded just as much as cash has to be. Checks can be easily forged by a person with bad intentions. Assuming the worst, blank checks must be locked away in the safe, to be removed only when a check needs to be written. Seven control issues concerning checks and check copies that you need to understand are listed below:

- *Preparing and issuing checks:* Just as in the case of petty cash, a check register must be maintained. Even a small notebook will do. You will need columns for the check number, the bank account on which the check is being issued, the amount of the check, the person to whom it is being issued, and the date of the check. Also, an additional column for reference details would be useful. Here, the person preparing the check should write down if the check was sent by mail or through a courier service or hand delivered and also note the date and time of dispatch. The check preparer should not be the one to sign the checks unless it is a very small business with the owner being the one to carry out both functions.

- *Cancelled checks:* Cancelled checks should be voided with lines drawn diagonally across the face of the check and the word "cancelled" written on it. The signature part of the check should be torn off and destroyed. The check register should be changed for the cancelled check number to read "cancelled" with a reason given for why it was cancelled. File cancelled checks with your accounting records for reconciliation as well as safe keeping so that they cannot be misused by unscrupulous persons who may lay their hands on these checks.

- *Depositing checks:* Checks received from customers should be sent to the bank for collection at the earliest possible opportunity. A deposit should be made either in the morning of the following business day or arrangements should be made to make two or more deposits daily depending on the store volume. A register needs to be maintained for incoming checks as well. Columns for writing down the details include the date on which a check was received, the invoice number against which the payment was made, the person from whom it was received and the amount of the check. Additionally, at the time of depositing the check in the bank, another column should be included for an entry to be made in the checks received register to indicate that the check has been deposited.

- *Copying checks:* From the time of receipt and until the time of deposit, checks received should be placed in the cash drawer or safe. A photocopy may be made of a check received for the business owner's records. These copies may be filed away with the accounting information. Also, duplicate copies of checks need to be regulated to avoid misuse. Lastly, never copy blank checks. This will create undue stress and needless liability for you.

- *Check Policies:* Controls on the issuance of checks should include clear guidelines for check requests, issuance and signing procedures. Checks are normally the most popular way of transferring funds into and out of bank accounts of small and medium sized businesses. Policies on check writing and issuance should be tied into the usage rules of the bank account of the business.

- *Signatures:* Put in place authorization procedures including authorized signers for all checks. All checks may need to be signed by two or three people as you think fit. Prepare an authority matrix assigning check signing powers to various individuals depending upon the value of the check and the functional level of the individual in your organization.

For instance a check to pay the monthly utilities billed up to $1000 may be signed by the treasurer and the accounts manager. You as an owner may want to sign any check bigger than, say $5000, yourself, along with your account payables manager, or treasurer. The payee bank needs to be informed of these rules so that checks which do not conform do not get withdrawn. The authority matrix you created should carry the designations of the person who are authorized to sign checks, as well as the names of the people who currently fill those positions. Either the bank will provide signature cards or you should provide the bank with copies of these signatures, and these cards should be updated from time to time. Every time an employee who is an authorized signer ceases to be an employee, the bank should be notified immediately and an alternative signing authority should be provided.

- *Check Requests:* Checks are usually requested by accounts payable or whoever handles the functions of accounts payables or the treasurer. Such requests are raised in response to a routine payment schedule coming due or in line with the credit period extended to the business by vendors. A request raised by accounts payable should be double-checked by the accounting manager or treasurer.

Accounts payables reports must be drawn up monthly and checked for due or overdue payments so that a payment schedule can be drawn up for the coming month. This also makes budgeting easy and allows the organization to take full advantage of the credit period offered without over extending its credit. All requests must be accompanied by invoice copies and an aging statement of the accounts-payables.

Check requests may be made by the treasury to keep the petty cash box at desired levels. It is imperative that the manager check the petty cash expense book as well as the actual cash available before granting the check request, especially if it is being asked for relatively sooner than normal.

Abiding by these control principles will guide you in managing your checks and check copies. This important documentation will help your financial operations to run efficiently and effectively.

Lastly, the check-clearing process is full of checkpoints that help to authenticate and validate the check. This process begins when the check is presented for payment and ends with accounts being credited or debited. Banking standards are strict as the check is imaged and validated for processing. When internally processing a check, you must have similar standards in place to protect yourself in the event of bad checks. Check verification services can help you with the verification process and are a worthwhile investment for your company. The following illustration provides a brief overview of the check-clearing process and is included to educate you on the fundamentals of this process.

Figure 5.2

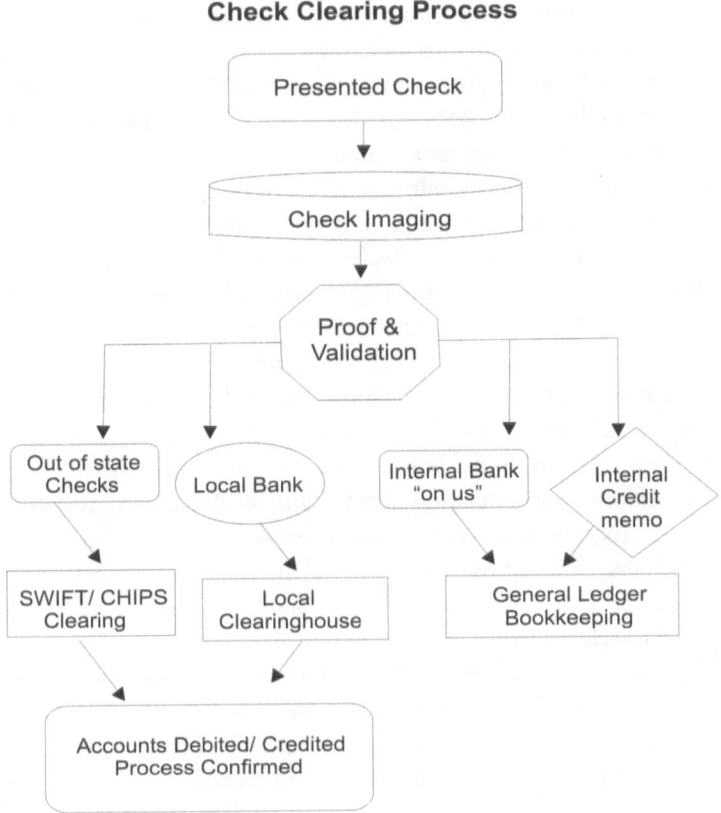

Check Clearing Process

Wire Transfers

Wire transfers may be made through the business's bank account or by using online banking. Maintain a wire transfer request form or use the bank's wire transfer form every time a wire transfer needs to be made.

Wire transfers should be authorized the same way that a check would be. Maintaining a paper trail for this authorization helps to track the payment. File away wire transfer details with other accounting records. Ensure that the form mentions the reason for transfer, the amount of transfer and provides the invoice or other supporting documentation to justify the transfer. There will be greater detail about online transfers shortly, when we deal with online banking.

Bank Reconciliations

Bank reconciliation is the process of matching the organization's accounting records against the information provided by a bank statement. The process of creating a bank reconciliation statement not only verifies the correctness of the bank statement itself, but exposes discrepancies in the business's cash and bank books, if any. It is desirable to repeat this exercise at regular intervals, such as weekly or monthly, or as often as a statement is received from the bank. These days with most bank statements being available online, it is possible to make bank reconciliation a continuous exercise. The purpose of this exercise is to ensure that the balance in the bank account as declared by the bank is the same as the balance shown by the business's accounting records. There are some typical reasons for which such differences arise. One common reason is deposits in transit, which are checks that have been recorded in the company's books but have not yet been received at the bank and hence do not show up on the bank statement.

Alternately, checks may have been issued by the company and disbursed but have not yet been cleared at the bank when the bank statement printed. Errors, either by the bank or by the business also become visible during reconciliation. As a result, bank charges, which may not have been accounted for surface in the bank statement, and may be another reason for a discrepancy. Bank reconciliation is therefore a good external check on your business's accounting functions and also on its cash and check recording functions.

To be effective as a control tool, a bank reconciliation statement must be completed routinely. It should be repeated at fixed intervals. Any accounting errors or discrepancies that arise during this process must be immediately rectified. The statement is then filed away with the accounting records for future reference.

Accounts Receivables Controls

Receivables, or accounts receivable (AR) are the amounts due to the business from sales or services rendered. Efficient and effective collection of these payments will ensure that the business has enough liquidity available to function smoothly.

Every sale that is made must be included in the recording process as this will affect inventory as well as collections. Also record all transactions at the proper values. If goods or services are sold at a discount, indicate original sales price minus discount. Tracking your receivables will allow you to determine your gains and losses and help you to adjust accordingly.

Invoicing

The invoicing process starts with the receipt of purchase order from a customer or preparation of a sales order by a salesperson. A sales order may or may not be a hardcopy document. In the case of a salesperson making a call on a customer, it is preferably to generate a paper sales order document. Such documents need to contain a controlled document number, an authorized signature of the sales person and the customer, formal approval for the credit extended, a part number and article description, sales price, shipping terms and an authorized billing address. In the case of a customer service agent answering a toll-free number the sales order would contain most of the above details. It would be keyed into a computer and each transaction uniquely identified. In the case of a retail business selling over the counter, there would be no record of a sale order, only the checkout clerk recording the order and payment received on the cash register.

Invoices are normally prepared when notice is received that goods were shipped. Some businesses however, find it convenient to prepare invoices in advance as long as records show that sufficient levels of inventory are on hand. Such businesses need to implement control procedures to ensure that the invoices are not processed until there is evidence of shipment. Invoices can be transmitted to the customer by preparing hardcopy documents and sending one to the customer or electronically transmitting the invoice to the customer.

Credit Controls

In the interest of increasing turnover, it is often necessary to extend credit to customers. This brings in a host of issues regarding the monitoring and control of accounts receivables. Extending credit is usually at a cost to the business of using borrowed funds to tide over liquidity problems if and as they arise. The terms of credit should be clearly written into the sales or service contract. Whether your business offers 30 day credit or interest free installments for a year, the process of collection should not be delayed until the customer has defaulted.

Formal credit approval policies should be implemented to minimize credit losses. Mail-order companies and companies taking sales orders through the internet often eliminated credit risk by requiring a credit card payment to be made before goods can be shipped. While credit cards eliminate credit risk, they add an additional cost to you in the form of percentages that you pay to the credit card companies for their services. You must decide if these levies are a reasonable cost for the convenience and if you can absorb them or if you need to price your goods and services to reflect the extra cost of accepting credit cards for payment.

The credit approval process typically includes a review of sales orders and customer credit information by a computer program to determine whether credit should be extended to the customer. The computer file should be regularly accessed to determine whether a sales order exceeds pre-approved credit limits. If it does, credit should be denied or be formally considered by the credit department.

As you evaluate your customer's creditworthiness, use some of the same tools the bank uses to evaluate your credit position. The most common tool is known as the *five C's of credit*:

- *Character*: What is integrity and reputation of the applicant as gauged by their willingness to pay? This element is part of "knowing your customer." Make sure you have a good idea how your client governs their business and how they treat their own customers and suppliers.

- *Capacity*: What current and future financial resources are available to meet current and long term obligations? This is measured in terms of liquidity rations and cash flow analysis.

- *Capital*: What long term resources are available? This looks at long term assets that could be liquidated to meet obligations.

- *Collateral*: What guarantees are available to secure the debt if payments cannot be met?

- *Conditions*: What are the current economic conditions locally, nationally and globally that could affect the credit position?

A periodic review of the credit policy by key executives or the owner of the business is a good control over the process. They can determine whether changes to the policy are necessitated either by current economic events or by deterioration of the receivables.

Duties in the credit department should be segregated to keep specific authorization to write off receivables separated from individuals who handle cash transactions with the customer.

Collections

The proper recording of all receipts is crucial to the ultimate valuation of both cash and accounts receivable. Thus, as part of the control structure over accounts receivables, control procedures to ensure the completeness and accuracy of cash receipt recording are important. An aging report will help you to keep priority collections at the front of the line, so to speak, and ensure that your receivables loss rate does not deteriorate your bottom line.

Online Banking

In spite of the immense popularity of online banking and its increased use by businesses as well as individuals, online banking is still open to the possibility of fraud and error. However the convenience that it offers of round-the-clock one-click banking from your desk far outweighs the risks, especially if you are able to install procedures to cover all possible risks.

Whether you use a traditional bank or an online bank with no physical offices, confirm that the bank is legitimate and your deposits are federally insured. Read vital information about the bank posted on its website in the 'about us' section. Review your bank's privacy policy which should also be available on the website. You can learn from this policy how much of your information your bank shares with others and you can change this, if you so wish, in most cases. Watch out for copycat websites that look the same or similar to your bank's website and use a web address very similar to that of your legitimate bank. Always check to see if you have typed the correct website address for your bank website before conducting a transaction.

Check the bank's website or approach the bank directly for information about its security practices. Some of the commonly used security features are encryption, passwords or Personal Identification Numbers (PIN) and other general security measures. Encryption is the process of sending private information over a secure socket to prevent unauthorized access. To show that your transmission is encrypted, some browsers display a small icon on your screen that looks like a 'lock' or a 'key' whenever you conduct secure transactions online. Avoid sending sensitive information such as account numbers or passwords through unsecured email. Passwords or PINs should be used while accessing an account online. Passwords should be unique to you and changed frequently. They should not be common information that can be easily guessed. Generally, a strong password will contain letters and numbers or symbols in a random order. Share the password only the people who are authorized in your business to operate the bank account.

General computer security such as virus protection and physical access controls should also be used and updated frequently. As was mentioned before, free antivirus and antispyware software is available for download and should be used before attempting to use or send sensitive information on the internet.

Accounting Documentation

The accounting system of any entity large or small is based upon documentation. A very small business may prefer to maintain hand-written books of accounts but as we continue to move toward a paperless world, tools are available to manage all accounts electronically. In such a system, there should be procedures in place to regularly back up the accounting data.

Documentation provides evidence of the authorization of transactions, the support for journal entries, and the financial commitments made by the organization. Documentation may be either paper-based or electronic. The following checklist is a guideline for developing reliable documentation and ensuring control of the storage of those documents:

- *Pre-numbered documents:* These facilitate the control of and accountability for transactions.

- *Timely preparation of documents*: This improves the credibility and accountability of the documents and reduces the probability of errors creeping in.

- *Authorization:* All authorization for a transaction, including electronic approval, should be clearly evident on the document.

- *Transaction trail:* The accounting system should capture sufficient information to facilitate the development of a transaction trail to provide information to respond to customer inquiries, facilitate returns or exchanges and identify and remedy errors. Information facilitating the development of a transaction trail includes the date of the transaction, location, outside parties shipped to or received from, products shipped or received, terms and dollar amounts involved.

- *Simplified designs:* The accounting system should use simple screens and forms which will facilitate ease and completeness of an entry as well as inspection of acceptable entries to minimize the possibility of errors.

Chart of Accounts

A chart of accounts is a listing of the names of the accounts that a company has identified and made available for recording transactions in its general ledger. This chart is designed by the business to suit its specific needs. It may be added to, deleted from or amended in any other way required from time to time when the need arises.

A typical chart of accounts carries two major classifications, namely balance sheet accounts and income statement accounts. Balance sheet accounts include assets, liabilities and owner's equity. Income statement accounts comprise operating revenues, operating expenses, other revenues and profits and other expenses and losses. The statement including assets, liabilities, incomes and expenses may be further categorized according to business function or production divisions.

The chart of accounts is a listing of all the accounts in the general ledger, each account accompanied by a reference number. To set up a chart of accounts, you first need to define the various accounts to be used by your business. Each account should have an identifying number. For very small businesses, a three digit code may suffice for the account number. In a larger business, more digits may need to be used. When the code is larger, accounts may be inserted while maintaining the logical order. An example of how the accounts may be coded is shown below:

1000–1999	Asset Accounts
2000–2999	Liability Accounts
3000–3999	Equity Accounts
4000–4999	Revenue Accounts
5000–5999	Cost of Goods Sold
6000–6999	Expense Accounts
7000–7999	Other Revenue
8000–8999	Other Expense

Providing for a large set of numbers for any given type of account allows for many new accounts to be added to any category while maintaining the general numbering order. Different types of business will have different types of accounts.

For instance in a manufacturing business the important accounts will deal with manufacturing costs, whereas in a retail business they will be concerned with inventory.

Accounting software packages often come with a selection of predefined account charts for various types of businesses. When you are designing your chart of accounts, remember that there is a trade-off between simplicity and the ability to make historical comparisons. Initially keeping the number of accounts to a minimum does help to keep the accounting system simple. On the other hand, splitting up these basic accounts into more specific classifications, as and when the need arises, will make it very hard to make historical comparisons. Hence, use foresight and common sense when designing a chart of accounts for your business.

Files and Records

Files and records are concepts associated with computerized database management. A file is described as a collection of records. A record is a single line of information pertaining to one transaction in the file.

For ease of understanding and communication when you are seeking information, keep in mind the difference between these concepts for they are not words that can be interchanged.

Year End and Month End

The accounting function consists of compiling quantitative data over a time period. For this data to be useful in analysis, this data has to be reviewed at frequent time intervals. This time interval is called an accounting period. An accounting period is usually one calendar year. Within that calendar year, a monthly accounting period review may be efficacious to expedite the year end reporting. In order for revenues and expenses to be reported in the time period in which they are earned or incurred, adjusting entries must be made at the end of the accounting period. Adjusting entries are made so the revenue recognition and matching principles are followed.

Accounting systems are designed to handle a large number of routine transactions during the year very efficiently, usually with the aid of computers and devices like cash registers with scanning capabilities, bar code inventory management systems and automatic credit card processing systems. An automated accounting system has the built-in capability to handle these items with little human intervention, creating appropriate journal entries, and posting thousands of transactions with little effort.

However, at the end of the year accountants must step in and prepare financial statements from all the information that has been collected throughout the year. This is called the "year end close." Although an automated accounting system is designed to efficiently capture a large number of transactions, this information is only partially in accordance to mandated Generally Accepted Accounting Procedures (GAAP). The information needs a small amount of adjustment at the end of the year to bring the financial statements in alignment with the requirements of GAAP. And this is where adjusting entries come in. GAAP also requires certain additional information, referred to as Notes to the Financial Statement. This is a combination of narrative and numerical information that must be prepared by an accountant. Computers can do many things, but the process of preparing financial statements requires professional reasoning and experienced judgment.

At the end of the year, or anytime before financial statements are prepared, accountants have to make certain adjustments to the books to make sure that all revenues and expenses are correctly recorded and reported. This is where adjusting entries, accruals and deferrals are made. Some companies make adjusting entries monthly, in preparation of monthly financial statements. This process is called the "month end close."

Adjusting entries fall outside the routine daily journal entries and activities of special departments, such as purchasing, sales and payroll. Accountants make adjusting and reversing journal entries in a way that does not interfere with the efficient daily operations of these essential departments. Adjusting entries should not be confused with correcting entries, which are used to correct an error. That should be done separately from adjusting entries, so there is no confusion between the two, and will ensure that a clear audit trail will be left behind in the books and records documenting the corrections.

Soft Copies

Data maintained in electronic format on a computerized information system is called a soft copy. Unlike a paper document, a soft copy is not tangible, is easy to duplicate and faces a greater theft of loss or destruction. This checklist defines common threats to computer data:

- *Computer viruses*: Viruses are malicious programs that enter the computer network and cause some sort of damage. This threat can be countered by using properly authorized and up-to-date anti-virus software.

- *Unauthorized use:* This threat may be external or internal, in the form of employees or third parties breaking into a network or employees gaining access to sensitive areas of the network. They can cause damage such as theft of data or customer information.

- *System failure:* The more your business depends on its computer system, the higher the risk of loss from breakdowns.

This checklist includes the following practical measures which could help control the risks to computer data and soft copies of important documents:

- *Routine risk assessments*: Carry out a risk assessment on the computer data systems. Use recognized information safety standards as benchmarks.

- *Security policies and procedures*: Create and implement policies and procedures to implement high levels of data security. Include clauses in employee contracts that cover information about confidentiality of propriety information.

- *Company safety nets*: Build safety into all company processes. Choose secure premises, create and implement thorough back-up procedures and enter into recovery agreements with hardware and software vendors to make the business more secure.

- *Software safety nets*: Use technology effectively. Virus protection software should monitor both internal and external communications and should be updated regularly. Firewalls and intrusion detection systems can alert you to ongoing threats to your computer network.

Financial Goals of Accounting Controls

In a very rudimentary sense, running a business involves the investment of money or other resources and employing these resources to earn the optimum returns. Management of money involves three questions which will bring you to three decisions that affect how you run your business: where to invest the money (the investment decision), how and how much to invest (the financing decision), and how much of the profits to pay out to yourself or to other investors (the dividend decision).

Financial management considers the answers to these decisions in regard to the size and composition of assets and the level and structure of financing. To make wise decisions a clear understanding of your financial goals is necessary. The goal provides a framework for optimum financial decision making. A financial goal is the decision criterion for the three questions involved in financial management. It implies that what is relevant is not the over-all objective or goal of a business but an operationally useful criterion by which to judge a specific set of mutually inter-related business decisions: namely investment, financing, and dividend policy.

Two approaches are commonly used to determine the standards for financial management; one of them is profit maximization. Simply stated, profit maximization declares that actions which increase profits should be taken and those that decrease profits should be avoided. In specific operational terms, as applicable to financial management, the profit maximization goal implies that the investment, financing and dividend decisions of a firm should be oriented toward the maximization of profits. The rationale behind profit maximization as a guide to financial decision making is that profit is a test of economic efficiency. It provides the yardstick by which economic performance can be judged. Moreover, it leads to efficient allocation of resources, for resources tend to be directed to uses which are most desirable in terms of profitability.

Profit maximization has been questioned on several grounds. The primary concern is that the term "profit" is an ambiguous concept amenable to different interpretations. Another problem with this approach is the differences in the time pattern of the benefits received from investment proposals or courses of action. Lastly, the quality aspect of the benefits associated with a certain financial course of action tends to be ignored.

The other approach used to determine the decision criterion for financial management is the wealth maximization method. The wealth maximization method is based on the concept of cash flows generated by the decision rather than accounting for profit which is the basis of the measurement of benefits in the case of profit maximization goal. The most important argument for the wealth maximization method is that cash flow is a precise concept with a definite connotation in contrast to accounting profit which is vague and amenable to varied interpretations.

The second important feature of wealth maximization is that it considers both the quantity and quality dimensions of the advantages of a singular financial course. At the same time, it also incorporates the time value of money. The operational implication of the uncertainty and timing dimensions of the benefits emanating from a financial decision is that adjustments should be made to the cash flow pattern first to incorporate risk and second to make an allowance for any difference in the timing of benefits. The value of a stream of cash flow with value maximization is calculated by discounting its element back to the present at a capitalization rate that reflects both time and risk. For these reasons, the wealth maximization method is superior to the profit maximization to use as a financial benchmark.

Calculating Break-Even

Break-even analysis is a technique for studying the relationship between fixed costs, variable costs, profits and sales. The break-even point represents the level of sales at which the operating income and operating costs are equal so that profit is zero.

Every business has fixed costs and variable costs. Fixed costs refer to those costs which have to be incurred to keep the company is business regardless of the level of production. Fixed costs do not increase when the volume of sales increases, nor do they decrease when the sales decrease. Examples of fixed costs are rents and rates, depreciation, research and development, administrative etc. Variable costs are the costs that are directly attributable to an increase in the volume of sales, and which increase when the volume of sales increase. They vary directly with the level of output. They represent cost of sales related input such as raw materials, direct labor, fuel and revenue related commission.

Another category of expenses is called mixed expenses or semi-variable expenses. These are, as the name suggests, partly variable and partly fixed. They can be split up into their fixed and variable parts and reclassified accordingly. *Break-even point* is the point at which the revenue from sales just about covers both the fixed and the variable costs.

Another important concept associated with break-even analysis is the "Contribution Margin." At any given volume of sales the contribution margin is the revenue less variable expenses or

$$\textbf{Contribution margin = Revenue – Variable expenses}$$

Contribution may also be measured in per unit terms where the contribution per unit is said to be the difference between the unit sale price and the unit variable cost of the product or

$$\textbf{Contribution per unit = Unit sale price – Unit variable cost}$$

Break-even point in terms of units can be derived by the formula below:

Break-Even point = Fixed Costs ÷ Contribution per unit

In other words, the break-even point in terms of sales revenue will be break-even point in terms of unit multiplied by sale price of each unit. This can be demonstrated by the following example:

> Ace Manufacturing sells a power drill for $100 per unit. The company's variable costs per unit for making the drill are $50. The fixed costs involved in making this product are $50,000. What would be the company's break-even point?

> Contribution per unit = Sale price per unit less Variable cost per unit, which is

$$= \$100 - \$50 = \$50$$
$$\text{Fixed Costs} = \$50,000.$$
$$\text{Break-Even point} = 50000/50 = 1000 \text{ units.}$$

> This means that at sales of 100 units of power drill Ace Manufacturing will incur no loss nor make any profit. It needs to sell more than 1000 units to make a profit or to "break even". The revenue from break-even sales in this case would be $100 x 1000 = $100,000.

Limitations of the Break-Even Analysis

Though the break-even point analysis is helpful in calculating the profitability of a business, it also has a number of limitations. One weakness of the break-even analysis arises from the assumption that there is a constant price and variable cost per unit irrespective of volume. In many cases, the firm's sales volume may influence the market price of a product. For instance, increased output may lead to a decline in market price. Moreover, variable costs are likely to increase as the company reaches its full production capacity. For example, costly overtime or more expensive input material may have to be used.

Another weakness of the break-even analysis is the difficulty of classification of costs into fixed and variable. But, the semi-variable or semi-fixed costs defy clear categorization. In some cases it may not be possible to divide these costs into fixed and variable components for break-even analysis. Moreover, break-even analysis assumes that costs classified as fixed remain unchanged over the entire volume range, but this range is limited by the physical capacity of the business. Consequently, a break-even analysis is relevant only for volume up to that point.

A third weakness of break-even analysis is the problem relating to multiple products. Break-even analysis is best suited for a one-product analysis. When there are multiple products, single break-even analysis cannon be used.

The information inputs for break-even analysis are usually based upon historical relationships. These relationships may not be stable over time. In the case of extreme volume changes, there may even be no historical precedent.

Finally the break-even analysis is of a short-term nature. It is typically applied to one year's project operations. The benefits realized from long term capital expenditures research and development outlays and so on are not likely to be realized during the period of time covered by the break-even analysis. Since the benefits of these outlays are not received in the current period, their inclusion in the fixed costs is questionable.

Benchmarks and Ratios

Profits alone are not a measure of the success of a business. Other qualitative techniques may be used such as benchmarking and ratio analysis to assess the performance of a business.

Benchmarking is a tool through which organizations evaluate various aspects of their processes in relation to best practices, usually within their own industry.[2] They can then develop plans on how to adopt such practices usually with the aim of increasing performance or some aspect of performance. Benchmarking may be either performed as a one-off event or as part of a continuous process of quality improvement. Benchmarking opens organizations to new methods, ideas and tools to improve their effectiveness. The advantages of benchmarking would be as follows:

- Benchmarking provides a better understanding of customer needs as based on market realities.
- It leads to better planning of the business objective due to processes, operations, etc., being measured against industry standards.
- Benchmarking leads to a better understanding of the production process from the point of view of what it produces. This helps to increase business productivity.
- New and improved practices that may be current in the industry but not followed in the business may be introduced as a result of the benchmarking process.

- Benchmarking can foster about sharper competitiveness thanks to a better knowledge of the competition in the industry.

The procedure of implementing benchmarking technique may be summarized as follows:

- *Identify the problem areas*: Performing benchmarking activities of a broad range of business processes requires a variety of research techniques. These techniques may include informal conversations with customers, employees or suppliers; focus groups, in depth marketing research, quantitative research, surveys, questionnaires, reengineering analysis, process mapping, quality control variance reports or financial ratio analysis.

- *Identify similar problems in other industries:* Seeking out examples of similar problems and analyzing how they deal with such issues will be helpful in solving problems that face all players.

- *Study the practices of market leaders:* Sometimes following the leader is a good thing and applying this concept to the business is another technique that may be used.

- *Conduct surveys:* Companies that specialize *in conducting surveys* may be used in the benchmarking exercise. These companies target specific business processes using detailed surveys of measures and practices and use these to identify business process alternatives from leading companies.

The nature of benchmarking is such that it can be an expensive exercise, but it usually fully pays for itself in terms of returns.

Benchmarking Financial Ratios

Financial statements provide a summarized view of the financial position and operations of the firm. Much can be learned from these statements if the information is presented in a manner feasible for analysis. The focus of financial analysis is of the key figures in the financial statements and the significant relationships that exist between them. The analysis of financial statements is a process of evaluating relationships between component parts of financial statements to obtain a better understanding of the firm's position and performance.

Financial ratios are a useful indicator of a business's performance and financial situation. The first task in this analysis is to select information from the financial statements that is relevant to the decision to be made. The second step is to highlight significant relationships.

Ratio analysis is a widely used tool of financial analysis. It is defined as the systematic use of ratios to interpret the financial statements so that the strengths and weaknesses of a firm as well as its historical performance and current financial condition can be determined. The term ratio refers to numerical or quantitative relationship between two variables.

Computing ratios does not add any information not already inherent in the financial statements; rather it reveals the relationship in a more meaningful way so as to enable s to draw conclusions from them. The rationale of ratio analysis lies in the fact that it makes related information comparable.

Liquidity Ratios

Liquidity, in the sense of the ability of a business to meet its current or short term obligations is a pre-requisite for the very survival of the firm. The short term creditors of the firm may be interested in its liquidity, but from a view point of fund utilization these funds are idle funds and earn little. A proper balance between liquidity and profitability is required for efficient financial management. The liquidity ratios measure the ability of a firm to meet its short term obligations and reflect the short term financial strength or solvency of a business. Examples of liquidity ratios are net working capital ratio, current ratio, acid test ratio; and turnover ratio.[3] There are three main reasons your entity must maintain sufficient cash:

- *Transaction requirements*: These are daily demands on cash outflows that are often uneven and difficult to synchronize. This may be caused by delayed inflows of cash, late payments, or slow sales.

- *Precautionary requirements*: Your liquidity reserves may be drained by unexpected demands and expenses seem to be ever present, even with the best planning and forecasting.

- *Speculative requirements*: There may be unplanned investment opportunities that you want to take the advantage. Such occasions may include the liquidation of a competitor, equipment surplus, and other needs. In early phases of your company life cycle this should be tempered with a conservative nature. Refrain from speculation as much as possible, remember your enterprise is still already high speculative, do not add more debt burden or draining cash until you can be assured a near term recovery of liquidity.

Cash Collection & Payment Floats

A key component of understanding liquidity is in knowing the nature of the collection float. You are familiar with the collection float process on a personal basis. For example, your car payment is due on the 25th of the month, it is now the 15th at which time you decide to write the check and mail it expecting it to get applied to your account well before the 25th. Technological advances now provide you with online banking options that enable you to wait until the day of the 25th to initiate the transfer. Once you have confirmation, you experienced the maximum benefit in using of the time value of money.

Now, apply these concepts to your business. Cash management in business is a well-established and slow-changing environment. If most of your personal banking is online, prepare to step back and expect that most of your customers, vendors and other interactions will be in paper check format. While this environment is changing, the small business environment still depends heavily upon paper checks and mailed invoices and hard copy documentation. In your business to business transactions expect hard copies; this will continue to change slowly due to the nature of liquidity float. Since this is the majority of your environment, work within these parameters and take the most advantage of the situation. A list of the types of floats that you should become familiar with include:

- *Collection Floats:*
  - *Mail Float:* This is the time interval between the day a check is mailed and the day it is received by the payee.
  - *Processing Float:* This interval measures the delay in processing the payee's check; this includes the time from receipt to the time you actually make the deposit.
  - *Availability Float:* This interval measures the time from the deposit of the check to the credit in your account of the collected funds available for your disbursement.
- *Disbursement floats:*
  - *Mail Float:* The same type of float as in the collection float area, which is the time interval between the day a check is mailed and the day it is received by the payee.

- o *Processing Float:* Again the same as with the collection float, which is where the interval measures the delay in processing the payee's check; this includes the time from receipt to the time you actually make the deposit.

- o *Clearing Float:* This type of float measures the time for the check to be processed and cleared including the time the depositor collects funds and the check clears back to the drawee bank account.

Working Capital Management

Working capital management is the process of decision making and strategizing required for the handling of current assets. Remember your current assets are mostly liquid assets including cash in accounts, short term equities, accounts receivables, prepaid expenses, and inventory.

Current liabilities, on the other hand, refer to the liabilities such as accounts payables, notes payables, accrued liabilities and other notes due within usually the next year or less.

Working capital is defined by this group of current assets and liabilities. Net working capital is defined as current assets less current liabilities. Your lenders and investors will be watching this ration closely while using some of the leaders in your industry to benchmark what your ratio should be. Typically a ratio above 2 is a comfortable place to begin. This means for every one dollar of current debt, you have two dollars of current assets.

Working Capital Cash Flow Cycle

You will need to monitor closely the interval between purchasing of inventory and your payments related to inventory to the time you collect payment. This includes the number of days of materials in inventory, the number of days to convert to finished goods and the number of days that finished goods sit in inventory until sold. A business can quickly tie up funds in working capital which emphasizes the impetus on materials management as a high priority control item.

Figure 5.3

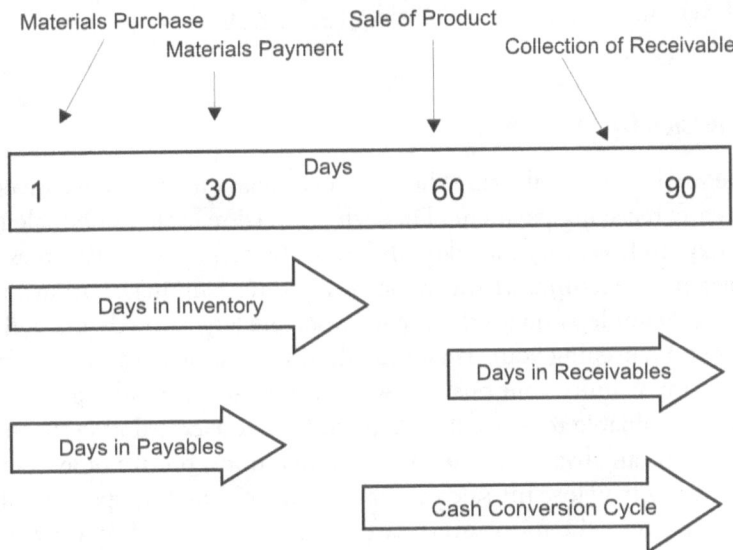

Working Capital Cycle

As this working capital cycle diagram illustrates, you can quickly turn large amounts of cash into working capital without receiving a return for an extended length of time. If your enterprise has too much money locked into inventory you can become cash-starved, while still being a profitable organization. This is the concern with growing too quickly.

Reality Check:
Uncontrolled Growth Can Kill

One tactic taken to kill weeds is by actually adding growth hormone to the leaves. Broadleaf weed killers are selective herbicides that work in lawns by targeting broadleaf plants (usually dandelions) that are growing in your grass. The most common broadleaf weed killer is 2/4-D. This compound is an auxin or plant hormone that, when applied to the leaf area, causes the plant to grow too quickly, actually rupturing cells and deforming the leaves and interfering with photosynthesis.

Small businesses often find themselves, after months or years of dedicated sales efforts, finally landing those large sales. However, the cash cycle and working management of inventory may leave them out of short term cash and unable to secure immediate bank loans while investors may suddenly find themselves seeking bankruptcy protection.

Source: Environmental Protection Agency, www.epa.gov.

Cash Conversion Cycle

This is the method for evaluating the time a company must finance inventory or product before receiving payment. The cash conversion cycle can be calculated by using the days in Inventory plus days in Receivables less days in Payables.

Here again we reemphasis the value of a strong banking relationship. Meet with your banker at least quarterly; if you anticipate large growth you will want to spend more time keeping your banker involved in your business success and what new growth opportunity your business will offer the bank. Working lines of credit become a very valuable resource during periods of accelerated growth. Anticipate needs early. You can always decline the borrowed funds, but if not available when most needed you may lose the sale you have been working for, upset suppliers and fail to make payroll (the most severe cases usually result in filing for bankruptcy protection).

Capital Structure Ratio & Leverage Ratios

The second category of financial ratios is leverage or capital structure ratios. Just as short term creditors are interested in liquidity ratios of a business, long term creditors will judge the soundness of a firm on the basis of the long-term financial strength measured in terms of its ability to pay the interest regularly as well as repay the installment of the principal on due dates or in one lump sum at the time of maturity. The long term solvency of the firm can be examined using leverage or capital structure ratios. The long term solvency of the firm covers two aspects, namely the ability to repay the principal when due and regular payment of the interest.

Accordingly there are two types of interrelated but different leverage ratios. The first are the type based on the relationship between borrowed funds and owner's capital like debt-equity ratio, debt assets ratio and equity-assets ratio. The second type of capital structure ratios are called coverage ratios and include interest coverage ratio, dividend coverage ratio total fixed charges coverage ratio, cash flow coverage ratio and debt service coverage ratio.

Profitability Ratios

Apart from creditors, who are interested parties in the financial soundness of a firm are the owners and management or the company itself. The management of the firm is naturally eager to measure its operating efficiency. Similarly the owners invest their funds in expectation of reasonable return. The operating efficiency of a firm and its ability to ensure adequate return to its shareholders depends on the profits earned by it. Profitability is a measure of efficiency and the search for it provides an incentive to achieve efficiency.

The profitability of a business can be measured by its profitability ratios. Profitability ratios can be determined on the basis of either sales or investments. The profitability ratios can be determined either on the basis of sales or investment. The profitability ratios in relation to sales are profit margin and expense ratio or operating ratio. Profitability in relation to investments is measured by return on assets, return on capital employed and return on shareholders' equity.

Activity Ratios

Activity ratios are concerned with measuring the efficiency in asset management. The efficiency with which the assets are used would be reflected in the speed and rapidity with which the assets are converted into sales. All things being equal, the greater the rate of turnover or conversion, the more efficient will be the utilization of assets. For this reason such ratios are also called turnover ratios. Depending on the various types of assets there are various types of activity ratios. Some of the more important ones are inventory turnover ratio and investment turnover ratio.

Thus ratio analysis as a tool of financial management has crucial significance. The importance of ratio analysis lies in the fact that it presents facts on a comparative basis and enables the drawing of inferences regarding the performance of a firm. Ratio analysis is relevant in assessing the liquidity, long term solvency, operating efficiency, over-all profitability, inter-firm comparison and trend analysis of a business.

Chapter Summary

This chapter began by looking at some of the different roles in accounting held by different staff members. In a small enterprise, you may be involved in most or all these roles. Later, we evolved around a discussion of cash handling and related sensitive documentation while being taught the basics of check and credit card bank clearing and some of the steps involved in those transactions.

The chapter material also highlighted some of the security concerns with cash, check and credit card management. Of course security is often not thought of until the damage has been done. However, if you can take some precautionary measures it could save some long term heartache. You were introduced to some of the standard monthly reports. Often viewed as optional by some entrepreneurs, get ahead by making visible reports part of your mission objectives. These reports will help you to study where you have been and where you are going as well as provide a solid roadmap of how your organization is performing relative to your strategic goals.

Finally, we discussed a number of commonly tracked ratios, perhaps more than you care to ever see. This discussion brought us around to a review of liquidity management. Get familiar with your working capital ratio and establishing criteria for your cash flow needs. Remember, liquidity is one of your keys to survival.

CHAPTER SIX

Control Systems in Practice

From previous chapters, you will recall that controls have been defined as systems that accomplish certain objectives. Specifically, operational controls maintain operational effectiveness and efficiency, trustworthy accounting and financial reporting and government compliance. Your efforts in becoming successful will depend largely upon your ability to keep a high growth and quickly evolving company under control. Many risks can be reduced with the proper systems put in place.

In the second chapter, you learned about projects and programs. To briefly review, each project stems from a need; this could be as simple as installing a company safe or as involved as implementing ISO 9000 certification. Once these projects are completed, many will become systems or programs, such as a new system for handling inventory or processing checks.

Whatever your situation, maintaining control should be a constant priority in running your business. Curiously, our human nature enjoys the thrill of watching someone cross a tightrope 50 feet off the ground without a safety net, almost certain to plunge to their death with a sudden slip of the foot. More curious is how many entrepreneurs operate their businesses in like manner, operating in very precarious positions at times without a safety net.

Controls function as a safety net to minimize damage if there is an incident of fraud, unauthorized invoicing or ownership disagreements. With proper controls in place, these situations will be temporary rather than chronic. There is no benefit in risking all your efforts just to see your business dashed away by a few rocks.

Controls build a solid foundation for trust as well. Developing and maintaining trusting relationships are very important in the business world. When founded on solid principles, controls reduce the probability that trust will be violated. Controls, when properly practiced, make sense of extraordinary as well as everyday events.

Integrated Framework of Control

As you prepare to incorporate internal controls into your organization keep in mind several guiding principles:

- *Broad in scope*: Internal controls is a broad system reaching beyond accounting and financial statements and includes the safeguarding of assets, efficiency and effectiveness of operations, and compliance with industry, environment and government regulations. Briefly, a review of each of these categories follows:
  - o *Safeguarding of assets*: Systems for the protection of enterprise assets including all physical and intellectual property.
  - o *Efficiency and effectiveness*: Operations should be managed to operate at optimum levels for maximum returns. Controls govern this objective.
  - o *Compliance*: Controls should include compliance to all governmental, environmental and industry regulations.
- *Responsibility of Management*: Internal controls are led and directed by the managing team. Entrepreneurs should instill a culture of compliance early and deeply into the company.
- *Flexibility*: Controls will evolve and move with the organization, not to be regarded as immovable anchors.

These principles will provide a framework in which to make the appropriate decisions when designing an internal control system that will function best for your company.

Company Organizational Chart

Organizational charts are a control tool in the workplace and a must-have in any place where teamwork occurs. This importance of this document should not be overlooked as it defines roles and reporting responsibilities, simplifying the communication process and becoming the map to implementing the necessary internal controls as well as successful growth and development. Often, when asked to put together an organizational chart, I face groans of resistance: *"We don't need an org chart! There are only three of us ... how complicated can this be?"* The good news is that the smaller the group, the less time it takes to put the chart together.

Drawing up this chart will provide a framework for future building. It will outline responsibilities and duties in the absence of one of the key members.

Also, keep in mind that this simple document will serve as the foundation for growth. As you expand and incorporate additional resources, where those resources fit in the organizational chart will serve as a solid structure for reporting and responsibilities. Additionally, interested third parties may request copies of your Organizational Chart. Bankers, vendors, auditors, attorneys, and customers alike will inquire about your organizational chart when asked to be involved in any way from financing to supplying to legal representation. This document provides a basic blueprint of your operations and gives them a quick reference of how reporting works and where different types of communication ought to be directed.

If you are a small organization, this should be a fairly painless exercise, and using word document or flow chart software, it should take only a few minutes. The ease of the process should not undermine the important fact that this chart becomes a cornerstone document for all your internal controls. It will also demonstrate to others such as lenders and employees that you take your business seriously. If you have known vacancies in your chart that one day you would like to fill, insert a placeholder position and outline the potential duties. While I have seen many small companies criticized for not even having a draft version of an organizational chart, I have yet to see anyone complain for inserting placeholder positions. This gesture demonstrates forethought and organizational skills.

Finance and Accounting

At the heart of every successful business enterprise is a free flow of reliable information by which owners, creditors and regulatory agencies make informed decisions about allocation of resources or the need for governmental action. Managers require reliable information on organizational performance, including compliance with organizations, policies and objective analysis of operations. This information is generated by the finance and accounting functions. Accounting systems capture, record, summarize and report financial data and supporting information.

Though simple in nature in small business, accounting procedures in larger organizations include multiple accounting subsystems, many of which are independent or only semi-dependant of each other. Being familiar with how the "big boys" do it can often spark your imagination as to how you may improve something in your own accounting system. A few basic examples from big business accounting include sub-systems such as sales functions, accounts receivable, accounts payable, cash disbursements, payroll, inventory and general ledger. Many other subsystems can be found according to the needs of the company.

Although each subsystem functions within the overall control environment, each one is unique and may vary in the strength of controls built into the system. All subsystems depend on key personnel in spite of so much that is automated nowadays. Many subsystems depend on the quality of information received from other, non-accounting departments of the organization. Internal control procedures for this function must therefore encompass the entire organization. In addition to maintaining a stable control environment for the whole company, controls need to be applied at the sublevels as well for each department, division or function within these subsystems.

At the ground level, this means examining each employee's duties within the accounting function and testing for level of independence of these functions on other functional inputs. This activity should be made easy by the information which you have already detailed in your organizational chart as described previously.

In a well-designed control system, job separation within each system is important. Using an example from a payroll system, payroll and timekeeping functions within the personnel department should be assigned to different persons or departments. Some items will be manually processed and other activities will be automated. Additionally, an independent or "outside" control should exist within the system. In the case of the payroll system, the employee receiving the check is himself a control on the payroll department's efficiency, since he would be verifying the check for his own purposes and will certainly report any errors, at least those that go in his favor. The system of recording the financial information should be verified to ensure that no errors creep in, and if they do then they may be easily detected. A transaction trail should exist. This means that at every stage of the process, documentation should be generated that leads up to the next stage in the process; this trail will allow documents to be checked and analyzed later, if necessary.

The quality of an organization's control systems affects not only the *reliability* of the financial data but also the *ability* of the organization to make good decisions and to remain in business. Many companies recognize that control systems must be designed to parallel the risks that are present in the industry and the entity. Understanding of the risks facing a business will help to assess the need for controls and the extent of controls required.

One of the goals of a control system is to safeguard the business's assets. This includes controls designed to protect against theft and unauthorized use, acquisition, or disposal of assets. Internal control is a process that starts with you, the owner, to achieve the desired results for your business, namely successfully staying in business. The control process must ensure that all transactions are properly authorized, recorded in the correct time period and valued correctly. You should also receive feedback on the effectiveness of the control procedure. Feedback is essential for keeping the control procedure on track. All of these activities will assist you in building a stable control environment.

Controls as Business Assurance

Uncontrolled procedures can lead to poor financial results and business failure. In the absence of a stable control culture emanating from the top, lax behavior and fraudulent reporting from employees can result. However, fraud is not the only reason for installing tight internal controls. Controls are part of accountability. Controls infrastructure should not be seen as a cost, but as an integral part of management. Controls makes good business sense as it helps identify risks and deal with them effectively. A steady internal control environment leads to more efficient operations and generates data on which several stakeholders can rely to make decisions.

The people who have an interest in the quality of an organization's control system are:

- Owners
- Management
- Government Regulators
- Internal and external auditors
- Suppliers and customers
- Investors and lenders

As the owner, you are interested in ensuring controls for all of the reasons mentioned above, including safeguarding your assets and achieving the business goals as related to the strategic vision that you have for your business. Regulators have found over the years that poor or relaxed controls predict of future financial woes. For this reason various industry regulators such as external and internal auditors are stepping onto the controls bandwagon.

External auditors are interested in controls as a basis for determining the probability of manipulations and mis-statements in financial reporting. Internal auditors, as part of the business' risk management structure, help monitor on a day-to-day basis the effectiveness of internal control procedures.

In a world where margins are thin and room for error is very small, business partners include both customers and suppliers as stakeholders in your business controls system. Your business partners need to be assured of the high quality of goods supplied by the manufacturing process, regular shipment schedules, stream-lined order placement and requisition systems, on-time recording of transactions and timely payments of receivables.

Lenders and investors need to be assured that the money which they have invested is safe, protected and used optimally to earn them a good return-on-investment (ROI). The presence of a well-structured internal control system provides this assurance.

All of these interested parties therefore have a good reason to follow through with or help to implement the internal controls system by working together and assuring that your business will succeed.

Survey the Environment

Controls exist in the business environment to help the organization better man-age risks. The controls range from broad policies to effective supervision, starting with you, the owner, and the top management which will continue to permeate through every level of the organization. As previously stated, recent research of financial fraud within companies shows a high correlation between fraud and a breakdown of the controls system at the highest levels. Controls weaknesses are pervasive in nature, affecting almost every aspect of operations. A strong control system indicates that the risks are being managed properly.

To review some of the key performance indicators that can give a good idea of the quality of the control environment in your organization, study the following:

- *Backlog of work in progress*: Good process control will provide valuable feedback about process defects and set in motion corrective actions to ensure that the process is on track. Effective inventory control can pro-vide data about revenue earning potential locked up in inventory.

- *Amount of items returned, overall and by product line*: An increase in goods returns indicates substandard quality, or not operating to specifications.

Operational controls are put in place to prevent this. Controls can help increase product quality, promote service delivery and keep customer promises.

- *Increased disputes regarding accounts receivable or accounts payable*: A rise in the number of disputes is an indication of a problem in the receiving or accounts department. Accounts payables disputes may arise when quantities received do not agree with purchase orders, or accounts payable and material receipts are not recorded in a timely manner. Accounting controls and controls over the cash in/out system help to plug leaks in profitability resulting from wrong payments and slow collections.

- *Outcomes of customer satisfaction surveys*: The results of these surveys will often point to gaps in customer service controls. You can build your business only through building a strong customer base and ensuring return customers. Effective customer service and efficient customer feedback is the key. Customer service controls can help build customer trust and ensure satisfied customers.

- *Rates of employee absenteeism*: Human Resource controls are a required component of a well-established controls system. HR controls are necessary to protect yourself against mal-intent and willful damaging activities by members of your staff. Clear HR policies and a generally strong control environment in the business will foster good employer-employee relations and discourage high employee turnover. Conversely employee absenteeism points to a lax control atmosphere and lack of adequate support to the control initiative from the top management and ownership.

- *Decreased productivity*: Productivity is enhanced by improving processes using better technology, ensuring on-time deliveries of raw materials and obtaining efficiency in procurement and usage of raw materials. Product quality can be impacted by positive factors such as sudden growth in business or increased production pressures due to market expansion. Product quality can also be affected by saturation of production capacity and may be responsible for bringing down productivity. A control and feedback system will provide the necessary information that management can use to put corrective actions in place and ensure that production and productivity can be flexed according to changes in market conditions.

- *Information processing errors*: A successful business needs to be backed up by a well-organized management information and support system. Management information can be reliable, speedy and easy to use if the collection and processing system is well-designed. Double-check that you have installed good accounting controls to provide the backbone for the rest of the control mechanisms in the business.

- *Increased delays in important processes*: Timely recording of information, timely execution of business processes and timely completion of business cycle point to a smooth and efficiently run organization. Slip-ups and delays only lengthen the revenue cycle. This means it takes a longer time to recover investments. It slows down the entire business process and reduces profitability.

All of the above indicators may not be suited to your own business, or you may need some or all of them in addition to still more indicators to ensure that you get feedback from all parts of your organization's control system. You can tailor your own indicators and keep a tab on them from time to time to obtain a quick overall check of the effectiveness of your control systems. These indicators should be designed to focus on management objectives and key processes. The control environment will evolve over time as the organization changes to meet its competitive forces.

The approach for assessing control risk in a computerized environment is not very different from the approach taken in a manual environment. You can begin by identifying critical accounting applications, as you would in a manual environment. The only difference is that in a heavily computerized environment, specific risks involved in electronic processing will also have to be analyzed.

Ethics Policy

The effectiveness of control policies and procedures is directly tied to the integrity and ethical values of the people who create, administer and monitor them. Integrity and ethical behavior are products of the business's ethical and behavioral standards, how these standards are communicated, and how they are enforced in practice. You may enforce ethical behavior by removing temptations that could prompt your employees to engage in dishonest or unethical acts. You may also communicate ethical values and behavioral standards to employees through policy statements and codes of conduct and by example.

Policy statements will clarify where the business stands on specific matters of ethics. Such a policy would lay down what an employee may or may not do as a representative of the organization. This policy also protects the organization in the event unethical behavior becomes a problem. In effect, an ethics policy spells out ethical organizational behavior. A Code of Conduct lays down a standard against which ethical performance can be measured. These documents such as the ethics policy and the code of conduct make it easy for you to develop an ethical environment in which everyone can feel thrive.

Financial Transaction Authorization

A fundamental control concept is that only properly authorized transactions take place and that unauthorized personnel do not have the access or the ability to change already recorded transactions. The specific implementation of authorization procedures varies among businesses and depends also upon the extent of automation present in the business in the recording of transactions. The following guidelines will be useful for all businesses:

- Authorization to enter into transactions should be consistent with the responsibility associated with the particular person's job or management function.

- The ability to commit the business to any long term plans with substantial financial impact should be reserved for the highest functional level in the organization, or maintained with the owner of the business.

- Spell out authorization policies, document them and communicate to all affected people in the organization.

- Blanket authorizations such as are made in a computerized environment should be periodically reviewed by supervisory personnel to determine compliance with the authorization procedure and to determine whether changes should be made to the policy.

- Authorization should be limited to departments that are assigned responsibilities for a particular function.

Figure 6.1

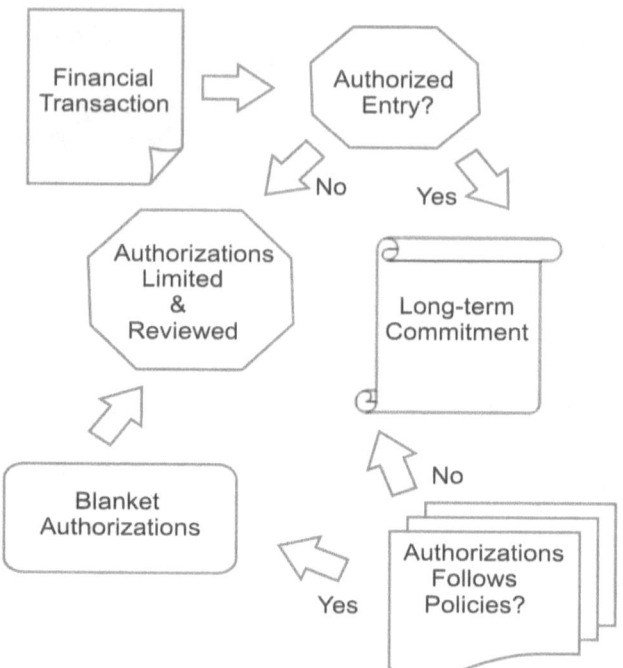

Financial Authorization Process

Conflicts of Interest

Conflicts of interest occur when a person's desire or duty to serve conflicting interests may undermine his neutrality or objectivity within a decision-making process. A conflict can arise when a decision maker represents multiple persons whose interests are at odds with each other. A conflict can also arise when a decision maker's own interests are at stake. Conflicts of interest can arise anywhere, in any situation and employees of a small business are not exempt. By putting in place a conflict of interest policy, you will be able to instruct employees on what constitutes conflict of interest and how they must act when situations or apparent situations of conflict of interest arise. Such a policy may mandate that an employee should not engage in activities that may create a conflict of interest or may conflict with the employee's duties and responsibilities towards the company. Employees should use good judgment in situations of conflict of interest, and make the best interests of the business their highest priority.

Nepotism

Nepotism is defined as bestowing favors and showing favoritism towards one's family members or friends. When an employee gives a job to a friend or relative who might otherwise not be suited for that job, which is an example of nepotism. Or if a vendor was used just because he was a family member but did not necessarily offer the best product, then that would also be nepotism. There is always a monetary gain to the friend or relative in a transaction involving nepotism. This can obviously affect a business negatively by bringing down organizational standards, missing out on the best deals from vendors or causing high levels of employee turnover. Large companies resort to policies that discourage relatives from working in the same department and from awarding contracts to relatives of employees.

While nepotism can be a source of problems in a large company, for a small business, nepotism can be a good thing. Small businesses are often family-owned, and your family and friends probably help you out in various capacities as and when they are needed. Employing family removes the problem of excessive employee turnover as family is usually loyal to the business. Family members may even be groomed and trained to take over the business in a kind of succession planning, so that the business does not end with its founder.

On the other hand, small business owners sometimes refrain from bringing in family members from the fear that the other employees may react badly to their appointment and professionalism in the organization may suffer. Also family members and relatives who do not deserve the job on merit may not be able to do a good job after all and may turn out to be a liability for the business.

These problems can however be tackled reasonably by ensuring that all employees are treated equally. Additionally, a formal employee procedure regarding hiring training, responsibilities, reporting and succession planning can be helpful for situations that deal with family employees. They should be prepared to conform to your environment, culture, dynamics and nature of business. After all, it is perfectly fair to groom family members to take over a business, and it is in the best interests of both the family and the business to make this transition a formal process.

Consulting Agreements

All of the control activities cannot always be performed in-house, either due to the lack of suitable expertise within your business, or for the sake of objectivity.

You will find that you may have to employ third-party assessors of risk and other services. Consulting agreements should be clear on the nature of the engagement, duration of the assignment, scope of work and terms of employment. It should also cover, among other things non-disclosure clauses and limits on usage of proprietary information. *(See A-1 Appendix:* Sample Consulting Agreements*)*

Engagement Letters

A letter prepared by the CPA firm appointed as your auditor is often called an engagement letter. You should have a mutual understanding with your CPA firm on the nature of the audit services to be performed, the timing of those services, the expected fees and the basis on which you will be billed, the responsibilities of the auditor in searching for fraud, your responsibilities for preparing information for the audit, and the need for other services to be performed by the CPA firm. The CPA firm should prepare an engagement letter documenting this understanding between the auditor and the client. The engagement letter clarifies the responsibilities of both management and the auditor as well as the nature of the audit engagement and audit report. Signing an engagement letter with the auditor eliminates potential misunderstanding with the auditor. The engagement letter serves to document the contractual duties agreed to by a CPA, or his or her firm, and the client's business. *(See A-2 Appendix:* Sample of Auditor Engagement Letter*)*

Related Party Transactions

Much has been said about related party transactions in the corporate world. A deal between two entities that have had some prior connection to each other, which may make the deal less than above-board will be called a related party transaction. For example, a contract for erecting a new facility between a public company and one of its major shareholders who is a contracting company will be a related party transaction, even if the deal is legitimate. The contracting company then must accept the burden of proof that the deal was above board or "at arms length". While most related party transactions are perfectly normal, the special relationship between the involved parties creates potential conflicts of interest which can result in actions that benefit the people involved as opposed to the owning interest. As you can see, the possibilities for fraud and misappropriation of business assets are very high in related party dealings.

The existence of related parties and related party transactions has the effect of weakening existing controls. Auditors, in testing an organization's internal control systems, will search for related party transactions. Related parties must be identified, and if the transaction is large enough to affect the financial reports for the year, the transactions must be examined to ensure their authenticity.

Cash Handling

The nature of cash makes it a risky asset. It can easily be misappropriated since individual amounts vary greatly in size. Cash as a financial instrument is instantly negotiable, meaning it can easily be exchanged for goods and services. It therefore has the potential to be used for unauthorized purposes. Cash transactions may be posted to the wrong customer's account or not recorded on a timely basis. Maintaining proper security and accountability during process is the primary concern in providing control over cash receipts. Segregation of duties, appropriate authorization procedures, proper recording and timely reconciliations are necessary to safeguard and ensure control of your cash assets.

Accounts Receivable: Checks and Receipts

Cash receipt transactions may include cash received from customers on account, cash sales and cash received from miscellaneous sources like disposal of assets, disposal of scrap and other miscellaneous cash receipts. An essential internal control required in the cash department is segregation of duties. This is true of both manual and computerized systems. Incoming customer checks and remittance advices are segregated on receipt and processed by different people. Posting to accounts receivable should be based on remittance advices and reconciled to the postings to Cash, which are based on checks received. Another additional control feature involving segregation is to have an independent group such as customer service department handle account balance queries from customers. The people who handle cash or record cash transactions should not perform the cash reconciliation function.

Sample procedure for cash receipts:

The mailroom clerk receives checks from customers. Mailroom staff then separates the checks from remittance advice and restrictively endorses the checks. The checks are sent to the cashier, while the remittance advices are used to prepare a pre-listing of checks. A copy of the checks prelisting is filed for future use, another is sent to the accounts receivable function along with the remittance advices and a third goes to the finance controller or treasury.

The cashier deposits the checks with the business' bank and prepares a summary of cash receipts. The cash receipts summary is used by accounting to record cash receipts and update cash receipts records.

Accounts receivable uses the remittance advice and prelisting of checks to post and update customer accounts. The final checks and balance come in the form of a verification procedure initiated by the controller, of checking check prelisting with deposit tickets issued by the bank, and tallying these to the cash receipts entry in the accounting records.

This procedure should be used not only for cash received from customers but for all cash receipts. Functioning in this manner will ensure that your cash assets are safeguarded from theft and fraudulent use.

Disbursements

Disbursement consists mainly of payments to vendors and to employees. When payments to vendors are due, accounts payable should pull the due vouchers and send them to the treasurer along with the relevant invoice, purchase order and goods received documentation. The treasurer will then prepare the check based on these documents and send the check to the vendor. The treasurer should then collate all the checks issued into a check summary. This check summary along with check copies and all voucher documentation should be sent to the accounts payable and another copy should be sent to the accounting department. Accounting will check the summary and record disbursements in the general ledger. Accounts payable will post the payables ledger and file documents for record keeping purposes.

Chapter Summary

In this chapter, we discussed some of the common control practices engaged in successful businesses. This material focused on organizational structure and duties in finance and operations as related to separation of responsibilities. We examined how to draw up an organizational chart and related why this chart is the foundation for a well-designed controls system. Also, security concepts were re-examined in relation to overall management.

Further attention was given to an overview of some of the elements of a company out of control, particularly dysfunctional operations and how to identify if your business is out of control. In review, the main indicators include: *backlog of work in progress; amount of items returned, both overall and by product lines; increased disputes regarding accounts receivable or accounts payable; outcomes of customer satisfaction surveys; rates of employee absenteeism; decreased productivity; information processing errors; and increased delays in important processes.* Maintaining your awareness in these areas of your business could help you to scout out potential weak spots where you could implement controls to get your business on the right track.

You were then given tools to assist you with the financial authorization process. The tools included definitions of nepotism, conflicts of interest, and related party transactions as well as letters and forms located in the appendix section at the back of this book. While your emerging business may not need all elements of the financial authorization process at this time, as your entity matures financial authorization becomes increasingly vital as risks grow in proportion to business growth.

CHAPTER SEVEN

Understanding Risk Management:
Evaluating Entrepreneurial Risks

By definition, risk is the probability of an outcome of a certain event. Traditionally, risk management has focused on the undesirable consequences of an event and how the organization may be impacted by the aftermath. Recently, the scope of risk management has expanded to include positive events contributing to the success of the organization. This chapter is directed toward managing undesirable events.

In large organizations, risk management teams often have strict boundaries from the operations of internal controls. An entrepreneurial enterprise has neither the time nor the resources to draw such distinctions. For this purpose, this text is dedicated to offering a solid understanding of risk.

Historically this same role of risk management has been limited to the insurance functions within an organization, serving as a liaison between management and insurance providers who transfer risks.[1] The evolution of risk management has progressed to encompass many of the processes also used to govern, control, monitor and manage the enterprise. The driving force behind risk management is to increase the probability of success and reduce the risk of failure. Risk management enhances the business strategy by integrating risk analysis with comprehensive objectives. In other words, long term plan will always have factors and events that could prevent your goals from materializing. All events related to the timeline and overall business design need to be reviewed for the probability of occurrence and the junctures needed if an undesired event interferes with your progress.

Most critics of entrepreneurial pursuits claim that such start-ups do not consider or plan for the risks involved with *not* accomplishing their objectives. Since the risks are never calculated, there is usually no contingency plan which can translate into fewer options available for survival in the event of a disaster whether financial, economical, physical or even emotional. This chapter will not only prepare you to meet your critics with a framework for risks and possibilities but will also give you the necessary tools to make risk considerations part of your culture.

Where there is risk, there is reward; but failure may be the final outcome without responding to the risks which threaten your objectives. As part of risk analysis, we will explore the different approaches to risk management, namely, Traditional Risk Management (TRM) and Enterprise Risk Management (ERM). TRM deals with loss prevention by assessing and identifying internally and externally driven threats while ERM approaches risk management by evaluating the potential threats to the asset portfolio of the organization and how to minimize the damage from risk by maximizing the efficiency of those assets.

Traditional Risk Management

As previously stated, the focal point of the Traditional Risk Management (TRM) approach is loss prevention. This method of assessment uses different tools to evaluate an organization's inadequacies and then produce a plan for protecting the organization from future exploitation of those weaknesses. The main theme for TRM is to stand at readiness at all times to prevent loss, both externally and internally.

External Threats

External threats are those which are initiated from outside the business and are part of your external operating environment. There are four commonly recognized environmental sources of risks: financial risk, strategic risk, operational risk, and hazard risk.

Financial Risk

Financial risk is one of the most fragile risks to an entrepreneur. A checklist of these risks includes:

- Interest rates
- Foreign exchange
- Credit

In a global economy, we are subject to daily market fluctuations not only in our own country, but in other countries as well. These irregularities and their impact on your company need to be assessed regularly to maintain cash flow. Interest rates change depending on broad economic changes and governmental responses. Entrepreneurs are often heavy borrowers and need to look at the impact of rate swings. Since most business loans are on an adjustable rate, this means each time the Federal Reserve increases interest rates you will pay more in interest. Look at your loan documents and see what types of caps are placed on your loan. If there are no limits, how would your company respond to an increase of 5% in interest on your present loan? Would you be able to meet the new payments? While you have no control over these changes, lenders will want to see that you understand the implications and could manage the extra debt burden that rate changes would create to avoid a liquidity risk.

Reality Check:
Liquidity Risk

In May 1984, Continental Illinois Bank was the largest bank in Chicago and one of the largest in the nation. Since the late 1970's, Continental had been issuing loans to oil and natural gas companies. However, with the increases in interest rates and relatively little money in retail accounts, the bank's foreign investors began pulling out. Faced with a liquidity crisis, Continental was near collapse when the U.S. federal banks became involved to avoid a nationwide bank panic.

Lesson learned: even banks are subject to cash flow risks and the many other risks that are common to all businesses.

Source: Federal Deposit Insurance Company, www.fdic.gov

Increasingly, as we become a global economy, entrepreneurial enterprises are directly impacted by foreign exchange. Nowadays, entrepreneurs have so many international options for outsourcing and resourcing. Today's interconnected market has expanded the realm of opportunity for businesses: there are programmers to pay in India, manufacturers for hire in China, marketers to retain in Canada. All of this variety was once reserved for only the largest of international companies. Is your business prepared to handle the ups and downs of foreign currencies? When used as a hedge against international currencies in offshore commerce, financial derivatives can be a powerful tool in reducing risk. Most would consider such financial instruments as increasing risk, and certainly risk is escalated when these tools are used for speculative financial maneuvers. However, using foreign currency forwards and swaps may be a viable option to reduce risk when dealing with foreign currency.

Your credit, as a business, is unlike consumer credit, and certainly for a new entrepreneur, how it is calculated and managed can be a surprise. Externally, your credit may be impacted by changes in banking regulations and other events that you must face when, on the other hand, you may extend credit to your clients. Recognizing that your business credit may not be enough in some cases to give you the leverage you need, you can prepare yourself for other options. In risk planning, you should ask yourself: *what if I win this deal but lack the purchasing power and the cash flow to fund the deal?* With some creative options, such as end-supplier agreements and customer inclusion, this question can be resolved smoothly and profitably.

When a contract is available, yet too large for your credit to handle, chances are your supplier may not want to lose the sale either and could make a direct wholesalers' agreement where you are given royalties on all purchases and the customer works directly with the end-manufacturer. Invest in your supplier relationship, work ethically and include them in your campaign. You can reduce your exposure by creating long-term partnerships with key suppliers who will respond with increasing lines of credit as you require. If you fail to see the risks before you win the account, at best you may be unable to deliver and you could lose an important client.

Strategic Risk

Risk in business strategy is displayed through several factors. A checklist to study the strategic risks of doing business includes:

- Competition
- Change in consumer demand
- Industry shifts

Becoming knowledgeable about the different strategic risks that exist makes you aware of potential difficulties in carrying out your business plan. *Know thy competition; know thy customer; and know thy industry* are the top three commandments to remember when combating these risks.

Nothing chases away potential investors, bankers or partners faster than the naive phrase, "We have no competition!" Certainly, everyone has competing factors even if that competition is to make no change, perhaps and most especially if you are trying to promote a change or to influence others to adopt a new technology. Your responsibility is to identify as comprehensively as possible all of the competitive risks that affect your business. Risks from rival breakthroughs are accelerating as new technologies are adopted and customer preferences evolve. Some foresight as an entrepreneur is required to direct your efforts, while not all evens can be foreseen, general responses to meet those changes can be documented and catalogued for later reference.

Reality Check:
When Shooting Stars Burn Out

The year was 1997, and the release of Billy Bob the Singing Fish® was the customer must-have prize of the holiday shopping season. After a year of so of a few good laughs these fish have vanished, only to be found in variety stores and novelty back shelves. What caused the decline? Was it poor product quality? Poor market execution? Too many competitors? The answer is, of course, no. It was one of the myriad trendy consumer products that sells heavily for a while and simply vanishes as boredom sets in and annoyance takes over. Similar responses can be seen in categories that range from breakfast cereals to rock bands. Businesses need to realize that fickle consumers have tastes and demands that change over time.

Although some shooting stars can break the mold, most just burn out. At that point, it is back to the drawing board to dream up a new "latest and greatest" product. While trends can certainly heat up your market, a mix of trendy and traditional products and services will give you a solid base on which to grow.

Insightful entrepreneurs will see the risks that threaten their businesses with consumer shifts long before others are aware of these fluctuations. Risk assessment in this area is especially sensitive for those involved in consumer products. Including consumer shift assessments in your risk plan will prepare you for both the rise and fall of the product and service lifecycle.

From the days of the Industrial revolution, change has been a by-product of technological improvement. Every new technology gives birth to a new industry and has the potential to kill off an old one. For example, growth in the communications industry in the middle of the last industry killed off the telegraph and traded it for the telephone. Presently, new advances in technology have made cellular telephony a must-have technology even in many parts of the underdeveloped world. Over the last two hundred years the metal-working industry has evolved from being a craft to being a heavy industry. Changes caused by improved technology cannot be controlled and often bring a business to the brink of closure. On the other hand, a business can anticipate these advancements in the industry and adjust accordingly.

Operational Risk

Operational risk spells out significant cause for concern in a couple of different areas for today's entrepreneur. A checklist of these operational risks includes:

- Regulations
- Social changes

In today's scenario of more new markets and inexorable growth of enterprise, expansion of regulatory regimes is a foregone conclusion. Self-regulation is no longer an option where market forces are complex and their effects and consequences spread worldwide. In such a bureaucratic system, there are not only risks of regulation but also risks in the failure to understand its significance and relevance. Meanwhile, the increased threat of litigation knows no bounds and its foreboding presence is ever prevalent in business operations. The objective is of course to avoid this operational risk in the first place, and this requires both practical and intuitive management of risk.

A classic example of how social change can put businesses at risk is the tobacco industry. No other industry has probably been affected as much by social perceptions as the tobacco industry over the past fifty years or so. From what was once not just an accepted habit but a socially desirable one, smoking has moved from the top of the 'A' list to the bottom of the 'D' list. Instead of being the habit to have, it is the habit to kick. This is for the most part due to a shift in the societal mindset owing much to media-driven awareness of new research on how smoking affects humanity. While most social changes drive consumer demand for products and services, being sensitive to social changes and anticipating the following trends will keep you perched at a bird's-eye view of what consumers want and will allow your business to soar.

Hazard Risk

Lastly, a checklist of hazard risks that pose a potential threat to your business includes:

- Suppliers
- Environment
- Contracts

Knowing your suppliers' weaknesses and having a predetermined plan if a key supplier fails to make deliveries could protect your business from this supplier-side risk. Simply because a supplier has been trustworthy and steady does not mean that they are resistant to risks that may be entirely unknown to your organization. This practice has nothing to do with trust and integrity, but is simply good business. Be familiar with second sources. If your key supplier were to vanish, have at least two or three potential alternates that you could contact today to fill your needs.

Your geographical environment is filled with unique risks that you will need to accept and for which you will need to create some alternative measures. Some disasters are so monumental for a small business that they may disrupt operations significantly. These types of hazards, including flood, fire and general liability, should be transferred to an insurance company. Unless you are financially in a position to self-insure your enterprise, make the sacrifice and buy a policy. In many cases, when such disasters occur you can build again and often comeback stronger and better by correcting many of the things you had always intended to improve in your operations.

There never seems to be an end to potential litigation within the business framework of legal documents, particularly that of contracts. Review all of your contracts carefully and slowly, and make arrangements to have your contracts examined by an attorney when feasible. Make every effort to keep your contractual commitments and have a solid network of attorneys available to advise you on various legal issues.

Internal Threats

Internal threats are those risks that present themselves within the organization itself. Developing a risk management framework assists the organization in the identification of internal risk and how to mitigate the problems that could occur if and when these internal risks manifest themselves.

Risk Management Framework

Managing risk is a continuous process as opposed to something that only happens once. Starting with the business strategy and considered throughout the organizational processes, managing risk impacts every step of the planning process. The way to handle risk is to approach it with a positive mindset as an opportunity and not as a threat. Managing risk is central to the task of managing the business enterprise itself. It is a need that is woven through every function of organizational behavior and essential for enterprise growth.

The external risks mentioned above are typical and most likely to occur in any business enterprise. Apart from this, your business could be open to specific risks, hence, internal risks that you will need to understand both in terms of how they will impact your general business plan and your daily operations.

The successful management of risk requires a rigorous approach that begins with a coherent plan of assessment. This means that while incorporating the organization's business objectives it also states the organization's approach under the following key headings. This assessment plan establishes the procedures for systematizing the process of risk handling. A checklist of the areas associated with risk handling includes:

- Risk Planning
- Risk Information Flow
- Risk Education and Training
- Risk Process Structure
- Risk Recording
- Risk Handling
- Risk Audit and Compliance

The success of the entire approach to the management of risk depends on the organization's ability to formally define risk. Additionally, a protocol needs to be introduced that will recognize risks on a continuous basis. The risk study should also recognize the role of people and machines. It should standardize and allow for the identification of risk. It should be able to evaluate potential risks in terms of their impact and the likelihood for occurrence. In addition, strategies for risk should be updated in the event of significant changes in the organization's strategic planning and circumstances.

The risk strategy should be managed and implemented from the top of the organization, starting with the Chief Executive Officer or owner all the way down through every level of operation. Risk awareness should become second nature for everyone. An openness of culture will also encourage understanding and feedback about the risk factors in practice. Risk should be integrated seamlessly into the overall strategy—clearly defined, communicated and understood by everyone. Ownership and accountability are as basic to risk awareness as to any other business processes. To a traditional risk manager, managing risk is more a matter of understanding and seizing the opportunity, thereby maximizing value and minimizing potential loss of value. Let us examine all of the steps in risk management one at a time.

Risk Planning

The overall purpose of risk planning is to effectively implement the business's strategies including those parts identified to take account of the risks. The risk management process should improve what the business already does. Being in business means making decisions and all decision-making involves risk. The only issue is the level of risk that you are ready to accept. Your aim should be to know as many of the risks to which your business is exposed. Also, how you handle risk when it occurs is of utmost importance. Moreover, the processes which you have created to understand risk and to learn from its occurrence to benefit you in the future are vital to the health and wellbeing of your organization.

Risk Information Flow

The management of risk is part of a continuous cycle of understanding, learning about, improving upon and informing others about the strategic direction. The processes for identifying, understanding, communicating and managing risks and opportunities should be common and consistent across the whole organization. The risk information system should allow all adverse events, consequences and control weaknesses to be communicated to every appropriate authority in the organization. Information is crucial to the promotion of any activity involving specific attention on risk issues. The flow of information needs and requires constant thought, logical design, deliberate action and must be suited to the organization's needs. This means that relevant individuals should have ready and rapid access to the risk information necessary to make timely and appropriate decisions.

This can be made possible with the use of new technologies that speed up response channels. The information made available should be relevant, timely and concise. Unreliable, inconsistent or apparently conflicting information can either undermine the quality decisions or lead to differential or even under-performance.

During the strategic planning process, information can be collected, analyzed and reviewed at a slightly more leisurely pace. However the implementation phase requires rapid, responsive, reactive, and relevant information, especially in respect to the anticipated risk factor or unexpected events and consequences. A risk factor would be any variable that could affect the outcome in general. The flow of risk information should be designed with the final objective of risk assurance in mind. This will help with the process of planning for each of the management for each activity. Risk information needs to be interactive with the daily management process and not be restricted to the audit processes.

Risk Education and Training

To create risk awareness culture, structure and an organized approach is necessary to get started. The key to creating a successful risk awareness culture is to encourage a climate of opportunity and open communication. Positive and insightful risk education starts with communication. The organization needs to demonstrate its commitment to managing risk from the top management downwards. Specific exercises that help do the job include risk brainstorming by the top management and developing a team that includes a broad spectrum of representation from within the organization, then breaking this main team into smaller study circles, again, with the objective of brain-storming.

One of the techniques used in risk education is simulation training. This refers to the process of finding one's own way to knowledge by understanding through participation, learning in a safe environment, and being able to experiment. Everyone involved should be aware of their role in every situation. Simulation training also enables the process of risk handling and its' management to be integrated throughout an organization by delivering business risk education to all levels. Whatever other process is used to promote awareness and understanding of risk and to introduce the management of risk into the mainstream management and business processes, communication will be central.

A solid way to ensure successful communication and understanding of information is to test the process. In order to introduce and sustain the management of risk in the mainstream of management and business processes in your organization, some skills need to be learned and developed. A checklist of these skills includes:

- Communication skills and the ability to facilitate learning and understanding
- Ability to promote holistic thinking across the organization and in all individuals
- Ability to promote quality management by learning from experience and by understanding the importance of the continuous cycle of improvement
- Financial, commercial and general business awareness
- A knowledge and understanding of the organization including its vision, purpose and direction

In addition to these skills, do not underestimate the value of having some people within the organization assigned directly to think and focus on the management of risk. Direction over the whole process of establishing risk training and education is an important task that will ensure the success of its implementation.

Risk Process Structure

Ideally, the process of risk management should be eventually absorbed into the overall management process. In spite of this, risk can be better managed when supported by the creation of a formally recognized structure through which risk can be identified at every stage of the management process. The risk management structure should be easily recognized and should be adaptable to all parts of the organization. The management of risk may be outsourced, or may be handled in-house. While looking outside the organization for risk advice, the level of service you may desire would depend on your business's maturity and readiness for change. Also, you should look for an external advisor if you do not have the experience and competency in-house to carry out risk assessments. In your search, you need to find a professional risk manager. If you desire extensive assessments and have challenging questions about the risks you face, find one who is particularly experienced with the risks that are unique to your industry.

When managing risk internally, it is also useful to use the expertise of your project manager to expand upon the lessons learned and knowledge gained in the execution of smaller projects and to be able to adapt these lessons as they apply throughout the whole organization. The techniques, disciplines and experiences of project management give good insight into risks and how to manage them and are readily transferable back into the core operations.

Risk Recording

At each stage of the management processes it is possible to identify and evaluate the relevant risks. The purpose of recording such risks, their possible consequences and a recommended course of action provides an opportunity to improve risk awareness and understanding, ensuring that the organization is effectively managing risk.

The processes need to be in place to ensure that risks are identified, captured as soon as possible, recorded and monitored. This framework also needs to include the agreed course of action of how best to handle the consequences of a certain risk. All of the above should be documented and approved including authorization for the course of action to be taken in dealing with the risk. The line of communication which has been established during the risk information flow planning stage can be referred to and relied upon to decide who else needs to be informed. The documentation produced by this exercise should summarize the other key risks facing the business at every stage including description of the impending risk; the potential impact of the risk on the organization; the likelihood of the risk occurring; the person directly responsible for managing the risk; the existing controls and actions required to reduce the risks and a timetable for the course of action in response to the risk.

Risk Handling

Risk handling is about the way an organization deals with the risk both before and after the occurrence of incidents. In risk handling, you plan your work in how it relates to the events of a possible risk are dealt with, and then you work your plan when and after these events occur. Risk handling does not, of course, begin when the incident has materialized, the ideal situation would be to proactively manage the risk to prevent the incident from happening. However, accidents do and will occur and risk management is concerned with minimizing such risk. As mentioned before, this is done through an awareness and understanding of risks inherent to the business. This awareness combined with the proper training and education can optimize the potential avoidance of fallouts from the risk event. Planning will help keep the organization in a state of readiness as if an incident were to occur. Through risk handling, the business is not only able to reduce the possibility of incidents emerging but also to minimize the consequences to the quality of service and long-term value of the organization.

At the macro-level, risk handling translates into disaster and contingency planning. However well-planned your risk management system, incidents can happen suddenly and often without warning. One of the benefits of having a business fine-tuned to risk is that you can trust that an objective approach toward risk is part of the management culture, and is integrated into the management processes. Further, the people concerned with supervising the event caused by the risk would have the right skills and experience to make objective decisions and that the best risk recording and handling systems are in place.

Risk Audit and Compliance

Risk audits ensure that you have adequate risk planning and management arrangements in place to anticipate the possibility of risks and to manage them. These audits also include providing evidence that policies and procedures are in place to minimize the consequences of incidents when they occur.

The function of managing risk overlaps the audit function where the review of things that went wrong is intertwined with a review of the processes intended to minimize the possibility in the first place. Compliance with the traditional risk management process should be about assured delivery of objectives and sustained long-term value creation, together with facilitating and improving a continuous cycle of enhancing the existing risk management system to prevent loss within an organization.

Enterprise Risk Management

Unlike TRM which focuses on loss prevention, the Enterprise Risk Management (ERM) approach works at improving efficiency by handling operational risks in respect to its entire asset portfolio. ERM is a different approach to risk management which brings together strategy, people, processes, technology and knowledge with the objective of continuously improving your business's risk management ability over a period of time. The assets which come under the purview of ERM are as disparate as customer assets, employee/supplier assets, and organizational assets such as products, brands, patented processes and innovative systems. The broad focus of ERM helps more than anything else to reduce the risk of reputation damage and enhances the valuation of the business. Uncertainties can be anticipated and managed in the following three ways:

- ERM paves the way for attaining competitive advantage. It does not compartmentalize risks; instead by integrating various views of risks it helps the organization become more alert and responsive.

- The cost of managing risk is kept at an optimal level through the use of ERP. This is done by combining risk acceptance and transfer decisions, eliminating redundant activities and identifying the level of risk that the business is willing to accept.

- Business performance is improved through the use of ERM techniques. These techniques focus on anticipating major events and developing responses to prevent those from occurring.

A checklist of practical solutions for ERM implementation follows:

- *Assess risk:* An enterprise risk assessment is a good first step in ERM implementation. It involves identifying and prioritizing the organization's operational risks and responses to these risks including information about the current state of capabilities. You can add value to your ERM by identifying gaps in the risk priorities classified in your business. This makes the ERM more organization-specific and can exponentially add value to the business.

- *Define the role of ERM in the organization:* A working group of senior executives should be assigned with the task of 1) defining the role of risk management and 2) defining the goals and objectives for the business as a whole. For this to be achieved, management should be supported by a good information system and a capability to manage risks. This capability is built-in with the help of policies, processes, competencies, reports, methodologies and technology required to execute the organization's response to managing its priority risks.

- *Improved handling of priority risks:* Like any other program, ERM has to begin somewhere and a good place to start is a high risk or priority risk area. These may range from regulatory compliances, financial risks or even process risks. Wherever you may start, the goal is the same, to increase risk management capabilities for the whole organization.

- *ERM infrastructure:* Working within the infrastructure refers to working with the set of organizational tools that can help advance risk management capabilities. These include policies and procedures, structures and reporting associated with the management of risk. You will need to identify the level and nature of ERM present in your organization, and then pinpoint the gaps that have been left where principal risks are not covered by the current risk management arrangements. ERM infrastructure establishes fact-based understanding about the enterprise's risk and risk management capabilities. Working toward this understanding ensures that there is ownership over the crucial risks. Closure of unacceptable risks is encouraged and leaves a very small percentage of uncovered risks. ERM infrastructure needs to be customized to suit each business's specific needs and should fit the organizational culture and the extent of coverage desired by the management.

- *Move to other key risks*: After establishing an ERM plan by completing the first four steps, the organization returns to step 1. This time the focus is to re-evaluate priorities and produce a fresh risk assessment based on the new critical risk management areas. In this manner ERM can slowly be extended to cover risk management capabilities to all the key risk areas and to broaden the managements focus to the entire organization.

A properly implemented ERM plan can help organizations pursue strategic growth opportunities with greater speed, skill and confidence by aligning the organization's risk-taking desires with its core competencies.

Best Practices in Enterprise Risk Management

Best practices is a management accounting term that has been defined as the most efficient and effective way of accomplishing a task, based on repeatable procedures that have proven themselves time and again in different situations for different people. This management idea asserts that there is always a technique, method, process, activity or reward that is more effective at delivering a particular outcome than another. When such a technique is discovered, it becomes the new standard, against which all future performance will be measured.

In relation to Enterprise Risk Management, best practice is considered to be a buzzword which describes the process of developing and following a standard way of doing a particular activity which then can be followed by all businesses in the same industry or by any industry carrying out a similar practice.

Corporate Governance

Large corporations have the benefit of a dedicated CRO, or Chief Risk Officer, who is professionally trained to analyze, calculate and respond to various risks within an organization. Small enterprises may not have trained specialists, but they can be trained to be skilled at recognizing and reducing risk. As was stated before, where there is risk, there is reward, but you, as the small business owner, must determine how much risk is appropriate in relation to ROI (return-on-investment). You will govern risk with one of the following four options:

- *Avoid risk*: Choose not to perform the activity.
- *Transfer risk*: Use third parties, insurance or hedge vehicles.
- *Mitigate risk:* Operational risk, reduce through preventative procedure and detective controls.
- *Accept risk*: Certain risks must be accepted to earn gains.

Figure 7.1

Govern your business on the principle that each risk must go through this analysis process. For example, you offer computer network consulting services and want to know what impact adding a new security monitoring service might have on your enterprise. You will need to ask yourself what risks could be avoided, transferred, mitigated or accepted. A typical thought process might look like this:

What are the risks of a lawsuit, damages, customer loss of data that could impact your ability to perform?

⇗ ⇘

Avoid risk mitigate risk

What are insurance costs for this activity?

⇓

Transfer risk

What risks are worth keeping in order to offer the additional service and what gains could be made?

⇓

Accept risk

Using the internal controls team that you have formed to share in the decision-making process would be a worthwhile inclusion. This controls team is the nearest functioning body that a small team can create to serve as your audit committee. Ask the members of this group to weigh in the probabilities and risks of a given event's occurrence. One option may be to assign one member of your controls team to also serve as your Risk Director, helping to determine which of the risks can be mitigated, transferred, avoided, or accepted within your operation.

Protecting Physical Assets

To protect important documents, valuables and perhaps even cash, you might be using a safe deposit box at a third party location. You may sometimes feel a pin-prick of fear about whether or not the safe deposit place is really 'safe'. Tackle this fear rationally by identifying the risk factors involved in this situation. First, there is the very obvious security risk, the risk of theft. This can be covered by ensuring that the provider of the service has a good watch system in place, both through organic security and electronic surveillance.

There is the element of risk involved in the consistency of service delivery. Before establishing your safe deposit box location, you probably made an assessment of how reliable your service provider is, by checking out his performance track record and client references. The organization's reputation and management profile can also serve to make you feel secure about the services rendered. Investigate the service provider's reporting system which may include an opportunity for you to audit the services received from time to time. This opportunity serves as a type of feedback and opens communication between you and your service provider and allows for building a trusting relationship which can assist in alleviating this risk.

The safe deposit box also faces the risk of situational hazards. The third party location may be subject to flooding, earthquakes, fires, arson and other unexpected natural and man-made calamities. This risk can be diminished by a scheduling physical tour of the premises and ensuring that the service provider has an adequate insurance clause written into your contract.

Instead of a safe deposit box, you may consider using a safe at your business location as your best bet in ensuring the safety of your precious belongings. Even with this choice, risks are present. There is the security risk, just as in the safe deposit box at the outside location. You can cover for that risk by setting up adequate security systems. A safe at your location poses the additional risk of pilferage by someone on the inside, perhaps one of your own staff, or an employee of one of your contractors. Implementing a control system here would safeguard against unauthorized access to the safe and to the security systems that guard it, at the same time. You can also ensure that the system is designed in such a way as to minimize the damage from connivance of two or more individuals. Additionally, you can insure the contents of the safe against theft, burglary and loss or damage from fire and natural calamities, and hence transfer some of the risk.

Protecting Inventory

You have invested large amounts of working capital into acquiring the assets that form the basis of your inventory. You inventory is, of course, worth more than dollars and cents since it is the life-blood that keeps your business operating so that you can meet and even exceed customer expectations. This automatically appertains to several elements of risk with inventory storage and delivery conditions. These risks can vary from business to business but there are a few general risks that apply in any situation. A checklist of these risks includes:

- Physical damage or theft
- Shrinkage
- Obsolescence

The risk of physical damage or theft is common in any business situation. This risk can be reduced by ensuring proper storage and access by employees only on a "need" basis. Setting up security measures will ensure a significant reduction in opportunities for this threat to manifest. Also, protecting inventory with an insurance policy will guard against total loss in the event of an uncontrollable natural disaster.

The risk of deterioration of inventory quality when in storage or shrinkage applies to businesses where fresh product is paramount to customer satisfaction. If your inventory is of the nature that it spoils with time, you probably already have systems to ensure that the oldest stock is used first, and nothing is allowed to waste by not being used before the expiration date. A fine example of where inventory control is needful is for the fresh flower inventory of a flower shop. To allow minimum shrinkage and maximum inventory usage, you could develop a system where you use color-coded buckets to rotate older flowers that still have use when new inventory is received. Regardless of how you set up this system, regular rotation of fresh product assures you that your customers will be satisfied with their purchase and you will generate repeat business by gaining a fresh reputation.

Lastly, there is the risk of obsolescence. Processes and products are always evolving and you are perhaps also constantly innovating so that your products remain technological superior and always on top. You inventory needs will also perhaps change with time, and you will perhaps be left with great quantities of raw materials or products that you know you don't need or may have a reduced demand. A good stocking system following the principles of just-in-time inventory and similar systems can alleviate this risk.

Legal Risk

It is common knowledge that no one is immune to legal risk and anyone can be sued at any time for any amount, resulting in staggering financial losses in most cases. Regardless of the merit of the case, you can prepare yourself to handle this risk and how to take appropriate action to protect your enterprise. As this following press release illustrates, you can be sued for any amount regardless of reason.

Reality Check:
$54 Million Dollar Pants

A dry cleaner in Washington, D.C., who was confronted with being cleaned out itself when it was sued for $54 million over an allegedly missing pair of pants, will not have to pay anything to its disgruntled customer, a Judge Bartnoff ruled. Instead, Roy Pearson, who sued over the missing trousers, may have to pay the store owners' legal fees. She also said that Pearson's theory that the owners owed him $54 million because they lost his pants despite a sign that ensures "Satisfaction Guaranteed" had no support in the law. "A reasonable consumer would not interpret 'Satisfaction Guaranteed' to mean that a merchant is required to satisfy a customer's unreasonable demands," Bartnoff wrote in her ruling.

Fortunately, reason prevailed, but it brings to mind the value of a working relationship with a quality attorney to protect your assets if you lose a customer's pants.

Source: Associated Press News, June 25, 2007.

If you do not yet have a relationship with a reputable attorney in your area, get one. It costs nothing to meet with most attorneys for the purpose of introducing yourself and inquiring about their services and fee structures. This will give you an opportunity in advance to have strong relationships that will protect you from future mishaps. It is unfortunate that our society operates on the premise that you should be compensated for any inconvenience. Nonetheless, prepare yourself with a strong business attorney that is not easily cowered into a corner during a confrontation.

Reputational Risk

One of your most valuable resources is the creation of your brand. Think of brands such as Coke, Kraft, Pepsi, Sony, Disney and Merck. The brand name alone for these entities is worth billions. Most people know these brands have had problems, but they also know these brands are time-tested and proven, and this very fact impacts the buying decisions in our fast-paced culture. Reputational risk is defined as "the potential that negative publicity regarding an institution's business practices, whether true or not, will cause a decline in the customer base, costly litigation, or revenue reductions."[2]

Do not let any ethical conflict harm your reputation as your efforts to build your brand will make your entire sales process easier or more difficult going forward. Consider the damage to a bank that has had persistent robberies or lost multiple accounts due to security or service issues. Any of those events would cause irreparable damage to that bank.

Reputational risk entails the damage that could be done in the event of unscrupulous activity, prolonged unresolved customer conflict, poor customer relations, or security breaches. Protect your reputation with a sense of fairness and customer concern. Resolve conflict immediately, reach out to your customers, and consistently give 110%. A little extra effort can go along way in preserving your reputation and building your brand.

Chapter Summary

In this chapter, the topic of discussion that has prevailed is the importance of understanding risk management and how it impacts your entrepreneurial endeavor. Risk management is not just about having enough insurance. It is the principal way to control the repercussions from unwanted and unforeseen events caused by risk. The different approaches to preventing loss and effectively managing measures to reduce the risk of doing business every day have been reviewed.

Traditional Risk Management is a general risk management concept with a centralized risk assessment of internal and external threats. The four ways to deal with risk include *avoidance, mitigation, transfer and acceptance*. Through the evaluation of risk, you can create a culture of risk awareness and help others in your organization be like-minded in reducing opportunities that open you to setbacks caused by undesirable events from those risks.

Enterprise Risk Management allows you to better understand the risks to your company and its assets as a whole and how to create more efficient use of those assets to avoid unwanted difficulty. Using the techniques of this method, you see the aggregation of your organization and how the parts all work together to produce the final reward of a successful business. While risk is inherent to reward, properly managed risk will not stand in your way of obtaining those rewards.

CHAPTER EIGHT

Customer Performance Controls

In today's hyper-competitive environment, your most precious resource is your customer. As an emerging business you need to focus on the customers who are going to help pay today's bills, as well as remember the needs of future customers who will provide future sales and new opportunities for growth.

This chapter will provide you with vital insight into the entire customer relationship and what controls are needed to make sure you identify and maintain your customer base. Without proper treatment of customers and systems in place to ensure quality performance and delivery to your customers, all other controls are ineffectual. Loyal customers provide dividend value which you need to use to estimate and modify your products and services accordingly.

Who Pays You?

Without any exception, one point that needs to be understood is that the customer ultimately pays you in terms of growth and profitability. Everything you do in regards to servicing your customer will be reflected in your sales; and your sales will ultimately affect your profits. At times your efforts may be fruitful; conversely, there may be times when you experience customer scarcity and for seemingly no good reason. You must accept that you will never control customer choice; only that you can control components of your business that will affect customer choice.

What customer controls do for you are to provide a way for you to measure your ability to give your customers enough choices that you become the best choice. Simply put, respect for your customer's need to choose and your customer will respect your need for sales.

The relationship between business owner and customer is, in its best form, symbiotic. The business owner provides a need either through products or services and the customer reciprocates by providing money in exchange for filling that need. If the customer harbors any suspicion of an arrogant, forceful or otherwise controlling or neglectful situation, in almost every instance your customer will find a new supplier.

While you do not control the customer, you need policies and procedures within your organization to procure present sales and protect future sales. There are procedures and protocol to follow, yet you need to accept that a customer may leave at any moment and prepare a way to cope with that possibility.

Customer Relationship Package

The area of customer controls is delicate in nature and a bit of a misnomer because you ultimately cannot control your customers' choice. The relationship package you present to your customers is one aspect of measuring profitability within your organization. Your customer relationship package holds a fine balance between the basic product and the service that surrounds the product delivery. Outside the basic accounting perspective, measuring customer profitability spans a much broader scope than simply at the individual product level.

With present database tools, organizations can quickly identify which products are gaining profits and which products are losing profits. What these database tools fail to recognize is that while some products and services show paper results of marginal or no profitability, they may be what clinches the deal and retains the customer. In that sense, these services and products are a valuable "tour de force" that cannot be quantified through formulas or procedures.

In the book, *Driving Customer Equity*, the idea of stimulating profitability through the customer relationship level rather than through the component or product level is expanded. The authors advise that when a business fails to recognize how the customer relationship is directly tied to profitability they enter a "profit death spiral".[1] The following events explain the customer profitability death trap:

> Company Z is earning excellent returns, a handsome market share and high market expectations. Moreover, the company now has the resources and history to exploit current database technology and powerful information tools.

↻

> Management decides to take advantage of current information and has identified several elements of the company's services that are either returning marginal profits or actually losing money. These services are eliminated.

↻

Some of the customers preferred the company's services exactly as they were because these services are eliminated; they now find themselves looking for another supplier.

U

Loss of sales now preempts more cutbacks in order to preserve the previous financial performance. The company begins targeting only what it sees as its "core services."

U

Customers continue to leave as service declines and choices are removed which in turn forces more cutbacks for the company.

This process continues until either the company has lost all its customers, the company is sold or the enterprise has a dramatic recognition of what has occurred and begins reversing the cycle and restoring and improving services to attract new customers and even win back old customers.

Note that the decline began when eyes were taken off the true source of all the company's success, the customers. Customers "allow" a business to make a profit because the services are meeting their needs as a package; usually the solution is not simply one element of product or service. The entire relationship produces the profitable results. When customers sense that the business has cheapened its services and offerings, customers begin leaving for different reasons. These reasons all point back to a forgotten sense of what the customer needs.

Establishing Metrics for Customer Valuation

Customers make a dual contribution to your business value through immediate sales and future purchases. When a customer walks away dissatisfied, you lose not only today's sales but future earning potential from that resource as well. The probability that an unhappy customer will defect to a competitor is very high.

We have all experienced poor customer service and sometimes have promised ourselves never to return. Though many of us have been forgiving enough to give them a second chance, typically we only try once more when given a compelling reason such as a promotion that was so good that despite the possible poor service this promotion made it worth the abuse just to get the discount. In your reluctant state, the sale is made; at which point you either decide the company is not so bad after all, or you further entrench yourself in your former commitment to stay away.

From a business standpoint, you can put certain controls in place to establish metrics for customer valuation that will preserve the relationship that you build with your customers and protect the balance between that relationship and your profitability. From providing refunds to handling complaints, there are procedures that can be applied to these situations which will lead to winning solutions for both you and your customer.

Customer Equity

Before you are introduced to customer controls that can preserve your VIPs, one more idea related to your customer relationship package needs to be further explored. Unlike corporeal resources such as inventory or office space or funding capital, customers are an intangible resource as they do not exist until you create them.

Customer equity is an ingredient in your overall intangible assets contained within your customer relationships, and perhaps the most significant intangible asset to your business. This abstract capital is affected by how it is treated, not unlike mechanical or physical equipment which when neglected and devoid of preventive maintenance, may experience accelerated devaluation. Likewise, customers that are not trusted, respected and valued as such will manifest in diminished return sales.

When an enterprise is overly concerned only with short term sales, long term earnings may be severely hampered. From a quantifiable approach, one way to think of customer equity is to look at the cost of capital: if a company is generating profits of 5% but its return rate on capital is 7%, then the capital is actually losing shareholder value. When you consider what happened with Arthur Anderson and their connection with the Enron scam nearly overnight, the loss of trust and credibility which resulted in the loss of their remaining customer base was simply incomparable.

The customer asset although intangible is very real working capital. It may be consumed over the course of business if abused; it may be replenished and renewed with proper care. Customers change their minds and shift loyalties with promises of greener pastures. Remember your customer base is constantly shifting and in transition; if you are to build your customer equity, you will need to win more long-term customers than you lose.

If we look at the metrics for demonstrating customer value, one of the most accurate tools for analysis is identified as Customer Equity. Customer equity can be divided into three governing concepts which measure the value of the relationship:

- *Brand equity:* This measurement demonstrates the customer's subjective assessment of the brand above its objective value. (This means if the shoe carries the "Nike" name, what is the value a customer confers to that shoe beyond the objective value of the shoe?). Another way of understanding this is to value a product, Brand X, objectively for its function and features; if the customer is willing to pay twice Brand X's objective value vs. Brand Y then it carries measurable brand equity, in this case two times the amount that Brand Y would command.

- *Retention equity:* This appraisal establishes the tendency of the customer to stick with a relationship above the product's objective value to use that brand. For example, the customer sticks with Nike because she had a good experience in the past.

- *Value equity:* This element of customer equity assesses the objective measure of the utility of a brand in reference to what must be given in exchange. Referring back to our Nike example, the customer desires the Nike name on his shoes because that brand name helps him to fit in: he objectively knows he is paying more than other comparable product brands and accepts that factor in terms of value returned for purchase of the Nike brand.

Using each of these three principles—*brand, retention, and value*—you can begin to understand the importance that customer equity plays in establishing value with your current and potential customers.

Customer Equity Application for Entrepreneurs

As an entrepreneur you may be asking yourself; how does this apply to me and to my business? This brief, hypothetic analysis will provide you with an overview of how customer equity pertains to you as an entrepreneur.

Making some simple assumptions about your emerging business to assess your brand equity, you may carry a unique product that fits a niche that has a bonus "coolness" factor that your customers are willing to pay for just to be associated with your brand. Additionally, make the presumption that your brand is readily identifiable and trustworthy.

Next, in ascertaining your value equity, also assume because of your introductory status within the market, that you hold a value proposition is again most likely.[1] This does not mean that your brand will need to remain in this emerging arena, only that as an entrepreneurial venture, it will take time to develop a loyal clientele that will stick with your products and services and are even willing to pay extra for the perceived benefits your product offers.

Finally, the subject matter comes to customer retention. This is the one area where your efforts will amass customer equity faster than any other means. In promoting customer loyalty, you will develop repeat sales by offering your customers more than your competition can offer.

Putting all these factors into play, you can develop a quantifiable idea of how customer equity is relevant to you as an entrepreneur, wholly contributing to the establishment, growth and profitability of your venture.

Building Value with Customers

As the U.S. economy continues to shift from manufacturing and developing raw materials toward offering service-based products, your relationship with your customer will become more and more reliant upon creating your own brand of value. In viewing your business from your customer's perspective, your potential opportunities to expand and improve will be noted and rewarded.

Since the opening of the first Target store in 1962, their philosophy has always been to expect more and pay less for quality items. This retailer continues to rise above the crowd as the "quality" discount leader, providing a higher standard of service the sets it apart from its other major competitors.

Target has accomplished a brand of value because it was able to view the market from the perspective of their customer base. Certainly, the task of discovering the needs of your customers is no small undertaking; often customers do not know what they want until that want in the form of a product or service is presented to them.

Reality Check:
Uncovering Desire

Customers in the early 1990's certainly did not know they wanted internet access, until they began to see the information on their computer screens and all the excitement of the availability of real time news, stocks and other resources. My first experience with the Internet came in 1993 working with a 9600 baud modem looking up car manufacturers. At the time, the internet was painfully slow and browsers were awkward; Moreover, finding a site was very difficult. Eventually, as improvements were made, more people discovered the desire to get "on line".

What customers see and experience, they begin to desire and eventually the want becomes a need. By offering new services or products, entrepreneurs create needs and help customers uncover those hidden desires.

It is your responsibility to continue to focus on delivering to customers what they want; trial and error is an acceptable delivery vehicle. As you continue to uncover the desires of your customers, incorporate those desires into your products and services; anticipate what they might like by taking opportunities to see your services from their perspective.

In the following illustration you will see the connection between price, quality and delivery in creating customer value.

Figure 8.1

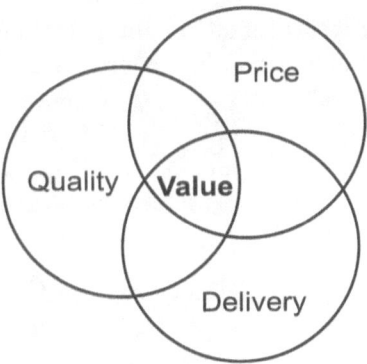

The perceived value of your product and service is directly impacted by the actual quality, price and delivery of your product. Keeping this in mind, you can create a customer relationship package that will provide a foundation for customer controls and assist in stabilizing the capricious nature of customer relations.

Control the Process and Expand Ideas

In developing customer controls, it's all about the process: never limiting ideas and making changes as needed. Create a framework where customers can be handled and changes can be adopted according to your customers' needs. Ensure that you distinguish between your customers' needs and your own needs as a business owner. As a for-profit enterprise, you wish to offer products and services with the highest yield per delivery as possible.

Because customers will want different things, part of the controls you will want to establish is identifying a target market. You cannot be all things to everyone; to attempt to do so will result in meaningless ambiguity. Focus your services toward a particular customer and determine what would offer the most value in their situation. That is what is meant by seeing your service from the customer's perspective.

Reality Check:
When Quality Kills a Business

You may not have considered that too much quality could be detrimental; however, it has and can lead to a company's demise.

The first small business winner of the Malcolm Baldrige National Quality Award in 1990 was Wallace Co. Inc. This business had spent large amounts of resources improving its services as a distributor of pipes and valves systems. In terms of quality, Wallace had it all: an automated delivery system, the latest information systems and an outstanding service team. What it did not have was a customer base that was willing to pay for the extra cost of the increased quality of service. Within two years Wallace Co. had filed chapter 11 bankruptcy.

Point being, when the focus is not on the customer relationship anything attempted in the way of quality will distance the business from the very success it is striving toward.

Source: Sixel, L., "Quality-Award Winner Files for Chapter 11." The Houston Chronicle, 1992.

Control Your Business Offering

As you fine tune your service offering, direct your attention and everything you do toward your customers. When examining your business's products and services and considering different solutions to improving quality, be careful that you do not lose the foundational vision of your business. Taking the customer's perspective may tempt you to offer various services and extended features of your product, but you must step back and make sure it will not detract from your core services and the perceived value that you have created. Many companies have been derailed by lack of control when it comes to developing quality services that they think will match the desires of their customers. In an attempt to offer more and more value to their customers, they overstep their competencies and end up distracted and unfocused.

One way that you can control your business offering and still adjust to your customers desires over time is using the Customer Lifetime Approach (CLA). This strategy accounts for all potential purchases to be made by your current customer base and all influences over other customers that your current customers will exert.[2] In responding to customer value with the CLA, there are four points to consider as you form your objectives:

- *Attract new customers*: As you begin your business venture your first customer challenge is getting customers to switch to using you, either from internal services or from a competitor. As you continue to build your business, you must continue to develop new customers in the same manner.

- *Increase customer retention*: You had to work very hard to build your customer base. It is in your best interest to keep them coming back. You will work at least five times harder to find a new customer as opposed to the amount of effort you will expend in retaining your existing customers.

- *Increase existing customer purchases*: Taking care not to distance yourself from core competency, you can grow within your current customer base. Do this by identifying the needs of your customers that are within your scope of services which their purchase history may not include. For example, a spa offers a variety of beauty services. They may have clients who historically have purchased only manicures. They could develop an offering of package deals on other beauty services to entice these existing clients to purchase additional services. No new services were added, yet additional sales could reasonably increase.

- *Improve customer profitability*: There are a number of goods and services that could be offered within the range of your core competency that will allow you to improve your offerings and make the persisting prospects of doing business even brighter. Explore options that enhance and improve your primary products and services then implement those services that will improve per-customer profits.

Considering these points, you will gain great insight as to which aspects of your business that can be streamlined or added upon to give you the customer-value profits that you desire without killing your business.

Who and What is Your Business?

To know *who* you are serving, you must know *what* you are serving. Once you know what you are offering, you must keep new service offerings within the core strategy of your business. Most businesses will identify themselves as services. Even utilities companies, often thought of as nothing more than power providers are now considering themselves to be in the "environment management" business. With this definition as their guide, they are allowing themselves to offer tools and services to their customers to extend beyond simple electricity to adding options such as green power renewable resources and power recycling systems. However, knowing the reaches of those services will facilitate controls over strategy and keep the enterprise on track and away from strategy drift.

Perhaps one example of strategy drift was PepsiCo's purchase of Taco Bell. In order to control the output of all soft drinks in Taco Bell, and to keep that market away from Coke and other brands, Pepsi bought the entire business, literally. While Pepsi may argue that it is in the "food" business and that Taco Bell certainly fits the bill as a food business, as is usually the case in conglomerate businesses, such a purchase may have proven to be a distraction. In reality, Pepsi is in the "beverage-experience" business, providing a range of soft drinks aimed at having fun! Using that definition, the purchase of Taco Bell was an unfocused attempt to capture customers and ward off other competitors. Keep your enterprise's vision broad enough to expand, but clear enough to know your limits.

Rules for Customer Relationship Conduct

Along with developing customer value, certain rules apply to the conduct that your business needs to incorporate to ensure that relationship boundaries are maintained. The following guidelines discuss appropriate behavior for the treatment and long term valuation of a customer:

- *Service from the customer's perspective*: This includes all the rules of good behavior, fairness and integrity that should be fundamental to any winning business. Employees should be trained and then expected to offer customers the highest service possible.

- *The most precious resource is customers*: Bear in mind that you are in business because customers allow you to operate; you are voted into office with their dollars. There are far too many choices for consumers for any business to forget that serving customers is the foundation of their business.

- *Preferential treatment of customers*: While certain preferences apply to the majority of your customers, each customer will have individual likes and dislikes. All appeals to the masses must be made at the individual level. Provide as much flexibility with your customers as possible, this will be respected and remembered as the customer returns for your help because of your attention to the individual needs he or she presented to you.

Understanding these guidelines for appropriate conduct when dealing with customers will provide your enterprise with a solid foundation for meaningful success.[3]

Anticipate Future Needs

If you really know your customer, you will know what they want before they ask. This mind-reading technique will certainly lead to significant improvements in delivery over time. The most common process of inference is extremely subjective and vulnerable to misinterpretation. Prior to launching any new business projects, approach customers and ask them if they could use this service or product. The answers from the customer's point of view, when directed in a specific area of your business, may surprise you.

You can also gain insight into customers' needs by comparing your business' ability to respond to those needs to how your competition is servicing those needs. Switching the discussion for a moment to business-to-business enterprises, those companies whose clients are primarily business entities themselves, these entre-preneurial ventures can quickly move in and out of the service industry. Use this timely phenomenon to your advantage to fulfill unmet needs and present your business as one who knows.

Watch closely your direct competitors, and perhaps even more closely than your direct competitors, watch your client's competitors. You will learn what potential direction and possible moves your competitor may take based upon what their competitors are doing in that market. If your client is a regional manufacturer of hardwood products, study your client's competitors to anticipate their future changes. Your extra insights and knowledge in their particular industry will be well regarded and will brand you as an expert of their needs.

No One Wants to Be a "Clone-Able" Customer

Many tools are available to assist you with the management and maintenance of your customer database. Before investing heavily into a new software system, take a step back and make sure that your customers really want a new marketing approach from you. Attempting to clone your customer relationship approach will frequently bring resentment as you use software to "sell" them on additional products and services based upon past purchases. Business is people and people are your business. If people feel software is being used to manage their "relationship," then most often they assume that a relationship does not exists and take no personal interest in your approach.

As our interactions have become faster and more complex we actually crave more personal contacts when available, not fewer, as would seem the case. No one wants to be thought of as a "clone-able" customer. A clone-able customer is defined as an individual who is identified by a set of algorithms that record the details of his or her life, work, home, marital status, and children to retirement and death and determine what those needs are based on the demographical statistics. We resent such simplistic approaches to humanity and what could be described as encroachment on our personal privacy. Make sure customer management tools do not violate privacy laws and overstep ethical boundaries. When using technology to assist with customer control functions, temper those approaches with the elements of human touch and personal service.

Customer-Based vs. Product-Based Strategies

Product-based strategies are businesses that are oriented on a product that they believe the customer will appreciate enough to purchase. The shortcoming in product-based strategies is that your focus is not on the customer, your focus in on internal engineering and design rather than an external focus on your customer. The introverted side of human nature causes us to fall into an introspective mode and occasionally to spend inadequate amounts of time and energy looking at the customer's needs and desires.

Indeed the very title, internal controls, seems to take on an entirely internal focus. This is perhaps an unintended ill effect of the very title *internal control*. Limiting behavior internally is all a business can do in governing itself. However, all this behavior should be governed in response to meeting and servicing external customer needs. Do not let the term "internal" customer control come at the cost of customer exclusion. Any internal controls that create distance between the organization and the customer are not achieving the core strategy of internal controls. Any customer neglect will fall far short of efficiencies and operational effectiveness if the end result decreases service and reduces performance.

Following Your Lead: Service For Better or For Worse

As you lead your culture, your team will magnify the characteristics of your own customer care philosophy, for better or for worse. If you gossip or complain about your customers, you can expect that your staff will do the same. This behavior does not last long until word gets back to your customer, one way or another. This becomes a sore spot and a potential reason to end the relationship.

On a better note, you can be a powerful influence in the lives of your employees as they observe you treating your customers fairly and kindly. The word also gets back to your customer, one way or another. This treatment will become a boon to your business and a potential reason for your customer to continue the relationship even if a misunderstanding arises.

As stated, the entire customer process is led by example, starting with the principle management team. As an entrepreneur, you have an exciting opportunity to make a considerable contribution to the present and future culture of your organization. Indeed, your organization will be an extension of your attitudes, biases and styles. The following are some of the behaviors displayed by successful businesses:

- *Directly interact with customers*: Do not let yourself get so busy with other activities that you fail to make regular time to talk to customers to learn their opinion about know how you are really doing and what you could do to improve your service or product.

- *Standards of performance*: Your enterprise needs to make certain that special customers are treated very special and regular customers are treated special enough that everyone knows there are no "regular" customers.

- *Taking the customer's perspective*: During conflict management, ensure that conflicts are resolved as favorably toward the customer as possible. There may be many non-monetary solutions available with some initiative and creativity.

Reality Check:
Know Your Customer's Desires

Fidelity Investments was severely criticized for its delayed adoption of internet services in the 1990s, and significant market share may have been lost in such an exploding market. However, Fidelity's unwavering customer services and desire for security allowed it to rebound and maintain its long term share of the mutual fund business. Service representatives are managed by the highest standards of professional behavior, with all recorded interactions between customers and employees this knowledge database was constantly employed to make improvements.

Certainly, Fidelity Investments knew the value of a customer. While not particularly chasing the bleeding edge of technology, Fidelity has held on to its service edge. Listen to your customer and develop relationships of trust that will last a lifetime.

Customers Worth Keeping

This chapter began with a focus on customer retention and understanding the entire customer package and also discussed the dangers of limiting service offerings simply on a profit basis because this may disrupt the very elements that attracted the customer base to your product or service. To put the finishing touches an all-encompassing customer relationship package that works for you and for your customer, you need to know how to recognize customers who are worth keeping.

Understanding when the relationship is simply not profitable is a strategic decision, and if it can not be improved, the relationship needs to be gracefully discontinued. As previously mentioned you cannot be everything to everyone, and some accounts will prove to be just too costly. When prospects are not profitable, the customer relationship needs to be adjusted in a way that good will is fostered and your good name is protected. You are, after all, operating a *for-profit* organization.

The customer relationship must help feed profitability to be a sustainable relationship. There is simply no other option in a for-profit enterprise. Your energy as an entrepreneur needs to be devoted toward creating profitable customer base and customer equity that will perpetually support your company so that you can continue to serve those customers. The Customer Profit Chain illustrates this point and can help you to visualize how the relationship between you and your customer is a mutually beneficial alliance.[4]

Figure 8.2

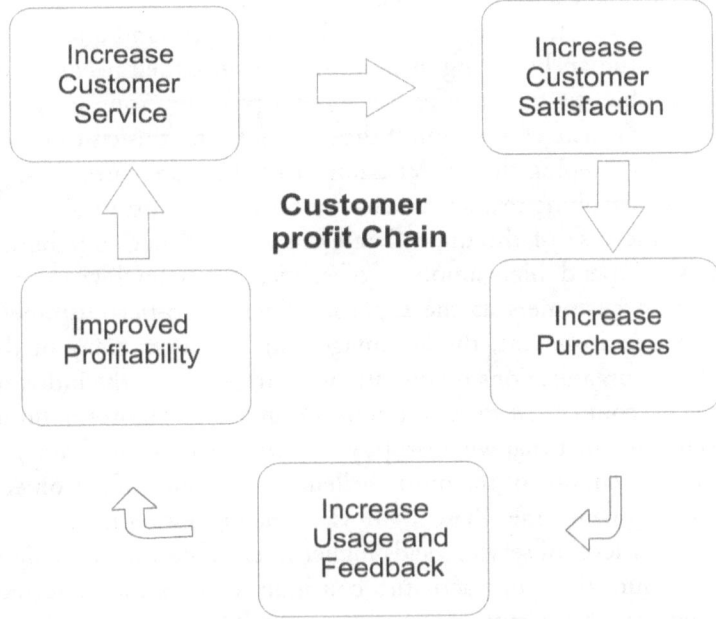

In studying the above illustration, you will discover how the Customer Profit Chain can be broken by either party and is a good indication that a change needs to be made. For example, if your increase in customer service and support does not result in increases in customer purchases, positive feedback and ultimately profitability, you probably need to discontinue the relationship.

There are two ways to discreetly turn a negative relationship around: either increase service or product prices or decrease service or product costs. On the cost reduction side, you may ask yourself: *If services which demand an excessive amount of time are reduced with this unprofitable customer, will the relationship become profitable?* If the customer doesn't notice, then you have made the right move. If the customer takes notice of the absence of that extra service, you could always take the price increase option. From this perspective, the alternative is to raise your rates. This customer may know they have taken much of the company's time and may be more than willing to pay for the additional services. More than likely, they were simply never educated about the cost of the extra benefits they have been receiving.

If the relationship still fails to change then discontinue the relationship with understanding that in certain cases, implications of negative feedback and disgruntled behavior are the weapons deployed on companies by unreasonable customers. In breaking a losing relationship, many customers will not understand your position. Explain simply and honestly that your business is unable to deliver the service in the way that they envision. Keep the focus and attention on your less felicitous customers by letting them know that since their needs are not being met to it would be best for them to use another provider. You may even recommend your least favorite competitor, if they did not refer this customer to you in the first place. By keeping the conversation focused on the customers, you leave no room for backstabbing retaliative behavior from those customers.

In light of the case of the unprofitable customers, what your business cannot afford is to spend high amounts of service levels on low or moderately profit-generating customers at the expense of your top-tier customers. In an entrepreneurial environment, the advantage you have over many of the larger, more established organizations is your attention to service at the individual level. Nurture those accounts that merit the time and resources; however, do not allow distractions in a manner that will disrupt your best (i.e. most profitable) customer relationships. Indeed, one of the most challenging demands of customer controls will be employing your time where it will yield the highest returns.

Finally, if your level of service yields higher levels of customer satisfaction and profitability, ensure that your activities continue to meet the increased benefit level in harmony with the customer's expectations. The customer should feel that all their additional involvement has been noticed and should see your level of service as reciprocating this relationship. This reciprocation creates the highest cycle for growth and profitability and is the highest objective of customer controls.

Chapter Summary

This chapter outlined the customer relationship package, keeping in mind that one never "controls" the customer. However, you need to have fair practices and procedures so that you do not end up in a position where customers take advantage of your services without fair compensation to you.

Some effort was directed to the customer profitability trap and the temptation to reduce services in order to maximize profits. While this is a solid objective of any thriving business, remember to consider that the reason for that existing customer base may depend upon some products and services which may yield lower returns in the short run, but over the long run provide greater margins when the entire relationship is considered. All revisions and discontinuance of services must be carefully considered from the viewpoint of the customer's expectations as well as the perspective of your company's profitability.

Also, customer equity was discussed in terms of brand, retention and value. Entrepreneurs will begin by creating the value and retention components of their brand until resources are sufficient to establish further branding. The culture that evolves regarding customer treatment will depend largely on your attitude as the owner and you can use that influence for better or for worse.

Finally we discussed the customer value chain, increasing and matching the level of services with the profitability of the customer. Additionally, some techniques for discontinuing poor performing relationships were offered. The core principle surrounding customer controls consists of establishing a mutually beneficial relationship where expectations of the customer and the business are met.

CHAPTER NINE
Becoming Your Own Internal Auditor

Recalling our discussion about fraud from a previous chapter, three concurrent events perpetuate internal fraud: a reason to rationalize dishonest behavior; an incentive to deceive the company; and an opportunity to carry out the fraudulent plan. When each of these activities is present, the likelihood of fraud is very significantly increased.

As a business owner, you can be proactively taking steps to track down possible breaches in the internal security of your company by personally auditing or overseeing the audits of various internal controls you have implemented. An internal audit is defined as an independent objective reassurance and consulting activity designed to add value and improve an organization's operations. It helps the business to accomplish the objectives by bringing a systematic, disciplined approach to evaluate and improve the effectiveness of risk management, control and governance processes.

Internal audit functions may be housed within the organization or outsourced to an outside service provider. Internal audits provide 'assurance' to various stakeholders including the top management, owners and operations management. The assurance may be in relation to any area of the business's operations. Through problem-solving methodologies, the consulting activity of the audit function seeks to improve the conditions of the organization. The scope of internal audits includes risk management and control evaluation, operational audits and compliance audits.

Audits are used to reassure you and those who have a vested interest in your company that current operations are efficiently and effectively carrying out the core objectives and goals and leading the company towards profitability. When procedures are ineffective and are producing dismal results, an audit can surmise the trouble and provide information which could lead to recovery.

As stated, there are many types of audits a business may encounter. At the core of all auditing is the capacity to uncover any inconsistencies between existing internal policies and actual implementation of these policies in everyday procedures. Also, audits can provide a way to detect any individuals who may be working outside the parameters of established ethical or legal conduct to take advantage of the company. Periodically, take time to peruse your accounting records and operations and try to see these records and activities through the eyes of an auditor: What would the auditor find? What weak points in the system could be exploited? Is it possible that you have already been the victim of fraud?

The objective of this chapter is not to make you an expert in auditing techniques, but to educate you about some of the auditing tools and indicators, particularly the tools used by larger businesses. These tools will provide a springboard of ideas for your own auditing needs. Also realize that the stringent auditing standards upheld by Sarbanne-Oxley compliance make these tools and indicators inherently more reliable for your smaller company.

While you are not required to provide a yearly, lengthy external audit, you can develop your company's philosophy around the reality that audits are included within the normal course of business. Let your employees know that you will occasionally be performing an audit of general business activity. As you elevate expectations within your own operations, your high standards and the information you retrieve from the audits will continue to serve as a fraud deterrent.

Four Elements of Audit Evidence

Auditors use a variety of information to assemble a body of evidence. With analytical evidence, information is built on the premise that relationships of information will be reasonably expected to continue and exist in their current state. For information to be used as evidence, that information should be sufficient, reliable, relevant and useful in providing a sound basis for reaching conclusions by any prudent person.

The "prudent person" principle essentially states that a reasonable person, under similar circumstances would form a similar opinion based upon the known body of evidence. The evidence gathered in your audit should provide reasonable grounds for all your opinions and conclusions. This implies that a prudent person, not simply a trained auditor, should be able to understand and make reasonable deductions from the information gathered.

As stated above, your information should contain the following four elements to provide conclusive evidence at the end of an internal audit:

- Sufficient: Adequate information should be compelling enough that the prudent person would be persuaded to reach the same conclusions. The greater the risk or claim, the stronger the body of evidence must become. Proving a mistake in accounts payable requires much less evidence than proving an employee is using false payables to embezzle money from the company.

- Reliable: Information is reliable when it can be duplicated by others. Methods used to gather data should be verifiable. Most reliable information is collected from third party external sources, corroborated by other information and original data.

- Relevant: Information that is relevant stays within the focus of your audit activity. If you're auditing your operations for efficiency, data collected from accounts receivables may not have any application in the situation. Relevant information should have a logical relationship with what you are attempting to prove.

- Useful: Gathered information is useful if it helps the organization achieve its auditing objectives and goals.

The following figure depicts these elements as they overlap to point to the best evidence that will support the desired conclusions. When all four elements are fixed and accurate evidence, then that evidence will be centrally conclusive in the outcome of the audit. These audit elements coincide with different types of audit evidence that will be considered as factual and genuine. Using a variety of audit evidence will strengthen the auditor's position as he or she presents opinions and findings at the end of the audit.

Figure 9.1

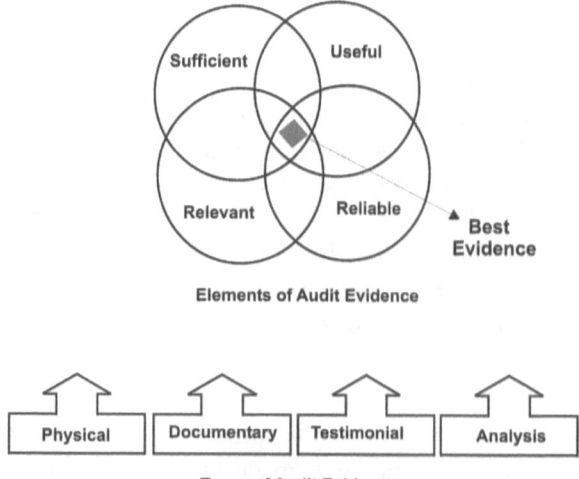

Elements of Audit Evidence

Types of Audit Evidence

Four Types of Audit Evidence

When building a case or opinion an auditor should use multiple types of evidence that incorporate the four elements as possible to support their claims. There are four types of audit evidence from which to gather information:

- Physical: This is direct contact with the people, property or activities of the business. An auditor regards a direct observation of a process as physical evidence, though the process is actually an intangible contact. Since physical evidence changes over time, it is recommended that two authorities view the same physical evidence.

- Documentary: Documentary evidence is the permanent record of a transaction such as a check, purchase order, sales order, government record, or etc.

- Testimonial: Written or spoken witness of an event or transaction that is relative to specific questions is considered to be testimonial evidence. Testimonies, viewed as the least conclusive form of evidence, should be augmented with other supportive evidence.

- Analysis: Analytical evidence is created from ascertaining relationships found in future, current and historical data and evaluated as cause and effect. Understanding relationships allows conclusions and reasonable assumptions to be reached; however, analysis is also a fairly inconclusive form of evidence that should be supported with other evidence.

Developing an understanding of how the different elements and types of audit evidence work together in providing you with solid information on which to base your conclusions is very important to magnify the strength of your audit discoveries.

Audit Evidence for Entrepreneurs

Another important reason for becoming familiar with the types of evidence available is that this knowledge will help you in your reasoning and in changing any assumptions you may have previously held regarding what is sufficient evidence to prove a point, suspicion, or opinion in any case, including audits.

All pieces of available evidence are not equal, nor equally weighted by a prudent person. In your enterprise, you need to educate your controls team on the basics of audit evidence. This training will help to bridge gaps in understanding that may arise when your controls team responds to a sensitive audit situation.

Employee Fraud Management

One area that is subject to audits is employee fraud. The following issues contain a high degree of sensitivity and subjectivity, especially in the area of human relations and employee. These issues deal with the employee relationship from the application process to hiring and firing and everything in between. Always approach any assumptions about people, customers and employees alike, with respect. Any concerns over procedures, treatment of situations or ethics should be deferred to professional legal council.

The following illustration maps out some of the corresponding issues surrounding employee fraud management. As you can see, prospective employees and current employees must be managed to protect your company from possible exploits resulting in fraud. Prospective employees can be reduced to a low risk through conducting thorough background checks and paying attention to the information gathered from these checks before completing the hiring process.

Figure 9.2

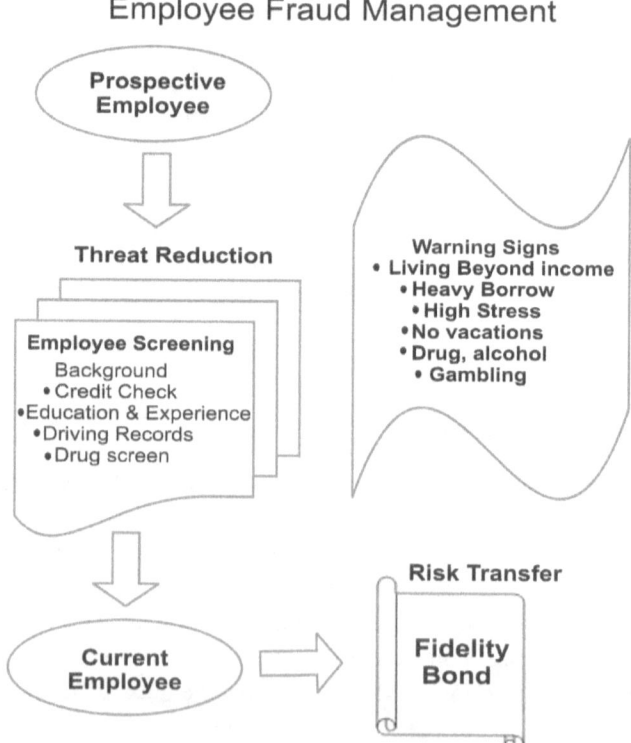

Employee Fraud Management

Prospective Employee

Threat Reduction

Employee Screening
Background
• Credit Check
•Education & Experience
•Driving Records
•Drug screen

Warning Signs
• Living Beyond income
•Heavy Borrow
•High Stress
•No vacations
•Drug, alcohol
• Gambling

Current Employee

Risk Transfer

Fidelity Bond

In dealing with current employees and managing those relationships to steer clear of fraud, you will want to pay attention to their everyday lives and keep up on certain events. When odd behavior is displayed, you may need to closely monitor the employee to ensure that the change is not a threat to the security of your company. Things like not requesting vacation, late nights with unproductive results, asking for loans or any signs of high stress should not go unnoticed. In a caring, non-threatening manner, you can approach employees and most likely find ways to resolve the difficulties they are experiencing in their lives. You will be respected and seen as a boss who cares.

Sometimes you may need to protect your company and transfer the risk of current employees betraying you with insurance through a fidelity bond. More detail about this type of insurance will follow.

Employee Screening

Depending on the nature of your business, one way to mitigate risk when hiring key employees is to run a background check. Most references are cordial though usually less than candid and, due to litigation concerns, most companies will not offer a reference good or bad of the previous employee, only verify the period of their work. How do you know you're getting an honest new hire? There is no fool proof method, but in your financial department it is certainly worth the investment to perform some basic background checks. These checks are not economically feasible for each position but they could save you from embarrassment and unpleasant situations later.

Some types of background checks can legally be performed in most states. While fees for these services vary, usually the price of a due-diligence private investigator's fee will save you from the cost of fraud in the workplace. Here is a list of legal background checks for you to consider when hiring key employees:

- Criminal Background Check: Criminal convictions are public records. A good application form will require references of prior felonies, and a basic criminal background check will verify residencies and prior areas where the candidate has lived.

- Education and Degrees: Asking colleges and universities to verify transcripts is an inexpensive way to see if your candidate is telling the truth. If the candidate cannot provide details or hesitates, a simple question to the registrar over the phone could save you a stamp for the transcript request.

- Credit Check: There are many agencies that offer credit checks for a nominal fee, such as Equifax, Experian and TransUnion. You will need to have the candidate sign an agreement allowing a credit check to be performed. Because this type of screening could give an indication of personal financial problems, it is a sensitive situation that should be handled with care.

- Social Security Number: It is also a good idea to verify the authenticity of the social security number provided. One common social fraud is to carry multiple social security numbers, collecting state unemployment and welfare benefits on one set of numbers and working with another.

- Driving Record: For any individuals running errands for the organization, this is a requirement. You need to protect your company from authorizing anyone to use a company vehicle who has a history of accidents or DUI offenses.

- Drug Testing: Often the knowledge that such tests are routine may keep users away. Drug testing is recommended for equipment operators, production and administration employees. If your company can afford the tests, all positions should require a drug test for safety precautions. There are many local laboratories that can provide such testing.

Reality Check:
Verify that MBA

Kenneth Lonchar held the position of CFO for the multibillion dollar Bay Area software company, Veritas Software, for over five years. When he was hired he claimed to have graduated from Stanford with an MBA, yet it was later discovered that he never attended the institution. What he did have, however, was an undergraduate degree from Idaho State University. Dismissal for lying on your resume is never a pleasant situation. Unfortunately, this high level ex-employee never got the memo on integrity when applying for the job.

Simple background checks do not have to be expensive. A few phone calls and a letter or two can verify information such as degrees, financial background, social security numbers and previous work history. Save yourself a headache down the road and verify that MBA.

Source: The Street, TSC Staff, October 3, 2002.

Using all or a combination of these background checks will help you identify the potential hires that will have the least amount of risk attached to their possible employment with your company. As portrayed by the above reality check, the embarrassment of having your CFO turn out to be less than honest is far more costly than a background check before hiring.

It is best to learn from this awkward situation and avoid having your perplexing problem. Verifying information on promising candidates will also reassure you that you can begin to build the working relationship based on mutual trust and respect. Most prospective employees are appreciative of background checks as a company hiring standard. They feel more assured coming into an environment based on trust and openness.

High Risk Indicators

There are certain types of behavior that should provide red flags for routine fraud committed against organizations when dealing with potential employees. Your responses to these behaviors should be extremely sensitive and take care not to make any accusations of illegal activity. Such incriminations could be subject to liable and slander and lead to possible legal action. There will be more information on these issues later. As listed in the previous figure, common patterns displayed as suspicious behavior include:

- Living beyond their means: Lifestyles which do not seem commensurate with their earnings should sound warning bells as indication that this money is coming from another source.

- Unusually compulsive: Employees that are extremely possessive of their work area and refuse help and view any intrusions with a high degree of defensiveness could be suspect.

- The borrower: This person is constantly borrowing funds from most employees and from the company, if permitted.

- Stressed out: Employees facing unusual stress in their lives may respond in ways they would not normally act given different circumstances. Be alert for those employees in situations that could become desperate.

- Refusing to take vacations: This is a unique pattern displayed by individuals who are concerned that their fraudulent activity will be discovered in their absence. They will not risk time off when their fraud may be exposed.

- Drugs and alcohol addictions: Employees with these types of challenges will do nearly anything to maintain their addictions. Counseling and care should be extended to these individuals. You should make sure they are not handling any financial or liquid assets.

- Gambling addictions: Be alert to individuals who spend unusual amounts of time at casinos, brag about winnings or discuss internet gaming. They may have overextended themselves and be placed in a compromised position.

One tip to assist in monitoring behavior is to verify where paychecks are being deposited. Checks should be cleared through a bank or credit union, signs of checks passing through directly to individuals, quick cash loans or pawn shops could be a flag for financial troubles.

Insurance and Bonding

One helpful instrument a small business may need to acquire is a fidelity bond. This bond offers a protection against a dishonest employee and is often required by companies with suppliers that frequently visit the facility such as security guards and janitorial services. If you are not actively managing your business as owner, a fidelity bond could save you from bankruptcy in the case of a corrupt president or financial officer. It may be less expensive to use a higher deductible policy since a bond's usage should be extremely limited to infrequent occurrences. As a deterrent to fraud, let the employees know that the insurance company assumes the claim and that criminal prosecution can be expected and that you as business owner will have no part in the legal proceedings.

Identity Threats

Identity theft and related crimes have seen an upswing in recent years as the number of face-to-face interactions reduces. It seems it is morally easier to rationalize stealing from someone you never meet than personally interacting with someone you are going to victimize. In other words, an increased percentage of people would steal from someone they have never met, than those that are in a position to exploit someone directly.

Identity theft occurs when someone takes your personally identifying information like name, social security number or credit card number without your permission and uses it to commit a crime. An estimated 9 million Americans fall pray to some form of identity theft each year. The cost of such theft can be very high and the recovery process tortuous. Identity theft starts with the criminals obtaining your personal identity information like name, social security numbers, etc. as mentioned above.

Various methods may be used to obtain this information. Thieves may skim through the trash looking for these details. They may steal credit card numbers using a storage device attached to the swiping machine when you swipe. They pretend to be financial institutions or companies and send spam or pop-up messages to get you to reveal your personal information on line. They divert your billing statements to another location by completing a change of address form. They steal wallets and purses; mail, including bank and credit card statements; pre-approved credit offers; and new checks or tax information. They steal personnel records, or bribe employees who have access. They use false pretenses to obtain your personal information from financial institutions, telephone companies, and other sources. Once they have your personal information, identity thieves use it in a variety of ways:

- Credit card fraud: They may open new credit card accounts in your name. When they use the cards and don't pay the bills, the delinquent accounts appear on your credit report. They may change the billing address on your credit card so that you no longer receive bills, and then run up charges on your account. Because your bills are now sent to a different address, it may be some time before you realize there's a problem.

- Phone or utilities fraud: They may open a new phone or wireless account in your name, or run up charges on your existing account. They may use your name to get utility services like electricity, heating, or cable TV.

- Bank/finance fraud: They may create counterfeit checks using your name or account number. They may open a bank account in your name and write bad checks. They may clone your ATM or debit card and make electronic withdrawals your name, draining your accounts. They may take out a loan in your name.

- Government documents fraud: They may get a driver's license or official ID card issued in your name but with their picture. They may use your name and Social Security number to get government benefits. They may file a fraudulent tax return using your information.

- Other types of fraud: They may get a job using your social security number. They may rent a house or get medical services using your name. They may give your personal information to police during an arrest. If they don't show up for their court date, a warrant for arrest is issued in your name. The best way to find out if you are a victim of this type of fraud is to monitor your accounts and bank statements each month, and check your credit report on a regular basis. If you check your credit report regularly, you may be able to limit the damage caused by identity theft by finding patterns early. Unfortunately, many consumers learn that their identity has been stolen after some damage has been done. You may find out when bill collection agencies contact you for overdue debts you never incurred. You may find out when you apply for a mortgage or car loan and learn that problems with your credit history are holding up the loan. You may find out when you get something in the mail about an apartment you never rented, a house you never bought, or a job you never held.

Awareness is the most effective weapon you can use to protect yourself from the risk of identity theft. As a business owner, be aware of how information could be stolen. Monitor your personal and business information to uncover any problems early. Allow only a few employees access to sensitive information to control the risk of fraud occurring internally. Make the practice of audits common knowledge to deter unwanted fraudulent behavior. By being proactively involved in lowering your risk factors, you can avoid such devastating events.

Payroll Threats

Payroll is an area that requires both computerized and manual controls since the human element plays a big part in the payroll department. Key control points of a payroll system are:

- Authorization of new hires and adding them to the payroll; terminations must be immediately removed.
- Authorizing wage rates and any changes in these rates.
- Tracking hours clocked per employee.
- Tracking jobs worked on by each employee.
- Generating payroll checks.

Ideally, the accounting data generated through a payroll system should be linked to the General Ledger and updated automatically as information is obtained.

Timekeeping

The timekeeping function should be kept separate from the personnel and payroll functions. The preferred timekeeping system should be automated. Automatic timekeeping devices range from the simple punch-clocks to the sophisticated swiping devices and a suitable system can be found by every business. An automated, tamper-proof system for timekeeping cuts away any risk of errors and frauds in the timekeeping process. The system should be so designed that reported employee time corresponds to time actually spent on the job.

Bogus Employees

The integrity of the payroll system is vital to ensure that pay is calculated for bona fide employees only. The control areas involved here are authorization at the time of hiring new employee, and the system by which a new employee is included in the payroll. Authorization for adding employees should be given by the personnel department. The employee will then get paid on payday only if the timekeeping function has recorded hours worked for the employee.

Similarly, the payroll department should provide the authorization to remove from the payroll records employees who have left or whose employment has been terminated. Records maintained by the personnel department should be checked from time to time with accounting records to ensure that there is no duplication of employee names and that there are no bogus employees.

Internal Auditing of Financial Statements

Internal audit of financial statements is in the nature of compliance audits. This type of audit tests the effectiveness of internal controls and provides assurance that transactions have been recorded properly and in the proper period. In a computerized accounting system, most controls are incorporated into the system and do not need repeat testing by internal auditors. For instance in a retail organization, a basic transaction such as a recording sale is well-controlled and these controls will be tested by an external auditor as well.

Accordingly, some aspects of an accounting system still carry major risk and need to be regularly tested by an internal audit, if one is carried out. These risks may be in the following areas:

- Information systems processing and controls.

- Accounting estimates: amounts falsely inflated or deflated not representative of full disclosure.

- Determining substance of the transaction and recording accordingly.

- Window-dressing of financial statements where the use of innovative methods, both legal and illegal produce financial statements that present a brighter-than-actual picture of the state of affairs within the company.

Reality Check:
Owner-Manager Controls,
Whether or Not You're in the Mood

Many small organizations lack the economic resources to maintain adequate segregation of duties. A person with access to a personal computer-based accounting system could make changes to account balances without review by a supervisor. The risk of control is therefore assessed high for these small businesses. This does not imply that there are errors in the system or that the employees are not trustworthy, only that the risk is present that material misstatements could occur which would not be detected by the normal functioning of the accounting system.

Owner-manager controls are very important in small organizations. The owner can create a better segregation of duties by performing a detailed overview of functions and setting the tone for employee operations. To be effective, they should be applied consistently and throughout the year, not sporadically when the 'mood' hits you right.

Source: Rittenberg, L. & Schwieger, B. Auditing Concepts for a Changing Environment, 3rd Edition, Harcourt College Publishers

---

Cash Transactions

Businesses need to handle cash for payments that are made with cash and when they receive cash from customers on account, through cash sales and through miscellaneous sources like disposal of waste, scrap, returnable containers and other sources. Documents normally associated with cash receipt transactions include:

- Cash receipts summary: The summary lists cash receipts contained in the daily bank deposit and is the basis for recording daily cash receipts.

- Receipted deposit ticket: This provides evidence of the daily cash deposit.
- Cash register tapes: These provide evidence of cash sales for the day.

The main concern in providing effective controls over cash receipts is providing security and proper accountability. Accountability is achieved by using locked in cash register tapes for cash sales. The controller's office or the owner of a small business would compare daily the receipted deposit ticker with the register tapes to determine that all incoming cash receipts are deposited in the bank every day. The monthly bank reconciliation prepared by someone having neither custodial nor cash-recording responsibility, provides further accountability over cash. In some cases, in a very small business, you may have to take over this function yourself if the resources are lacking to support segregation of duties.

Security over cash sales receipts can be obtained by installing cash registers with locked-in tapes. Fixing custodial responsibility over cash and requiring that cash receipts be deposited daily is an added security measure.

To achieve segregation, the cashier is not given access to accounting records and the accounting personnel have no access to cash receipts. Postings are made from remittance advices and cash register tapes rather than from checks and currency. Segregation of duties set up like this can prevent not only misappropriation of cash, but can also detect concealment through manipulation of accounts. Additionally, the function of recording cash receipts should also be kept separate from the function of posting customer accounts and postings to the general ledger. A chart of accounts, accounting manuals and use of competent persons to record cash receipts are good controls to ensure proper recording. Recording errors occur more frequently in transactions other than collections from customers and should be watched carefully. Filing cash receipts, cash summaries and deposit tickets will provide an audit trail to track transactions and control areas in the future.

Separation of Duties: Cash Handling

A summary of division of duties in relation to cash and bank payments in listed below:

- The cashier should not be recording accounting transactions other than cash disbursements. He should not be given custody of securities, titles deeds or negotiable instruments other than cash.

- The person preparing checks should not be an authorized signer of checks. Conversely, an authorized signer should not have the authority to prepare checks. This requirement may be overlooked in a very small business where the owner is the sole signatory, and may prepare some or all of the checks himself.

- Supervision over functional activities should be adequate.

Reality Check:
Avoid Temptation, Use Separation of Duties

A bank branch had a system of the head teller opening the night depository vault along with another teller each morning. Each teller punched in half the combination, as a security measure. However, both tellers were always present together when the vault was opened. The night vault security camera was only turned on at 8:00 AM every morning, after the bank opened for business. The head teller was the person who opened and closed the vault every morning.

One morning the head teller arrived at work before the other employees and before the bank opened for the day. She accessed the night vault by using the other teller's half of the combination, which she had memorized the previous night. She removed a couple of deposit bags and smuggled them out of the bank in her personal tote bag. The theft wasn't discovered until the next day when two customers of the bank complained about cash deposited by them the previous night not being credited to their accounts. The crime was eventually pinned to the head teller by the bank's audit investigator.

In a small business environment it may not always be possible to separate duties; make sure transactions including cash are shared between employees and owners. All too often partnerships are destroyed when easy access tempts one of the partners to take the money and run. Keep yourselves and others in a position to be above any suspicion.

Source: Internal Auditor, Oct, 2005 by Toby J.F. Bishop

Check Safety

One of the most urgent places where controls are needed is protecting your check stock. This is perhaps the most common element where a lack of controls is found in a small business setting. Checks can easily facilitate fraud and embezzlement when not properly controlled. Employees who can locate the check stock may take a blank check from the end of the stock so that the sequence numbers may go entirely unnoticed. Place your check stock in a secure safe with lock and key and provide access to few employees.

When checks are properly handled, the occurrence of fraud and misuse lowers dramatically. Here are some procedures that you need to handle with the proper controls to ensure check safety:

Check Voiding Procedures

- Prepare Check Void Form: this is a very simple document that can be quickly created and provide a permanent log of activity. (see A-7 in Appendix: Voided Check Form)
- Write VOID in ink across front of check.
- Tear or cut the signature line of the check.
- Write on back: DO NOT DEPOSIT.
- Staple voided check to Voided Check Form.

Signatures

The authority for check signing should be kept segregated from the function of recording disbursements, posting creditors accounts or reconciling bank accounts. Although this is generally true, in a small organization the owner may involve himself in more than one of these functions so that the others can be kept segregated. Another reason this makes sense is for better control. For example, the owner may sign all checks himself and make all bank reconciliations while assigning others to record payments and post accounts.

If there is more than one owner in your small business, it is a very good idea to issue two signature line checks. Two signatures will lower the chance of suspicion between partners because all signing partners will also be required to review any business expenditure before authorization. Using multiple check signatures, such as two signature checks, also makes it more difficult to commit forgeries and check fraud.

Transfers

All checks, as soon as they are received must be promptly and restrictively endorsed. This ensures the security of the checks since they cannot then be paid to anyone but into the accounts of the business. If you were not issued a check endorsement stamp by your bank when opened your account, then order one. As soon as checks are received put the individual in charge of opening mail responsible for endorsing checks.

Stop Payments

Stop payment instructions are usually authorized when an issued check is reported lost or is untraceable. It is important that the accounting function immediately reverses the original entries made when the check was issued. The check should be appropriately marked as cancelled on the check stub or the check issue register.

Reality Check:
Control Your Checks

A privately held company was notified by its bankers that they were returning several phony checks drawn on the company's general cash account. All of these checks had already been cashed as payroll checks by local check cashing services that bore all the loss from the transaction. Investigation revealed that fraudulent checks appeared as reasonable check amounts, similar check paper and layout and the information was very similar to legitimate checks. The checks resembled similar check number patters and made detection difficult.

The criminals used different check cashing services and limited their fraud to a few checks each week. It was later discovered that the criminals entered the building in the mail room and were able to steal actual blank checks. Detectives were convinced that partners in the theft used an inside partner to provide check information and check number information.

One obvious form of prevention that was implemented was to begin locking checks in a safe only accessible by authorized personnel. Further, the mail room was locked and automated pay system was established with the bank. Hopefully this story demonstrates the significance of controls and security measures, especially for something as basic as checks.

Source: Internal Auditor, April, 1996 by Donald K. McConnell, Jr.

Lockbox Controls

Lockboxes are used to speed up cash collections and reduce risk of fraud when cash has to be collected at diverse locations. Customers send payments directly at a specified post office box number which is a lockbox at the business's bank. The bank receives and opens the remittances and prepares a list of cash receipts. This list is sent to you the business owner, and your bank account is credited. You can then use this list to update your accounts receivables and your bank balances. Using lockboxes eliminates the need to set up your own elaborate cash collection processes, as all the risky parts of the process are transferred to the bank. Lockboxes can be established at multiple locations to further reduce the delay between the time the check leaves the customers office and is deposited into your bank account.

Controls should be established to ensure recording of all transactions as reported by the bank in the business's books. Remittance advices should be received from the bank to facilitate follow up if the customer has any questions. You should total up and reconcile regularly the remittance advices received from the bank with the cash deposits as recorded by the bank.

The downside of lockboxes is usually the cost for this service, charges from 0.50 per check and higher, plus a monthly minimum fee are typically required. While worth looking into, most small businesses are not in a position to take advantage of this service.

Remote Deposit

One relatively new technique that may provide significant security as well as expedited deposit needs is a point of deposit where check images are scanned at your office and the image is sent to the bank and deposits are made immediately. This prevents any delays in deposit time and accelerates your cash cycle.

Credit Cards

Use of corporate credit cards for paying for purchases can save a great deal in terms of payment processing costs. At the same time, they also possess a control risk. As we have seen before, corporate credit cards should be given the same level of security controls accorded to cash and checks. When credit cards are issued to employees or to geographically removed business locations to use for business purchases then effective internal controls need to be implemented.

Reality Check:
Credit Card Abuse

At least 13 employees of University of Arizona have been caught since 2000 for misusing corporate credit cards for personal purposes for a total of $112,000. Dishonest employees used the cards to buy gas, download songs from the internet, buy themselves airplane tickets and in one case, to furnish a home. Some of the abuses were not traced for months because supervisors did not check monthly purchasing reports.

While using credit cards has lowered business costs for the University of Arizona, a small percentage of employees are still committing fraud, about 0.02%. However, lapses in the system are still worrisome and the university has worked to strengthen controls. There is a proposal to add an 'internal controls' category to employee performance reviews.

In your small business remember to provide segregation of duties and ensure that someone other than the holder of the credit card performs the reconciliation.

Source: The Arizona Republic, July 8, 2007

Accepting payment through credit cards is an attractive option to quicken your collections, even if it means paying a fee for merchant services. It eliminates risk of loss from non-payment, and eliminates the cost of offering credit. Credit card companies transfer funds to your accounts within a week, and that can be welcome news for your cash flow. Also in a consumer-oriented business or with online selling, credit cards are must-haves.

However, there are various risks associated with handling customer credit cards, which need to be controlled to ensure your safety. Remember merchant accounts carry an enormous risk with abuse of merchant account theft as a federal crime. There are many types of fraud committed on merchant accounts, both simple and complicated schemes. Ensure your authorization security codes are well protected and that transactions are prescreened prior to acceptance. Credit card charge backs for vendor mistakes carry multiple levels of transaction fees and drastically reduce your profitability with credit card purchases.

Reality Check:
Fraudulent Returns

A part-time shoe salesman worked in a department store for nearly five years before it was discovered that he had pilfered thousands of dollars by recording fictitious returns. He exploited weaknesses in the store's customer credit procedures, and shared the loot with family and friends.

The fraud was discovered when the shoe department started to lose money due to an extremely high rate of returns. Upon investigation it was found that around the end of each month, certain credit card numbers would be credited for a return of approximately $300. No corresponding sale could be found for the returns, and each credit card number appeared only once in the month, so that anyone examining only one month's data would not discover the card numbers.

Most of the returns were traced back to one part-time employee who credited 200 credit cards belonging to about 110 people to the tune of $2000 to $3000 each week. He simply punched in the returns to the cards of his accomplice and they in turn paid him up to 50% in commissions. This fraud was possible because the original store receipt was not required to accompany store refunds.

Internal controls regarding refund policies should include presenting original receipts with merchandise. These receipts act as a reference and can discourage fraud among employees who handle returns.

Internal Auditor, April, 2005 by Toby J.F. Bishop

Financial Statement Fraud

Financial frauds usually begin with aggressive financial targets and an unforgiving expectation to meet them. This is not a crime limited to publicly traded companies as small businesses are very vulnerable to these types of schemes. Also present are vague areas of financial reporting such as revenue recognition issues. Many financial statement frauds start small and grow over time. Financial statement fraud can be grouped into five major segments:

- *Fictitious revenues*: Falsifying revenue is the most popular fraud category. It means recording higher revenue than actual sales figures, with a view to perpetrate fraud. There are three ways this fraud is accomplished. Sales may be increased quite simply through an accounting entry that credits sales and debits accounts receivable. However, this type of fraud can be easily detected in the next accounting period, when the accounts receivable age, and the inventory position doesn't match sales on record. Another method is by creating actual fictitious sales to real clients. Fraudulent documents are crested, and normally the clients chosen are large businesses or government agencies, where the fraud will not be easily discovered. Another method is by making false sales to fictitious clients. The address is usually the give away here, since it is almost always a fake.

- *Fraudulent timing differences*: This system is also used to show false profits. Fraud in timing differences, also called cut-off fraud, normally involves one of two basic techniques: recording revenues early and/or recording expenses and liabilities late. Revenues from sales accrue when the earnings process is complete and the rights of ownership have passed from seller to buyer. Revenue recognition frauds can be subdivided into three categories: holding the books open past the end of the accounting period, recording revenue when services are still due and shipping merchandise before the sale is final.

- *Concealed liabilities and expenses*: Sometimes, liabilities such as accounts payable or advances from customers may not be recorded at all. This will boost the asset values in the balance sheet and make the business look good for a while. You should have a solid understanding of each liability in your enterprise. If there are any liabilities which are unclear ask questions and keep searching until you are satisfied you have a valid answer.

- *Improper or fraudulent disclosures or omissions*: Generally accepted accounting principles (GAAP) concerning disclosures require that financial statements should include all relevant and material information in the financials or footnotes and that these should not be misleading. Most fraudulent disclosures involve purposeful omissions, which normally fall into one of four categories namely liabilities, significant events, management fraud or accounting omissions.

- *Fraudulent asset valuations*: Misstated asset valuations account for nearly half the cases of fraudulent financial statements. Most of these misstatements are in the form of overstated inventory. A combination of several methods may be used to commit inventory fraud including declaring outright fictitious inventory, manipulating inventory quantities, not recording purchases or fraudulently capitalizing inventory. All these elaborate schemes have the same goal of illegally boosting inventory values.

Bank Reconciliations

Bank reconciliations can help you to detect check frauds of every type. Checking account reconciliations should be performed monthly so that fraudulent or doubtful items are not overlooked. A regular deadline for reconciliations should be set and then maintained. If the volume of transactions passing through the checking account is large, then the bank reconciliation may have to be made every week or even daily instead of every month. Segregate the functions of check issuing from check reconciliation. Communications between accounting department and treasury department should be smooth and quick, so that Treasury is also aware of any likelihood of check fraud as soon as it is detected. Incorporate a bank reconciliation procedure and include steps to be taken if a doubtful item is found during reconciliation.

Reality Check:
Job Segregation Could Have Saved the Day

This case of fraud examines a reconciliation accountant who re-issued checks to herself that had never been cashed by the original, genuine payees. The stale-dated checks were tracked and cancelled by the reconciliation clerk, so that she could use genuine check numbers, amounts and payee names on the check request forms. She made out check request forms and presented them personally to the check issuer, and the checks were issued without obtaining authorization, in breach of company policy. Also, on her request, the check issuer directly returned the checks to her for disbursement.

A year-end audit revealed that a lot of the manual checks were made out to a single payee name or other similar names. Deeper investigation revealed numerous old items, represented in the total as one item. The reconciliation clerk who had carried out the scam had since moved, and the new appointee could not identify the items. The bank reconciliation had not been prepared promptly, so old items had never been identified and resolved.

The reconciliation accountant had apparently accepted another job and left the area when the new supervisor began to plug the loopholes in the bank reconciliation process. She was later confronted with the crime and confessed. The loss to the business was over $20,000 over a 30-month period.

In your small business make sure the individual responsible for reconciling the account is someone other than the person who will write the checks. Segregation of these duties could have saved this company money.

Source: Internal Auditor, April 2001, by Kate M. Head

Electronic Data Interchange

Automated transfers are a way of transferring funds electronically without any physical cash or negotiable instruments having to move or be moved to affect a transfer. For an electronic transfer system to work well, your business, as well as your customers, must have the capability to make the system work. Also, it is better to enter into a cash transfer agreement with the customers who will use this method. Such an agreement would include a process for the customer to notify you of any payments made directly to the bank. Furthermore, there should be automated or manual reconciliation procedures between your business and the bank. These procedures will create a trail that can be followed whenever any information is required about a particular payment made by a customer.

Fraud Response

If you suspect your business has become the victim of fraud there are some Dos and Don'ts that are extremely important. Following these rules will keep you safe as you investigate what went wrong and proceed to prove that fraudulent activity occurred. Failure to pay attention to these procedures may cost you money, lose the conviction and bring a potential slander lawsuit against your business. The Dos and Don'ts for handling suspected fraud are as follows:

Do:

- Contact an attorney familiar with employee fraud.
- Contact a CPA with fraud investigation experience.
- Protect all original documents containing suspected fraudulent information; provide copies to attorneys and CPAs as requested.
- Contact local law enforcement under the direction of legal or insurance notification.
- Change computer passwords, locks and safe combinations. Fraud may have extended beyond suspected employees to involve other organized members.

Do Not:

- Make any accusations and do not allow attorneys and law enforcement to make any charges at present. Even if you are convinced your evidence is solid, refrain from direct conflict as you probe.
- Discuss details of the situation with other employees. Advise any other employees that are aware of the situation to refrain from any rumors or details of the case.
- Allow the situation repeat itself; learn from your controls system failure.

Adhering to these simple rules will protect your company from premature retaliation that could retard the resolution process. Making accusations of fraud is a very serious matter and should be treated with professionalism and sensitivity. While you will be emotionally charged in such a situation, remain calm and keep a level head. Resist the temptation to panic and give more attention to the situation by hyping the details. Remember, this too shall pass and resolution will follow investigation.

Investigation Procedures

There are some investigative procedures that you need to understand to prepare you in the event you need to handle a case of fraud within your company. These procedures include:

- *Privileged Information*: The right to legal privilege is available where legal action is going to result from the investigations being conducted. The principle of privilege protects communication between lawyer and client and any other confidential communications that are made for the purpose of actual or prospective legal proceedings. If right of privilege is to be sought it is important to establish that the goal of the investigation is to pursue proceedings. Along with the right to privilege goes the right to confidentiality. At the beginning of an investigation procedures should be adopted which protect confidentiality, by limiting the people involved, if necessary.

- *Fact gathering*: The goal of the investigation determines the amount of evidence that will be required in gathering the facts. Nevertheless facts in the form of records are very important. Some of these records like accounting records and transaction records would already be available to you. Discrepancies found here may pinpoint the fraud but not necessarily the perpetrator. For this purpose it may be necessary to investigate records of communications from members of staff, information which may be in your possession but to which you are not privy. In planning with foresight, well-written contracts at the beginning of the employment process which give you rights of investigation will be helpful. In the absence of these documents, distributing a general notice to all staff regarding investigations to be conducted and providing a chance to object will not hinder the success of the investigation.

- *Employee interviews*: Interviews with employees, especially when they are suspects, are in every danger of going awry and should be handled in a professional and sensitive manner. Also, information obtained during a private investigation may be discredited by the due process of law. It is not necessary that the interviewees have their own lawyers present, or for you to caution them to obtain legal advice. However, if your legal advisors are present, make it clear that they act only for you. If the interviewee requests to consult his own lawyer, this request cannot reasonably be denied.

- *Employee Investigation*: During the course of an investigation you may want to suspend a suspect employee. While your reasons for suspension may include a desire to protect your company from further fraudulent activities, unless your employment contract expressly allows this, you may need legal advice. Suspending an employee without pay while being suspected of fraud may harm your investigation and cause irreparable damage, even more so than the suspected fraud. Never make reckless statements during the probing process, and even after suspicions have proof, never let emotions provoke wild accusations. On the other hand, if people are potential sources of evidence it may be necessary to provide them with some information. Be calm and straightforward in your communication. If you appear to be baiting the situation, you may not receive the cooperation you desire.

In the process of the investigation, you may establish reasonable grounds to sustain your suspicions, and having reasonable evidence of misconduct you may decide to dismiss an employee. However you need to be able to prove that all criteria of a reasonable investigation were met to protect you from being accused of false accusations and slander against the dismissed employee.

Getting Outside Help

All cases of fraud require professional help. You cannot uncover fraud and then hope that it will just go away and leave you alone. Fraud is a very serious matter that needs to be resolved with the help of CPAs, attorneys and local law enforcement. Should you attempt to take care of this delicate situation in a private investigation and resolution, you may leave loopholes open for the fraud to perpetuate itself.

Certified Public Accountants

The first person you should approach with your situation is a Certified Public Accountant. Find a CPA who is specially trained to audit for fraud and can help you to determine the validity and depth of your concerns. An audit will be considered as one of the pieces of evidence to prove that fraud has occurred and the extent of the damage that has been caused by the fraudulent activity. From there, you can continue to receive advice regarding the next steps you must take to resolve the issues surrounding the uncovered fraud, including recovery of lost assets and protection of remaining assets.

Attorneys

When contacting an attorney, make sure that you have retained one who is experienced with fraud and the laws and investigative procedures surrounding fraud. Legal advice is paramount when the goal is to prosecute. Even when prosecution is not necessary, ongoing involvement of lawyers will be useful in several ways.

They can offer advice on the importance and value of evidence gathered and whether that information meets the relevant standards of proof. They can assist in matters of employment laws and employee rights and can set you straight if the mode of investigation infringes upon any the rights of employees or others who may be involved who are under investigation. They can also assist with property recovery issues and help to protect remaining assets.

Local Law Enforcement

Whether or not to report an employee who is suspected of fraud to the police can be a difficult decision. Some employers may involve the police in every instance. Others may fear loss of control of the investigation, since the police are primarily concerned with prosecution, and not recovery of lost property. Generally, the police have the power to conduct a better investigation than the private one that you may undertake. If there are any doubts, contact your CPA and your attorney to assist you in making the choice to report the fraudulent activity.

Chapter Summary

Over the course of this chapter, we have examined the types of audit evidence which include documentary, testimonial, analysis and physical evidence. These forms of evidence are weighed into an audit and are valid based upon the degree that the evidence is reliable, sufficient, useful and relevant. These types and elements of evidence forms the framework of audit evidence.

The focus on becoming your own auditor is to get entrepreneurs thinking about the processes and procedures to elevate their business activities and protect themselves from fraud. We discussed elements of hiring, insuring and bonding of employees as well as the warning signs of potential candidates that may be more susceptible to committing fraud and embezzlement, including a number of high risk characteristics that may help you to identify possible perpetrators.

You were reminded of some of the basic components of check safety and maintaining segregation of duties especially in the area of check safety, cash management and reconciliation. Finally, you were given a list of specific dos and don'ts in the event that fraud is actually suspected. Remember to seek professional and legal advice in these delicate situations. Do not make a bad situation worse by attempting to resolve fraud and the surrounding issues without professional help.

CHAPTER TEN

Bridling Your Business Environment

Creating a controlled environment is not a binary on/off option, it is a complicated process that will involve time and resources and will vary in degrees of performance as the organization matures and processes are implemented. Many companies fail to make the required changes and as a result, simply fail. This chapter will outline some of the reasons why organizations fail to implement controls and how to avoid these pitfalls. As you review your own organizational procedures, take time to note your weaknesses and to be open to your own vulnerabilities. Later in the chapter, the focus will shift to ideas on how to communicate your vision and implement a new control cultural change.

Each enterprise will have its own blend of weaknesses. Tackle your weaknesses and gain control of your enterprise. Greater peace of mind and success await you as you make your control systems permanent and create an environment where controls deliver the ability to thrive.

Common Failures When Implementing Controls

The most common reasons for failing to implement a new controls system and create a new, controlled business environment can be categorized as *a lack of purpose, poor communication, missing mission, a lack of urgency, and little or no sense of accomplishment.* Separately and collectively, these different areas that contribute to overall failure can work against even the most promising circumstances regarding controls implementation.

Options abound to help you navigate through these limitations, yet the most important thing to understand is that you cannot combat a lack of purpose or clarify a missing mission until you recognize these weaknesses and how they are affecting your plans to bring your business under control. To turn your head away as if nothing is wrong or as if whatever is wrong will go away is destructive and will lead you to decline and eventual failure. Once you know what is broken, then you can use the proper tools to fix the problem. First, let's more closely examine these characteristics that coincide with failure to implement a new controls system in the business environment.

Figure 10.1

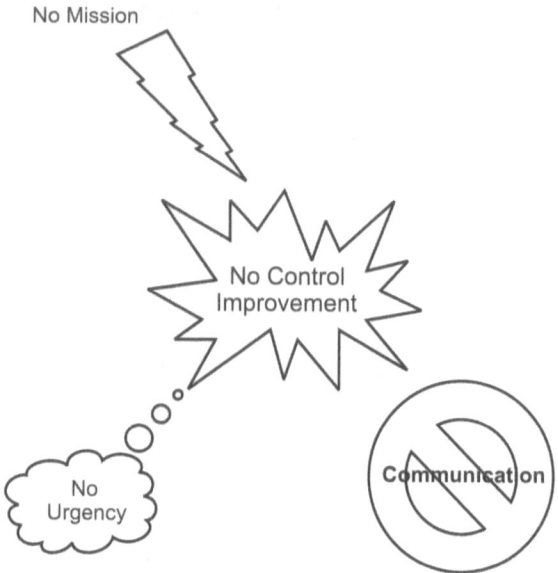

Poor Communication

Most small organizations struggle to share what it is they hope to accomplish by establishing the new system of controls. Unless you have the team bought into the value, they will not want to modify their prior routines. Often the organization thinks it's doing well enough and simply refuses to listen to any changes. Dynamic companies are in constant transition, to overhaul their basic routines is often an unwelcome disturbance. Other groups would like to make changes but simply lack the education of what is necessary to adopt the changes. Left with vague expectations, control projects never get launched, procedures never revised.

Missing Mission

The mission and vision for controls needs to be clear enough that the organization will be inspired and motivated to make a cultural shift. Knowing that routines and behaviors will have to be modified, the enterprise is going to need to know this is not simply a short-term "band-aid" to fix a larger problem. The group needs to know you are making these changes for everyone's long term wellbeing. This is not communicated through long drawn-out meetings, but simply a new control objective that will be created throughout the organization, ultimately providing for a fairer, more ethical and secure future for all stakeholders. If the organization senses any lack of direction, these fears will be magnified by the rest of the team. One preferred control statement comes directly from the COSO standards: "Controls will provide for effective and efficient attainment of our objectives, fair and accurate financial reporting and compliance with state and local governments."

Lack of Urgency

A grave error in implementing controls is presenting the message without a sense of urgency to make the needed changes and begin the required projects. Few others may see the dangers caused by lack of controls. Although you may not wish to expose existing vulnerabilities, your team members need to see your urgency to push forward in making the necessary adjustments. Unless you draw them out of complacency, the resistance to change will persist. Pushing people out of comfortable routines requires energy, and without a sense of anxiety that needed changes must happen immediately, status quo will usually prevail. Some may contend that there are no pending threats and those changes can be delayed. Delaying a needed course correction will put you in a perilous situation for when a company is lacking critical controls often the results are become evident in reduced productivity, profits and customer retention.

Communicating the Control Message

Your greatest ability to transform your environment will be generated when your entire team shares the same vision and sense of direction. Often negotiating the need for controls is sent with mixed messages including a long list of "dos and don'ts." Attempt to involve your team in the creation and implementation of each control. Allow them to create the project and implement the change. Often this may rest upon your shoulders depending on the depth of your organization, and that is perfectly acceptable.

The message will need to remain clear. Maintain focus on the big picture and allow each participant to improve his or her respective area. Communicating that message frequently enough to instill your dedication to the goal will help ensure that controls begin to integrate into the organization. One of the challenges in communication will be getting others to hear what they do not particularly care to hear, especially in the case of changing controls and that some or many changes will be happening to many common and familiar procedures. When conveying this message you will need to have a solid list of your priorities and how you see those best handled for your future success. Implementation is the process of carrying out the vision you have created.

Several elements will help you communicate the significance of controls.

- *Lead by example*: Demonstrate that your efforts are sincere and begin by changing your own behavior.

- *Repetition:* Let the team know that a control environment is being created as a permanent part of the culture, and then remind everyone often.

- *Simplicity*: Keep your message clear and limit distractions that keep others from understanding specific control procedures.

- *Clarify*: Explain any inconsistencies in the new procedures. There will be activities that may seem to impugn one or several employees' behavior. Explain that this is not the case; these controls will help keep them above reproach and keep the company away from those dealings that may disadvantage the company.

- *Be open*: Listen to what other team members have to offer, your situation has unique conditions that apply only in your environment. Adapt as often as needed to meet the needs of the enterprise.

- *Demonstrate benefits*: Look for applications of controls in your situation, take specific examples and apply them to your environment to provide a verbal image of the benefits that are derived from theses applications.

Your industry will have unique jargon and lexicon used to quickly convey information to others within the group. Make sure you convey the message of controls limiting any jargon or terminology that may confuse a newly hired employee or outsider, such as banker or capital partner. You are creating a cultural change and it is imperative that the message arrives clearly enough that there are no reasons why these controls are not instituted.

Vision for Control Leadership

There is a tendency to believe as a small entrepreneur that you must personally prescribe and institute all control changes. This thinking is flawed by the many stories of the mighty accomplishments of such characters as Sam Walton, Dave Thomas, Andrew Carnegie, and Jack Welch and on and on. These individuals seemed to be able to make everything happen and keep tight reigns on operations under their inspiring leadership. Do not make the mistake of thinking this was done alone, these leaders were great only because they were able to motivate other great people and recruit the help they needed to accomplish great objectives. They knew who to trust and more importantly they learned how to create systems that would act as safety nets in the event that trust was violated. You simply cannot go it alone. As you grow others will help form your team, they must be trusted but let that trust be directed not on the personality in particular, but rather in their ability to create systems that instill confidence and include checks and balances.

It is important that you realize that your vision for a controlled environment will provide the leadership to get your enterprise to higher levels of success and security. The use of micro-management and decrees well may cause confusion and frustration for your business. As you clarify what needs to happen in your mind, share these ideas and insights with trusted members of your staff. Encourage their constructive input and show that you value their input by taking time to listen and rephrase what you have understood from that input.

> ### Reality Check:
> ### Success = Controls + Respect
>
> Hatim Tyabji's, founder of VeriFone, one of the nations leading payment processing providers, created what he calls the "blueberry pancake" business structure. The people at VeriFone are like the blueberries—"they're all equals with respect to their importance to the company. The batter is the company infrastructure, the processes, the things that bind the employees together ..."
>
> Under Tyabji's leadership, VeriFone grew to over $600 Million in sales in less than 9 years. Through his philosophy of respect and equality he was able to generate enormous returns in the highly sensitive area of credit card information. Solid controls tied to mutual respect were the foundations of his tremendous success.
>
> *Fast Company*, 1995 January edition.

Feasible Goals

Establishing controls may be intuitive for some, while for others it is a foreign language. Create controls on a project basis. As discussed in Chapter Two, the value of project management is in creating a team that will evaluate, design and implements control systems within your enterprise. Taking part in leading the organization will help the team feel that the object for "robust internal controls" is clear and attainable. Breaking down your control objectives will help this vision to become even clearer. As you work with your team keep the purpose of the desired controls in mind. Keep in mind if the goal is not attainable then it is merely fluff. Formulate concrete objectives, and then expect realistic results.

The Controls Team

As you create a team to help you develop your controls system, there are four components to remember that will assist you in successfully selecting team members who will be best suited to guide you through the planning and implementation of your controls system. These components consist of:

- *Credibility:* Members should have enough respect so that their recommendations are taken seriously by others.

- *Leadership*: This team should have proven leaders that can drive the changes through the difficulties and discomfort that are certain to come.

- *Expertise*: Members should have experience relevant to their fields to know what will be expected and offer key insights.

- *Empowerment*: The team should be able to require the adoption of controls as mandatory and not simply recommendations.

If your enterprise consists of members from accounting, production, sales, and operations you may want to create control team that will handle the implementation of each desired control as a project. Appoint one main person to be the responsible project manager for that particular control function. For example, if the controls system you are instituting is in inventory controls, then select an individual who is capable of setting the standards. Use this text and perhaps other materials on inventory controls to serve as guidelines when setting up inventory and insuring the process is under control.

This same inventory team should include a representative each from management and accounting. From each representative you will receive input as to what is and what is not under control for your situation. Questions should be asked to review the status such as: *Is inventory sitting around too long? Is there too much safety stock? Are lead times recognized and monitored? Is product inspected upon arrival for compliance?* The list of appropriate questions goes on, and this team will be critical in handling and responding to the information gathered from these inquiries.

Encourage the team to establish a priority checklist of those items that may prove most vulnerable to the organization. You may know of certain concerns and should broadcast this to the team. For example, you may know that your materials represent 70% of your costs of goods; you may also know that gaining tighter controls in this area will add or protect the bottom line of the business more than any other area. This is an excellent starting point if you are not sure where to begin the process.

Alternately, another business may have the same 70% in vested raw materials ratio, but due to upcoming compliance issues they need to switch from a lead based solder to silver/tin alloy. The potential fines if compliance is not resolved could jeopardize the entire company. This point could serve as the springboard to pull together in this situation.

In another business, there may not have been recording of accounts receivables as deliveries are made, as a result recording and collection of some sales have been lost. This is a frightening and all too common situation. Start with the recording issues, today, if this represents your current circumstance.

Each enterprise will be unique and have its own priorities. You can use financial concerns, compliance issues and intuition as governing gauges to get process started. As you move down the list of priorities, there may be changes over time, so be flexible and allow for evolution of the process. Remember, this is a learning process and the knowledge gained is directed toward the success of the entire business.

Handling Frustrations

A productive approach would suggest handling one area of control at a time, simply for the reason that most entrepreneurial efforts simply don't have the time or resources to handle multiple projects and establish multiple processes synchronously. If you stretch your team too thin and plan too much too soon, enthusiasm will dwindle and frustration will set in. Some frustration is normal as each project will pass through some periods of disturbance. Expect frustration and resentment of the changes. Tensions will often build as area weaknesses are identified and sometimes extra steps and documentation may be required. There may be withdrawal from the group as negativism sets it.

As you lead the team, try to channel the energy toward positive emotions by reminding the group why these changes are entirely for the betterment of everyone involved. Encourage the group to maintain the focus on their objects and the controls that are best for the business. One way to do this is to ensure that control projects are broken up into small tasks and phases. These will offer some measure of satisfaction in moving toward the goal. This will also help prevent the team from feeling overwhelmed and at a loss for what to do or how they will be successful. Keep things small enough to achieve measurable progress and celebrate these milestones.

Small Victories

One of the most common distractions for the establishment of controls success is the "No-Win" perspective. Most quality control experts that have worked for a traditional organization will recognize that the quality control department never *wins,* they only *lose*. The familiar tale of "defects start coming out of the procedure, so there must be a problem with the quality control department" is an easy excuse and keeps real responsibility at bay but does nothing to fix the problem. Fortunately, most organizations have recognized the value of total control management where the entire organization is engaged in looking at the process of quality. You are going to be applying those same skills and abilities now regarding quality, not only to product quality, but to the quality of controls within the entire business.

What if controls are established and then not followed? In this case, it would seem the control team did not set up the proper program and thus failed. Although these thoughts are disheartening, your vision and desire to push ahead with the changes at all costs will help remove this traditional and nasty stigma. Controls are designed for the benefit of the entire organization. Establishing controls will take time and reiteration of the importance of establishing these goals will have to happen from time to time as well. As projects become adopted into programs, celebrate!

Unfortunately, there is no foolproof system to protect your company, and a group of conspiring people can evade even the best detection as set forth in even the tightest control systems. However, if your controls are in place and responding to the issues, an individual problem should be isolated enough to not harm the entire company. Each time a priority control project has been tested and consequently found to be functional, find a small way for the team to feel a rewarding sense of satisfaction.

These small victories will lead to encouragement and continued desire to succeed thereby pushing progress on to the next level of the controls priority list. These victories should provide recognition for the team. Measurable performance here consists of adopting control projects which are now ready for testing as programs. Do not wait for perfection to celebrate and recognize hard work. As soon as the group believes the program should be implemented, recognize this as a milestone of success.

Refresh the Team

Everyone should be able to acknowledge their efforts and feel positive about the future success of the enterprise. Human nature responds by becoming invigorated when the need adapt, the challenge to change and an opportunity to overcome obstacles presents themselves. When any of these trials have been surmounted, the group should feel a sense of satisfaction and be recognized for efforts expended. Some ways to show positive feedback include the following:

- *Pat on the back:* The controls team should all understand that these projects are not extra compensation packages, but requirements for the health of the team. Financial incentives should not be expected, but certainly praise and positive feedback are imperative. A pat on the back or even a letter of genuine complement regarding successful efforts will renew the desire to continue onward.

- *Show the value:* Demonstrate to the team how valuable their efforts are, ensure that they can see and measure results. As control programs are adopted, show them how their efforts have directly made the company ultimately better and they can all expect to benefit from their labors.

- *Subdue the critics:* For those naysayers who thought these projects were not valuable and would not change the security and health of the business, tactfully show them that they have been proven wrong.

- *Build momentum:* Others will see the value of the programs working in other departments when their area is directly impacted with new controls. See results will keep minds open to change and willing to work with the team.

Driving Forward

Once the first project is up and running, you will need to continue to check off your priority control list. Remember that resistance to changes in the existing systems will persist. There will be a constant need to push and drive for further controls. Do not let up on your efforts as you must continue to expect delivery of projects outlined and programs in position. If you send the message that the top few controls are working well and the balance of controls are not necessary, you will sabotage your progress and perhaps revert to old systems and lose the controls which were previously in place.

Beat the System to Strengthen Controls

If an employee discovers how to bypass the system, encourage them to demonstrate how they beat the system and let this employee be recognized for his or her resourcefulness. Of course any illegal activity is not acceptable, nor should any employee carry out an activity that may be detrimental to the organization. But employees that spot weaknesses in a control system should be recognized for their ability to identify problem areas and sought after for insight while making the required system changes to avoid future exploitations.

One business recognized employees at monthly staff meetings for identifying of system vulnerabilities that had not previously been addressed. Employees were awarded gift certificates to a local restaurant, and the business was given something even more valuable, the recognition of a potential system weakness that could later cause greater problems. When the program was initially launched there were so many vulnerabilities it seemed that nearly the entire staff was getting gift certificates for dinner. As the months rolled along and controls became tighter, the staff members had to struggle more and more to find and identify new vulnerabilities. Using creative energy protected the business long term and offered an environment of stability. Instead of complaining about a weakness this business took the stance that they would celebrate the person who could identify the problem.

Urgent Call for Controls

When taking a drive to instill controls in an organization, most people will outright reject the need for control systems. They will retort that the business has operated fine without these controls for this long, so it will be fine tomorrow without further changes. This type of attitude will drive a business into eventual disruption.

In order to get cooperation you will need to drive a sense of urgency. Control projects will not be launched without an expense of energy. A leader must be prepared to fight the negative drag. As you convince the team of the urgency of the situation, these controls will help promote the business to the next higher level, without them you remain exposed and may never grow as intended. If others do not share that sense of urgent need, time will bring back old habits and new controls will be bypassed with yesterday's routines. This will create some frustration, prepare for it and respond accordingly. You will be faced by those that admit some weaknesses but will respond that progress is being made. Whether that progress is satisfactory or not is irrelevant. If there are inherent weaknesses that could eventually disrupt operations, or that are dragging down efficiency or have fallen out of government compliance, then controls need to be implemented and you must use your influence for the good of the company to drive that principle home and convince your counterparts to make that change.

All too often business is governed by whomever barks the loudest, whomever is the most forceful in meetings. If such is the case in your company, ally that "barker" on your side of the desired control changes; it would be a mistake not to get their full input and buy-in prior to launch. We often like to think that we operate business more diplomatically in our modern era. Sadly, this is only a facade, so go to those who carry the most referent power and enlist their help to make it happen. If that individual is you as entrepreneur, then still make it happen.

Do not be misled into thinking that those unwilling to change current routines are somehow ignorant or apathetic. This is often not the case; it is not because they are so incompetent that they do not see the case for controls. They all too often know the value but are distracted by the many pressing concerns of the day. This is particularly true of the entrepreneurial venture where too many entrepreneurs find themselves burdened and hard pressed for time to deal with controls projects.

To demonstrate the simplicity of controls when they have been established, and the reason you need these controls just ask yourself why you brush your teeth twice a day. In response, it is because that is what you were taught as a child and have implanted in your head as a requirement for healthy teeth. Tooth brushing is a control activity, a preventative control against plaque and tooth decay. A system (toothbrush, floss, mouthwash, toothpaste) was put in place, parents, a dentist, a girlfriend or someone must have instilled a sense of urgency for you to develop that routine. If a young person with all their teeth in place does not see the urgency in brushing teeth, not many weeks and months roll by without discovering some damage that may be irreversible. This type of urgency to establish a system is exactly what you will need to do for your finances and operations. You are creating a system that will fight off financial plaque, keep out bacterial payables and prevent inflamed operations.

The following is a list of reasons that challenge the process of establishing controls, breaking old routines and redefining performance:

- *No emergency:* Most controls are preventative in nature and there is no current crisis to respond. Humans are typically generous and helpful during times of challenge and duress, in comfortable environments members will find more urgent matters which to attend (customer complaints, sales goals, employee recruiting, etc.).

- *Historical success:* The business is attaining a level of success so need for controls is not a priority. The common philosophy behind this reason is that the company should enjoy its position and let others worry about those matters. Remember, though, it wasn't raining when Noah built the ark.

- *Indifference to available tools:* This is reminiscent of the story of the marble worker, who, accustomed to his wooden mallet, refused to accept the concept of the new and improved metal mallet and consequently, he never attained the greatness he desired. Our wooden mallets may have worked for our forefathers, but we need to learn to use the new tools that will improve the process to achieve greater things. We need to build upon the success of our fathers and the only way to accomplish that is change and progress.

- *No measurement standards:* Many companies who are unwilling to change are also unwilling to measure their performance, or at least measure their effectiveness in terms of productivity and financial controls. Lacking the desire to know where they are, they fear what they may find. This may sound ridiculous, but this sentiment is much more prevalent in small businesses than you may believe.

- *Denial:* Some companies deny that controls have merit. If someone wants to "rob us blind" then they will. The fatalistic attitude that controls cannot stop the inevitable is fallible. Realistically, you will probably never be robbed blind unless your eyes are poked out. But you are cheating yourself and your success if you do not open your eyes to the opportunities and tools that exist to protect your business and procure your success. Fortunately, most entrepreneurs are optimists by nature and can be persuaded to believe in the value of change.

Leading boldly, you need to see the potential disruptions caused by lack of controls, yet as a small business you cannot afford to learn extra lessons that have already been learned by others. Business is too complicated and too risky for you to simply allow your enterprise to suffer a preventable setback. Be the driving force that will get the team together. The control team will be charged with working off the priority list, either created by Control Self Assessments or as directives from senior management. Make sure this team feels the significance of their position and that progress and results are expected within a specified time frame. As a leader you are responsible to motivate this team as well as yourself to get operations under control. Emphasize to the team the exposure the business faces each moment these controls are lacking.

As your control priorities begin moving down the list and changing as projects are implemented into programs, continue to push through until all priorities that can be addressed are installed. Set a short timeline from project to program, controls need to be in place "yesterday." This approach may weary the employees but this type of preaching establishes a cultural change, and change is exactly what is needed in the formation of controls.

Code RED: Simulating Emergencies to Stimulate Activity

To create the need for controls without allowing disruption to your enterprise you may need to simulate an emergency. In this situation you let others know that you are aware of a needed change in operations. You could run "what if" scenarios such as: *What if a bogus invoice just came through? Even send one to your own business, and then ask—do you know how it would be processed? Would someone enter the invoice into the system? How would it be sent for payment?*

Remember, if operations are not performing as efficiently as they could be, your company is losing money. *Period.* You need to let your partners and employees know that the organization cannot continue to lose money. A good leader will know how to instill urgency without producing panic. You do not want a massive "jump-ship", but you do need enough help on board to create the control systems and improvements necessary for your business's welfare.

Four Essential Habits for Constant Control Improvement

As entrepreneur you need to create habits that will carry your enterprise forward to new heights. In establishing controls you will feel a great sense of satisfaction in your ability and peace that comes from knowing you are taking every precaution to protect your goals, dreams and safeguard the assets entrusted to you. These four essential habits will help you to improve your business environment:

Figure 10.2

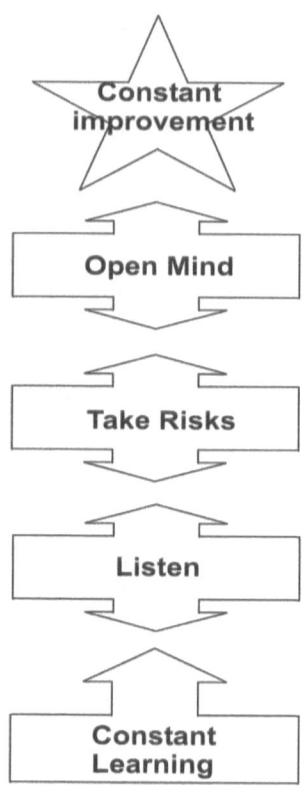

- *Constant learning:* Make continued education more than a nicety. Establish a set amount of time each week for continued professional development.

- *Careful listening:* Take time to listen and absorb what others are telling you. Politely probe and postulate the other person's position before you craft your own response.

- *Continued risk taking:* As an entrepreneur who is moving forward, you are already taking risks. "Progress always involves risk; you can't steal second base and keep your foot on first."—Frederick Wilcox. Keep taking risks and while you do, enlist others to share the risk with you.

- *Keep an open mind:* Be willing to make changes and adjustments as needed. Develop controls that will be dynamic and adjust to your business environment. Respond to changes and remember that it is okay to acknowledge weaknesses and imperfections.

By establishing these four essential habits into your management style, you will find that the internal controls development process will become an exciting adventure of discovery and growth for you and your company.

Chapter Summary

We discussed the natural tendency to fail to help you fully understand to need to establish a controls system. Realize that to make any sort of improvement to your business you will need to take action. Begin by building a mission statement and a message of your desires for a controlled environment. Communicate that mission with the team and keep it in a visible place. Once communicated, create a sense of urgency. While most controls will not be pressing or urgent, these steps build a strong foundation for solid performance. Create change. By proactively setting the standard for change, you will achieve success in changing your existing environment.

Use several tools to create a controlled environment: lead by example; repeat the message; keep objectives simple and clear; remain open to suggestions; and demonstrate benefits. These tools are drivers for change. If controls are to have any measurable duration in your organization, you will need to revise how and why you do the things you do.

Provide your controls team with the four components for successful implementation: credibility, empowerment, expertise and leadership. Your controls team can be as small as just two members or as large as twenty. Just remember that this will serve as the core of all future success. However large your organization and team, resolve to implement your control systems. Encourage your team with pats on the back, motivating tactics, building on your gains and subduing the cynics.

Avoid the traps that will prevent changes, lack of urgency, past success, failure to learn, no metrics and denial. These negatives will stall your progress and keep you in your present condition. You do not have time to lose, so push forward and accomplish the goals you and your team have set.

Incorporate these four essential habits into your management style: *constantly learning; listening to others; taking chances and keeping an open mind.* As you actively participate in planning and executing your internal controls plan, you can expect constant improvement and success in your venture.

APPENDIX

Resource Materials

A-1 Sample Consulting Agreement

Consulting Agreement

This Consulting Agreement (the "Agreement") is entered into this [specify date] by and between [Name of Consultant], an individual, ("Consultant") and [Name of Company] (the "Company").

The Company is in need of assistance in the [specify] support area; and

The Consultant has agreed to perform consulting work for the Company in providing [specify] support and consulting services and other related activities as directed by the Company;

NOW, THEREFORE, the parties hereby agree as follows:

1. Consultant's Services. Consultant shall be available and shall provide to the Company professional consulting services in the area of [specify] support ("Consulting services") as requested.

2. Consideration.

A. RATE. In consideration for the Consulting Services to be performed by Consultant under this Agreement, the Company will pay Consultant at the rate of [specify rate] per hour for time spent on Consulting Services. Consultant shall submit written, signed reports of the time spent performing Consulting Services, itemizing in reasonable detail the dates on which services were performed, the number of hours spent on such dates and a brief description of the services rendered. The Company shall pay Consultant the amounts due pursuant to submitted reports within 14 days after such reports are received by the Company.

B. EXPENSES. Additionally, the Company will pay Consultant for the following expenses incurred while the Agreement between Consultant and the Company exists:

All travel expenses to and from all work sites

Meal expenses;

Administrative expenses;

Lodging Expenses if work demands overnight stays; and

Miscellaneous travel-related expenses

Consultant shall submit written documentation and receipts where available itemizing the dates on which expenses were incurred. The Company shall pay Consultant the amounts due pursuant to submitted reports within 14 days after a report is received by the Company.

3. Independent Contractor. Nothing herein shall be construed to create an employer-employee relationship between the Company and Consultant. Consultant is an independent contractor and not an employee of the Company or any of its subsidiaries or affiliates. The consideration set forth in Section 2 shall be the sole consideration due Consultant for the services rendered hereunder. It is understood that the Company will not withhold any amounts for payment of taxes from the compensation of Consultant hereunder. Consultant will not represent to be or hold herself out as an employee of the Company.

4. Confidentiality. In the course of performing Consulting Services, the parties recognize that Consultant may come in contact with or become familiar with information which the Company or its subsidiaries or affiliates may consider confidential. This information may include, but is not limited to, information pertaining to the Company [specify] systems, which information may be of value to a competitor. Consultant agrees to keep all such information confidential and not to discuss or divulge it to anyone other than appropriate Company personnel or their designees.

5. Term. This Agreement shall commence on [specify date] and shall terminate on [specify date], unless earlier terminated by either party hereto. Either party may terminate this Agreement upon Thirty (30) days prior written notice. The Company may, at its option, renew this Agreement for an additional One (1)

year term on the same terms and conditions as set forth herein by giving notice to Consultant of such intent to renew on or before [specify date].

6. Notice. Any notice or communication permitted or required by this Agreement shall be deemed effective when personally delivered or deposited, postage prepaid, in the first class mail of the United States properly addressed to the appropriate party at the address set forth below:

    1. Notices to Consultant: [specify address]

    2. Notices to the Company: [specify address]

7. Miscellaneous.

7.1 Entire Agreement and Amendments. This Agreement constitutes the entire agreement of the parties with regard to the subject matter hereof, and supersedes all other agreements or understandings, whether written or oral. No amendment or extension of the Agreement shall be binding unless in writing and signed by both parties.

7.2 Binding Effect, Assignment. This Agreement shall be binding upon and shall inure to the benefit of Consultant and the Company and to the Company's successors and assigns. Nothing in this Agreement shall be construed to permit the assignment by Consultant of any of its rights or obligations hereunder, and such assignment is expressly prohibited without the prior written consent of the Company.

7.3 Governing Law, Severability. This Agreement shall be governed by the laws of the State of [specify]. The invalidity or unenforceability of any provision of the Agreement shall not affect the validity or enforceability of any other provision.

The parties have executed this Agreement as of the date first written above.

[COMPANY:]   Date

Authorized Signature

[CONSULTANT:]   Date

Authorized Signature

A-2 Sample of an Auditor Engagement Letter

Jack Trent & Associates
1111 XYZ Drive
Here, Now 12345

July 1, 2009

Mr. John Doe
Shark Manufacturing Co.
Main Street

Dear Mr. Doe,

Thank you for choosing us as the auditors for upcoming audits of your business. We will audit the consolidated balance sheet of Shark Manufacturing Co as of December 31 2009, and the related consolidated statements of earnings, retained earnings, and cash flows for the year ended. Our audit will be made in accordance with generally accepted auditing standards and will include examination, on a test basis, of evidence supporting amounts and disclosures in the financial statements, accessing the accounting principles used and significant estimates made by management, as well as evaluating the overall financial statement presentation.

The objective of our engagement is the completion of the foregoing audit and, upon its completion and subject to its findings, the rendering of our report. As you know, the financial statements are the responsibility of the management and board of directors of your company, who are primarily responsible for the data ad information set forth therein as well as for the maintenance of an appropriate internal control structure (which includes adequate accounting records and procedures to safeguard company's assets). Accordingly, as required by generally accepted auditing standards, our procedures will include obtaining written confirmation from management concerning important representations on which we will rely.

Also as required by generally accepted auditing standards, we will plan and perform our audit to obtain reasonable, but not absolute, assurance about whether the financial statements are free of material misstatement. Accordingly, any such audit is not a guarantee of the accuracy so the financial statements and is subject to the inherent risk that errors and irregularities (or irregular acts), if they exist, might not be detected. If we become aware of any unusual matters during the course of our audit, we will bring them to your attention. Should you then wish us to expand our normal auditing procedures we would be pleased to work with you to develop a separate engagement for that purpose.

Our engagement will also include preparation of federal income tax returns for your company for the year ended December31, 2009, and a review of state income tax returns for the same period prepared by your accounting staff.

Our billings for the services set forth in this letter will be based upon our per diem rates for this type of work plus out-of pocket expenses; billings will be rendered at the beginning of each month on an estimated basis and are payable upon receipt. This engagement letter only includes only those services specifically described in this letter, and appearances before judicial proceedings or government organizations such as the Internal Revenue Service, the Securities and Exchange Commission, or other regulatory bodies, arising out of this engagement will be billed to you separately.

We are enclosing an explanation of certain of our Firm's Client Service Concepts. We have found that such explanation helps communicate our commitment to the highest level of customer service.

We look forward to providing the services described in this letter, as well as other services agreeable o us both. In the unlikely event that any differences concerning our services or fees arise that are not resolved by mutual agreement, we both recognize that the matter will probably involve complex business or accounting issues that would be decided most equitably to both parties by a judge hearing the evidence without a jury. Accordingly you and we agree to waive any right to a trial by jury in any action, proceeding or counterclaim arising out of or relating to our services and fees.

If you are in agreement with the terms of this letter, please sign one copy and return it for our files. We appreciate the opportunity to work with you.

Yours,

Jack Trent

The foregoing letter fully describes our understanding and is accepted by us.

Shark Manufacturing Co.

Date

John Doe

A-3 Sample Code of Conduct and Ethics Statement

JACK TRENT & ASSOCIATES
CODE OF BUSINESS CONDUCT AND ETHICS

I. Introduction

Jack Trent & Associates ("JTA") has adopted the following Code of Business Conduct and Ethics ("Code") for directors of JTA. The Board intends the Code to promote: honest and ethical conduct including the ethical handling of actual or apparent conflicts of interest between personal and professional relationships; full, fair, accurate, timely and understandable disclosures in public communications made by JTA; compliance with applicable governmental laws, rules and regulations; prompt internal reporting to the appropriate persons identified in this Code of any violations of the Code; and accountability for adherence to the Code.

This Code is intended to serve as a source of guiding principles for directors and employees and other internal members. All members are encouraged to bring questions about the application of the Code to specific transactions to the attention of the Chairman of the Board or the Chairman of the Audit Committee, who may consult with legal counsel as appropriate. Directors who also serve as officers of the Company should abide by this Code in conjunction with the JTA's Code of Ethics and Conduct for Senior Financial Officers and Executive Officers as well as JTA's Code of Conduct and Standard of Ethics applicable to all employees.

Any violations of this Code may result in disciplinary action. An employee seeking a waiver of this Code must make full disclosure of the particular circumstances to the Board of Directors. Only the Board or the Board's designated committee(s) may grant waivers of this Code. JTA will publicly disclose amendments or waivers of this Code in accordance with applicable law, regulations.

II. Honest and Ethical Conduct and Conflicts of Interest

The directors will promote—by their words and personal examples—honest and ethical conduct on the part of all employees of JTA, including the ethical handling of actual or apparent conflicts of interest between personal and professional relationships. A "conflict of interest" occurs when a director's personal interest interferes or appears to interfere with JTA's interests. All directors shall exercise sound judgment and seek advice when appropriate to avoid all conflicts of interest.

III. Confidentiality

JTA provides its directors with access to confidential information about customers and employees as well as JTA's business plans, financial performance and services. Directors, acting in their capacities as such, may also acquire confidential information about JTA and its customers and employees from third parties. Such information is a valuable asset of JTA and directors must treat it as strictly confidential. Directors shall never use confidential information for personal gain or to compete with JTA.

IV. Disclosures

No director or employee shall knowingly misrepresent or cause others to misrepresent material facts about JTA to others whether within or outside JTA, including JTA's independent or internal auditors, governmental regulators and self-regulatory organizations or conceal a material mistake in JTA's financial reporting. Any director who discovers such a material mistake or misrepresentation must act promptly to disclose the mistake or misrepresentation to the Chairman of the Board, the Chairman of the Audit Committee or the full Board, as appropriate.

V. Compliance with Laws, Rules and Regulations

Directors and employees will comply with all laws, rules and regulations applicable to them as directors of JTA, including insider trading laws and the rules and regulations of any self-regulatory organization. Directors shall promote compliance by JTA and its employees with all applicable laws, rules and regulations.

VI. Reporting of any Illegal or Unethical Behavior

Directors shall promote ethical behavior and create a culture of ethical compliance that (i) encourages employees to talk to supervisors, managers and other appropriate personnel when in doubt about the best course of action in a particular situation; (ii) encourages officers and employees to report violations of laws, rules, regulation or any of JTA's codes of conduct and codes of ethics; and (iii) will not permit retaliation against officers and employees for reports made in good faith. The Audit Committee is responsible for applying this Code to specific situations in which questions are presented and has authority to interpret this Code. Any director who becomes aware of any existing or potential violation of this Code shall notify the Chairman of the Audit Committee promptly. The

Audit Committee shall determine whether violations of the Code have occurred, in consultation with the Company's Chairman and Chief Executive Officer, General Counsel and/or such external legal counsel as the Audit Committee deems appropriate. The Audit Committee shall report its findings of violations to the Board of directors for further action

I acknowledge and understand this code as established and agree to follow all its terms and conditions.

Employee Signature   Supervisor Signature

Date   Date

A-4 Sample Vendor Application Form

SAMPLE VENDOR APPLICATION FORM

Company
Name _____

Address_____

City/State/Zip_____

Phone_____ Fax _____

President Name _____

CEO Title _____

Federal Tax ID Number _____

COMPANY INFORMATION

Organization Type: Sole Owner ___ Corporation ___ S-Corp. ___

State of Incorporation? _____ Nonprofit? ___Yes___No

Other Socioeconomic Factor(s)_____

Domestic/Foreign Owned? _____

Is your company owned by a parent company? ___Yes___No

Parent Company Name _____

Parent Company Addres_____

Parent Company Tax ID _____

Are you: ____Small Business? ____Minority-Owned Business?
____Veteran-Owned Business? ____Women-Owned Business?
____Veteran Disabled-Owned Business? ____Other Socioeconomic Factor(s)?

Does your company accept credit cards? ___Yes___No

Primary Standard Industrial Code _____

Additional SICs _____

Primary North American Industry Classification System Code (NAICS)
_____

Did your company have a name change in the past 12 months? ___Yes___No

Name _____

Company Contact _____Quality Assurance Contact _____

GENERAL INFORMATION

Area in Sq. Ft.: Manufacturing ___   Office ___   Total ___

Number of Personnel: Manufacturing _____   Quality Assurance ___
Engineering _____

Are clean room facilities used for manufacturing product? ____Yes____No

What percentage of present work is: Government _____ Commercial _____
Other _____

Describe any special processes that you perform (e.g., plating, painting, soldering, welding, wire wrap, etc.). _____
_____
_____

Are you ISO-9000 certified? ___Yes ___No   ISO Certificate Type_____

Registrar _____ Certificate Number_____

Expiration Date: ISO READY/Not Certified _____ Date of Certification_____

Registered or certified to any other Quality Management System or model?
_____ Mil-I-45208 _____ Mil-Q-9858 _____ Other

QUALITY MANAGEMENT SYSTEM

Do you maintain operation policies and procedures for your quality management system? ___Yes ___No

Is an internal audit program maintained that reviews compliance with all aspects of the quality program? ___Yes ___No

Does the organizational structure define quality responsibility and authority? ___Yes ___No

Does the organizational structure provide access to top management? ___Yes ___No

Is the health and status of your quality management system periodically reviewed with management? ___Yes ___No

Do you have a documented employee training program? ___Yes ___No

Is the quality organization responsible for acceptance of product and services? ___Yes ___No

Are records of inspections and tests maintained? ___Yes ___No

Are quality data used in reporting results and trends to management? ___Yes ___No

Are quality records available to support customer certifications? ___Yes ___No

DESIGN INFORMATION

Do procedures cover the release, change, and recall of design and manufacturing information, including correlation of customer specification? ___Yes ___No

Do records reflect the incorporation of changes? ___Yes ___No

Does quality control verify that changes are incorporated at the effective points? ___Yes ___No

Is the control of design and manufacturing information applied to the procurement activity? ___Yes ___No

Is there a formal deviation procedure? ___Yes ___No

PROCUREMENT CONTROL

Are procurement sources evaluated and monitored? ___Yes ___No

Are quality requirements and inspection procedures specified? ___Yes ___No

Is a documented system maintained for the evaluation of purchased materials? ___Yes ___No

Are incoming materials identified and segregated until acceptance? ___Yes ___No

MATERIAL CONTROL

Do procedures exist for storage, release, and movement of material? ___Yes ___No

Are materials in storage identified and controlled? ___Yes ___No

Are in-process materials identified and controlled? ___Yes ___No

Are materials inspections identified and controlled? ___Yes ___No

Do storage areas and facilities provide control to protect material from degradation? ___Yes ___No

Do you have an electrostatic sensitive device protection program? ___Yes ___No

Are nonconforming items identified, segregated, and controlled? ___Yes ___No

If required, do you have the ability to provide tractability? ___Yes ___No

A-5 Sample Purchase Requisition

Sample Purchase Requisition

Requester's Name:	E-mail:
Phone Number:	Buyer's Name:
Cost Not To Exceed:	PCard Order No.:
Req. No.: Req. Date:	Approved By Supervisor:
Date Needed:	Project I.D.:
Req. Entered:	Approved vendor Yes/No

Vendor/Seller:

_____

_____
Street
_____
City   State   Zip Code
(_____)_____   (_____)_____
        Phone Number   Fax Number
Deliver to: _____
Bldg./Room: _____
Notify: _____ Ext: _____

Item   No.   Catalog

Number   Item   Necessary Specifications

Qty   Estimated Unit Cost   Total Cost

A-6 Sample Purchase Order

Sample Purchase Order

Company Details   Purchase Order Number

                                Order Date

Vendor: Shipping Information:

Terms: Sales Tax Exemption Number:

Item No./Part No./Description/Qty/Unit Price/Total Cost

Ship via: Freight Charges

Authorized Signature   Confirmation Signature

A-7 Voided Check Form

Voided Check Form

Date:

Check number: Check Date:

Check Amount:

Reason for Voiding:

Requested by:

Approved by:

Date:

Chapter Resources

Chapter One

[1] Merriam-Webster Dictionary (July, 2004). Merriam-Webster, Incorporated, New York, NY.

[2] Thomas, R. David (1992). Dave's Way. The Berkley Publishing Group, New York, NY.

[3] The Committee of Sponsoring Organizations of the Treadway Commission. (2005).

[4] Ibid.

[5] Cannon, D.L. & Bergmann, T.S. & Pamplin, B. (2006). Certified Information Systems Auditor Study Guide. Wiley Publishing, New York, NY.

[6] Wilson, Fred. Science and Human Values Aristotle. Rochester Institute of Technology.

[7] American of Institute of Certified Public Accountants (AICPA). http://www.aicpa.org/.

[8] The Committee of Sponsoring Organizations of the Treadway Commission. (2005).

Chapter Two

[1] Gray, C.F & Larson, E. W., *Project Management: The Managerial Process* (2005). McGraw-Hill Irwin, New York, NY.

[2] Robert N. Anthony & Vijay Govindarajan, Management Control Systems— Eleventh Edition, Tata McGraw Hill

[3] Hamburger, D.H. (1990). *The Project Manager: Risk Taker and Contingency Planner*. Project Management Journal v.21.

[4] Gray, C.F & Larson, E. W., *Project Management: The Managerial Process* (2005). McGraw-Hill Irwin, New York, NY.

5   Maciariello J & Kirby C., Management Control Systems—Using Adaptive Systems to Attain Control, Prentice Hall

6   ibid.

Chapter Three

1   Duffied, G. & Grabosky, P. (2004). *Psychology of Fraud.* Australian Institute of Criminology.

2   Association of Certified Fraud Examiners, 2004

3   Silverstone H. & Sheetz, M. (2007). Forensic Accounting and Fraud Investigation for Non-Experts. 2nd Ed., Wiley & Sons, Hoboken, NJ.

4   Rittenberg, L. & Schwieger, B. *Auditing Concepts for a Changing Environment,* 3rd Edition, Harcourt College Publishers

5   The American Society for Quality (2000). Quality Management Systems, Milwaukee, WI.

6   United States Sentencing Commission Guidelines Manual. (1991) *Sentencing of Organizations.*

7   Statement on Auditing Standards 99 (2006). The American Institute of Certified Public Accountants.

8   Management Antifraud Program and Controls (2002). The American Institute of Certified Public Accountants.

Chapter Four

1   Rittenberg, L. & Schwieger, B. *Auditing Concepts for a Changing Environment,* 3rd Edition, Harcourt College Publishers

2   Brinkley, Douglas G. (2003). *Wheels for the World: Henry Ford, His Company, and a Century of Progress.* Penguin Books, New York, NY.

Chapter Five

1   *Tips for Safe Banking over the Internet (2006).* Federal Deposit Insurance Corporation.

2   Khan M. & Jain P., (2004) *Financial Management* Second Edition. Tata McGraw Hill Publishing Co., New Delhi

3   Warren C. & Reeve M. (2007). Managerial Accounting. 9th Edition, Thomson Publishing, Mason, OH.

Chapter Six

1   Rittenberg, L. & Schwieger, B. *Auditing Concepts for a Changing Environment*, 3rd Edition, Harcourt College Publishers

2   Encyclopedia of Small Business 2nd edition 2002, Thompson Gale, New York, NY.

Chapter Seven

1   Crouhy, M., Galai, D. & Mark, R. (2006). The Essentials of Risk Management, McGraw-Hill, New York, NY.

2   Federal Reserve of Chicago (2007). www.chicagofed.org

Chapter Eight

1   *Roland T. Rust & Valarie A. Zeithaml (2000).* Driving Customer Equity: How Customer Lifetime Value is Reshaping Corporate Strategy. *The Free Press, New York, NY.*

2   ibid.

3   Peppers D. & Rogers, M. (2005). Return On Customer. Doublday, New York NY.

4   *Roland T. Rust & Valarie A. Zeithaml (2000).* Driving Customer Equity: How Customer Lifetime Value is Reshaping Corporate Strategy. *The Free Press, New York, NY.*

Chapter Nine

1   Federal Trade Commission, www.ftc.gov.

2   Konrath, Larry F. (2001) Auditing Concepts and Application, 4th Edition. Southwestern College Publishing.

3   Association of Fraud Examiners (2006). *Fraud Examiners Manual.* Austin, TX.

4   National Commission on Fraudulent Financial Reporting (1987). The Treadway Report.

Chapter Ten

1   The Committee of Sponsoring Organizations of the Treadway Commission. (2005).

978-0-595-46326-8
0-595-46326-6